A Visual Catalogue of Richard Hattatt's Ancient Brooches

Reprinted from his fourth book
'Ancient Brooches and other Artefacts'

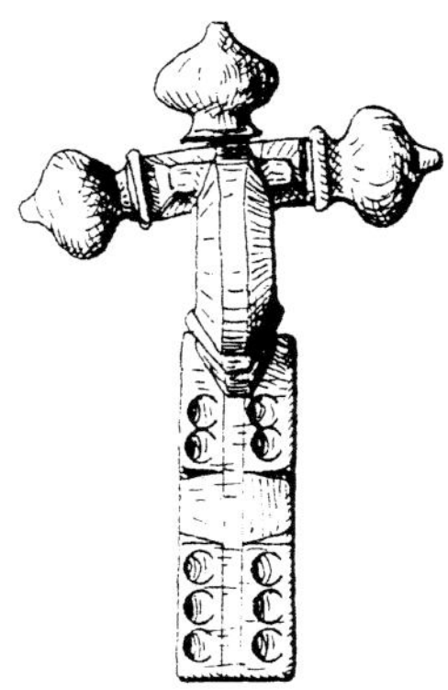

Oxbow Books

First published in the United Kingdom in 1989.
Reprinted as a paperback in 2000. Reprinted in 2007, 2012 and 2020 by
OXBOW BOOKS
The Old Music Hall, 106–108 Cowley Road, Oxford OX4 1JE

and in the United States by
OXBOW BOOKS
1950 Lawrence Road, Havertown, PA 19083

Paperback Edition: ISBN 978-1-84217-026-7
Digital Edition: ISBN 978-1-78297-801-5 (epub)

A CIP record for this book is available from the British Library

For a complete list of Oxbow titles, please contact:

UNITED KINGDOM
Oxbow Books
Telephone (01865) 241249
Email: oxbow@oxbowbooks.com
www.oxbowbooks.com

UNITED STATES OF AMERICA
Oxbow Books
Telephone (610) 853 9131, Fax (610) 853 9146
Email: queries@casemateacademic.com
www.casemateacademic.com/oxbow

Oxbow Books is part of the Casemate Group

Richard Hattatt

Richard Hattatt had a lifelong interest in archaeology, and when he retired from his family firm he devoted himself to the study and collection of antiquities. These ranged from flints and pottery collected locally near to his home in the New Forest and in Wiltshire and Dorset to Greek vases from the Mediterranean, but his interest soon focused on brooches, and he rapidly built up an important collection. The lack of easily obtainable reference books prompted him to write his own. His first book was published in 1982, and, as his collection grew, further books appeared in 1985, 1987 and 1989. Each brooch is described in detail and illustrated with a meticulous drawing, and there are lots of additional notes on comparable types.

Richard Hattatt died in 1992. He had already deposited parts of his collection in the Ashmolean Museum in Oxford and in the Devizes Museum, and sold other parts at auction and privately; so his collection is now dispersed. But his four books remain – a record of the collection and an endless source of reference and interest for those who follow him. The 'Visual Catalogue' reprinted here was a last-minute addition to his fourth book; he prepared it originally for his own use, and realising how often he used it, he decided to include it the book.

Richard Hattatt's four books are:

Ancient and Romano-British Brooches (1982)
Iron Age and Roman Brooches (1985)
Brooches of Antiquity (1987)
Ancient Brooches and Other Artefacts (1989)

Visual Catalogue of Brooches

This 'visual catalogue' was prepared by Richard Hattatt to aid the identification of brooches and for speedy reference to the drawings in his four books. It is reprinted here with the original pagination, and with a supplementary index providing the locations of the brooches.

The brooches are arranged, not by reference number, but by class, as indicated in the following list of contents. Each brooch bears its original number, and while the drawings are here reduced by varying amounts, the actual size of each brooch, together with relative information and discussion, can be ascertained by reference to the original drawings and text in one or other of the books, through which the numbering runs consecutively.

A few types remain unrepresented in the collection, but they are not very common and most can be seen diagrammatically in BoA Figs 116–118.

In the interests of economy, where the profile is comparatively unimportant, space has been saved by a number of the brooches being illustrated frontally only in this particular context.

Brooches from the collection already placed in museum custody are indicated by symbols following their reference numbers. A dot signifies the Ashmolean Museum at Oxford; an asterisk the Devizes Museum in Wiltshire. A small number of brooches other than from the present collection, mainly hitherto unpublished, have been included in the books, and these are indicated with a hyphen on each side of the number. These entries appear thus:

In Ashmolean Museum custody	603•
In Devizes Museum custody	1275*
In other ownership	–1386–

The metal of brooches other than bronze is signified by the following symbols:

AV = gold	AR = silver
fe = iron	p = pewter

Scales

The drawings in the visual catalogue are reduced by varying amounts (mostly about 67% of full size); actual measurements are recorded in the original publications.

References

The full description of each brooch will be found in Richard Hattatt's original publications referred to in the bottom right hand corner of each page of drawings. His books are abbreviated as follows:

ARBB	*Ancient and Romano-British Brooches (1982)*
IARB	*Iron Age and Roman Brooches (1985)*
BoA	*Brooches of Antiquity (1987)*
ABOA	*Ancient Brooches and Other Artefacts (1989)*

Visual Catalogue – Contents

Bow Brooches

Plate Brooches

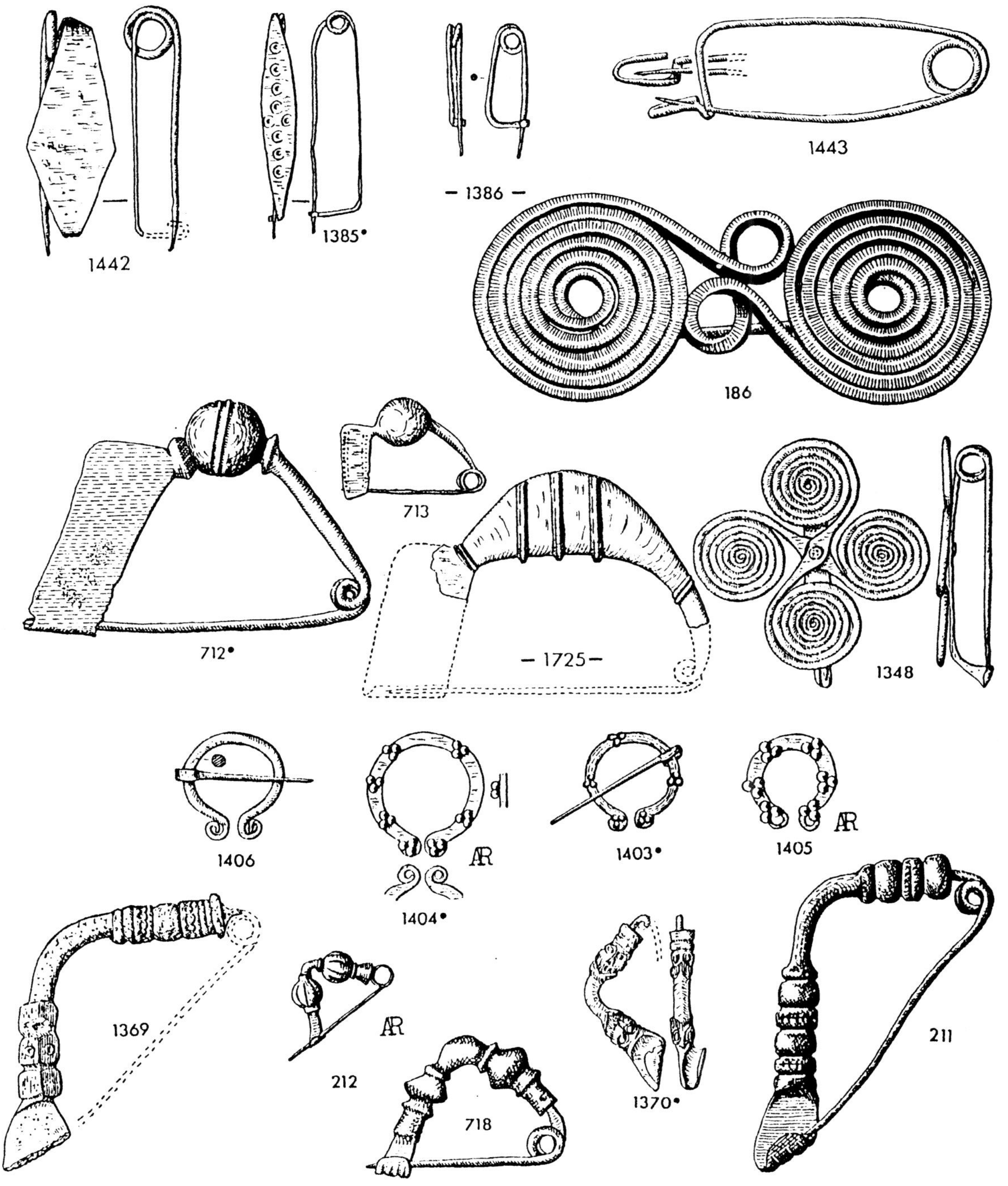

1–212 in ARBB
213–718 in IARB
719–1441 in BoA
1442–1729 in ABOA

Fig. 140 Bronze Age/Iron Age brooches. Top row, Violin bow type; 186 and 1348, Spectacle type; 712–1725, Greek bow brooches; remainder, Persian.

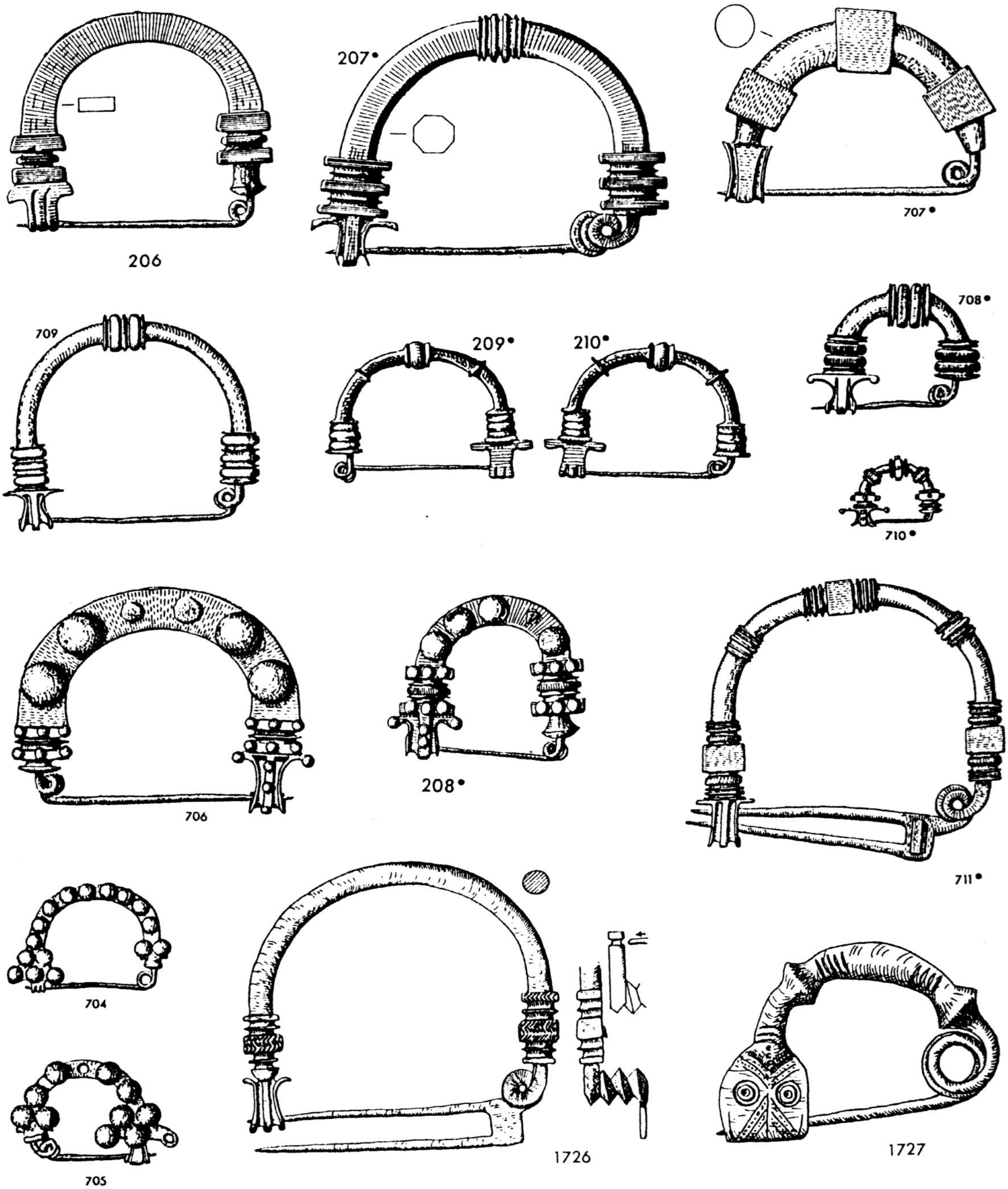

1–212 in **ARBB**
213–718 in **IARB**
719–1441 in **BoA**
1442–1729 in **ABOA**

Fig. 141 Phrygian brooches. C. 8th-7th century BC. Bottom right, a variant of the type.

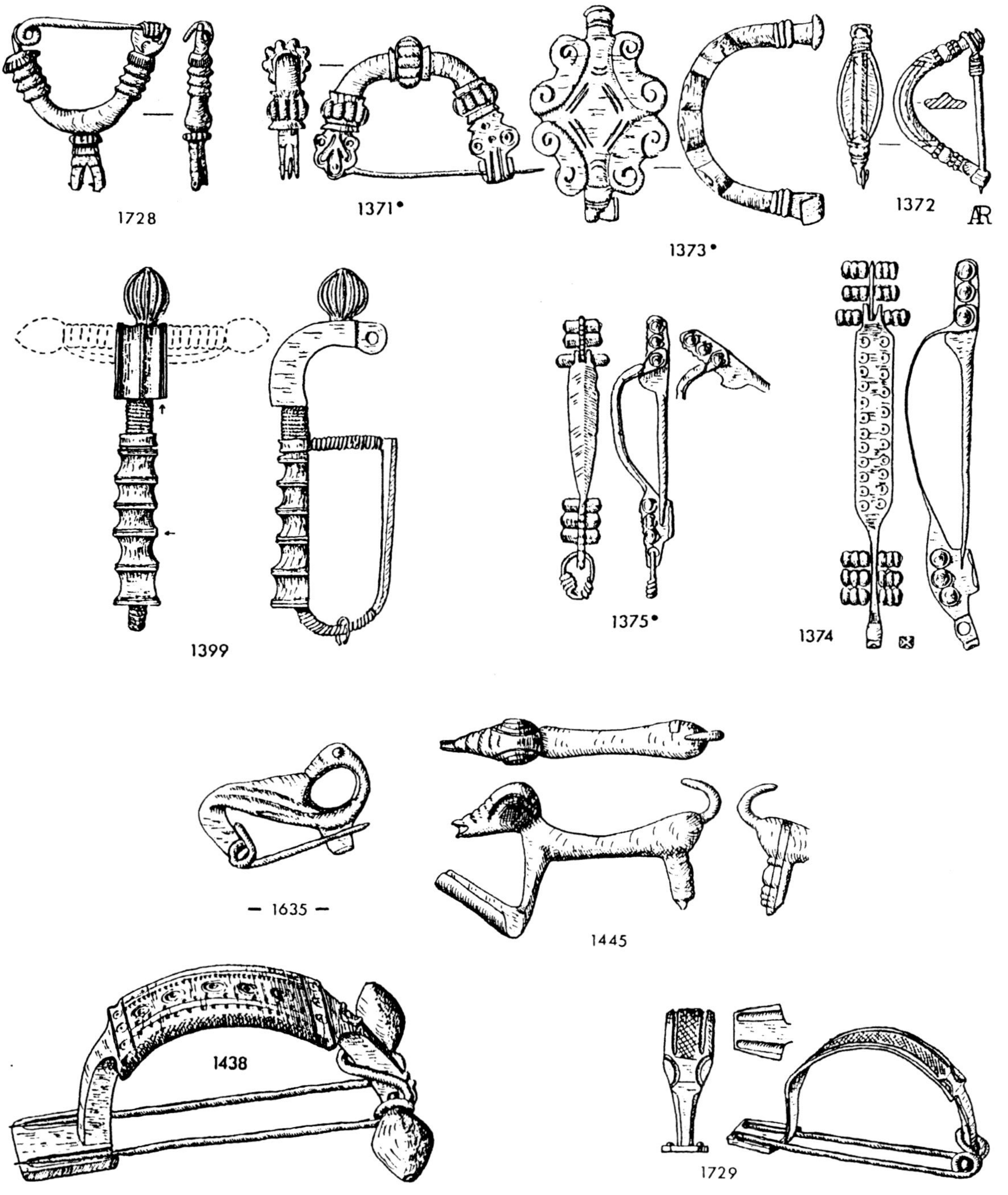

Fig. 142 East Mediterranean early brooches of various dates; and Mid-European Iron Age Animal brooches.

1–212 in ARBB
213–718 in IARB
719–1441 in BoA
1442–1729 in ABOA

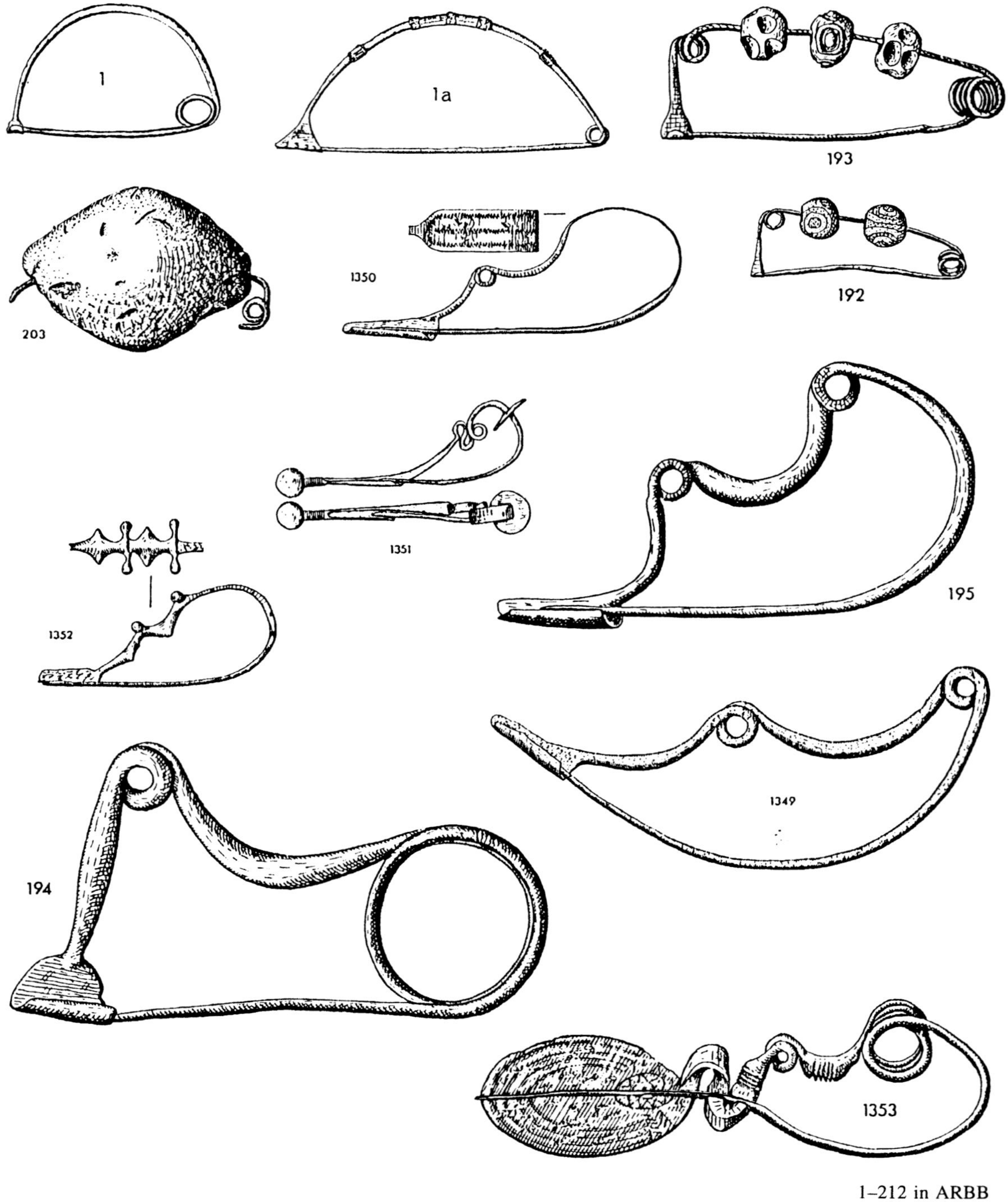

1–212 in ARBB
213–718 in IARB
719–1441 in BoA
1442–1729 in ABOA

Fig. 143 Italian brooches. 10–8th century BC.

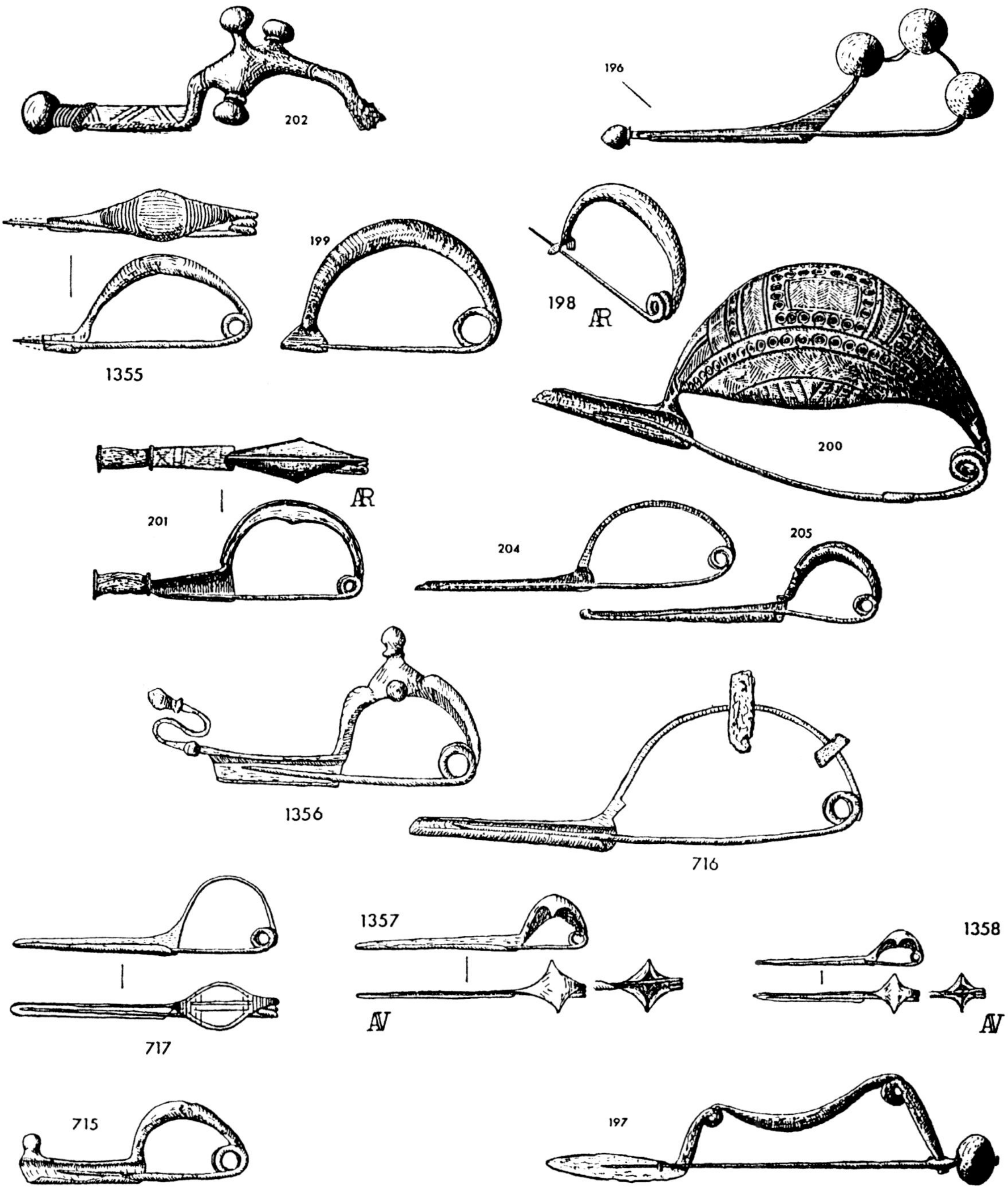

1–212 in **ARBB**
213–718 in **IARB**
719–1441 in **BoA**
1442–1729 in **ABOA**

Fig. 144 Italian brooches. 8th–5th century BC.

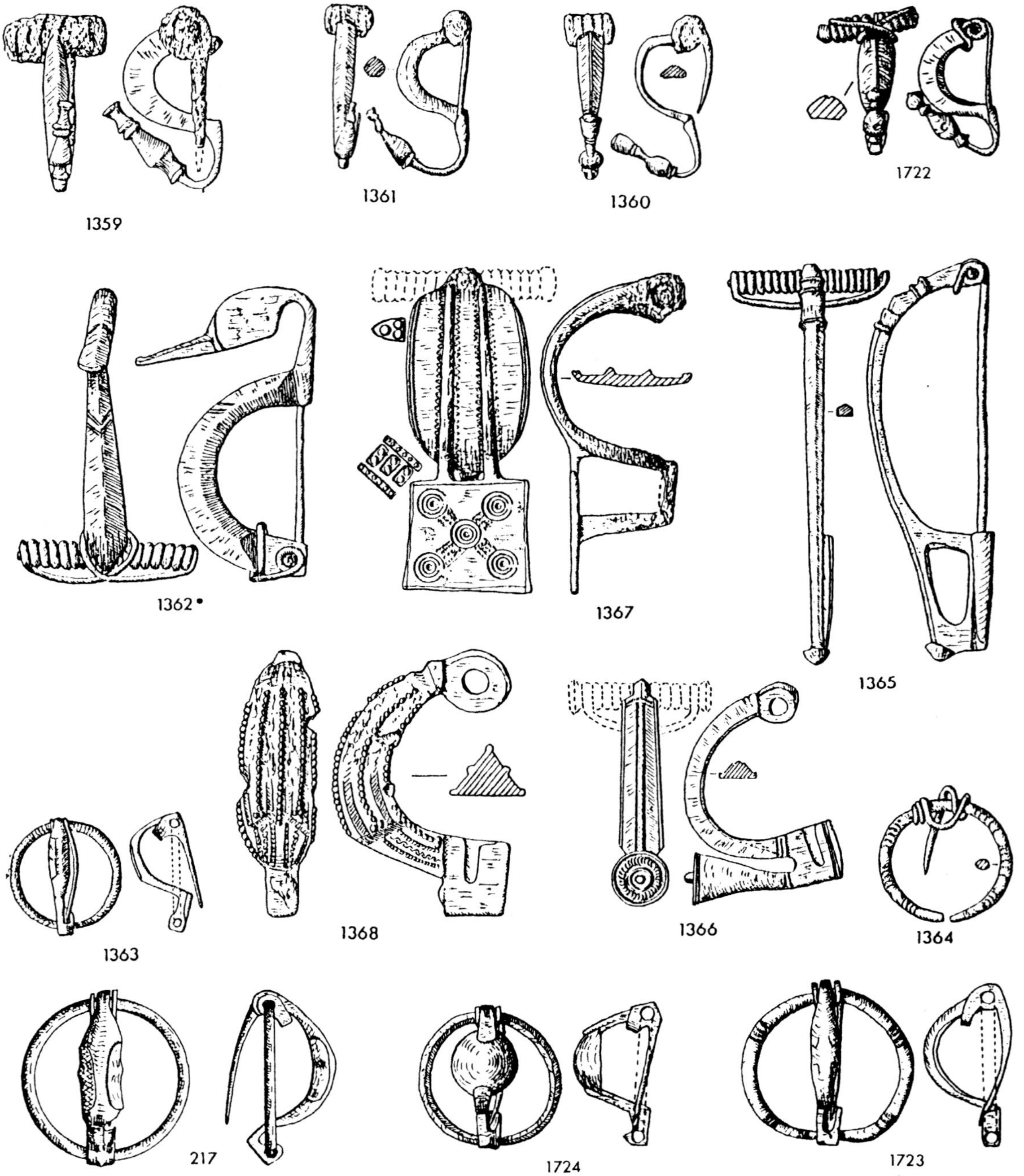

1–212 in **ARBB**
213–718 in **IARB**
719–1441 in **BoA**
1442–1729 in **ABOA**

Fig. 145 Iberian Iron Age brooches. c. 6th–3rd century BC.

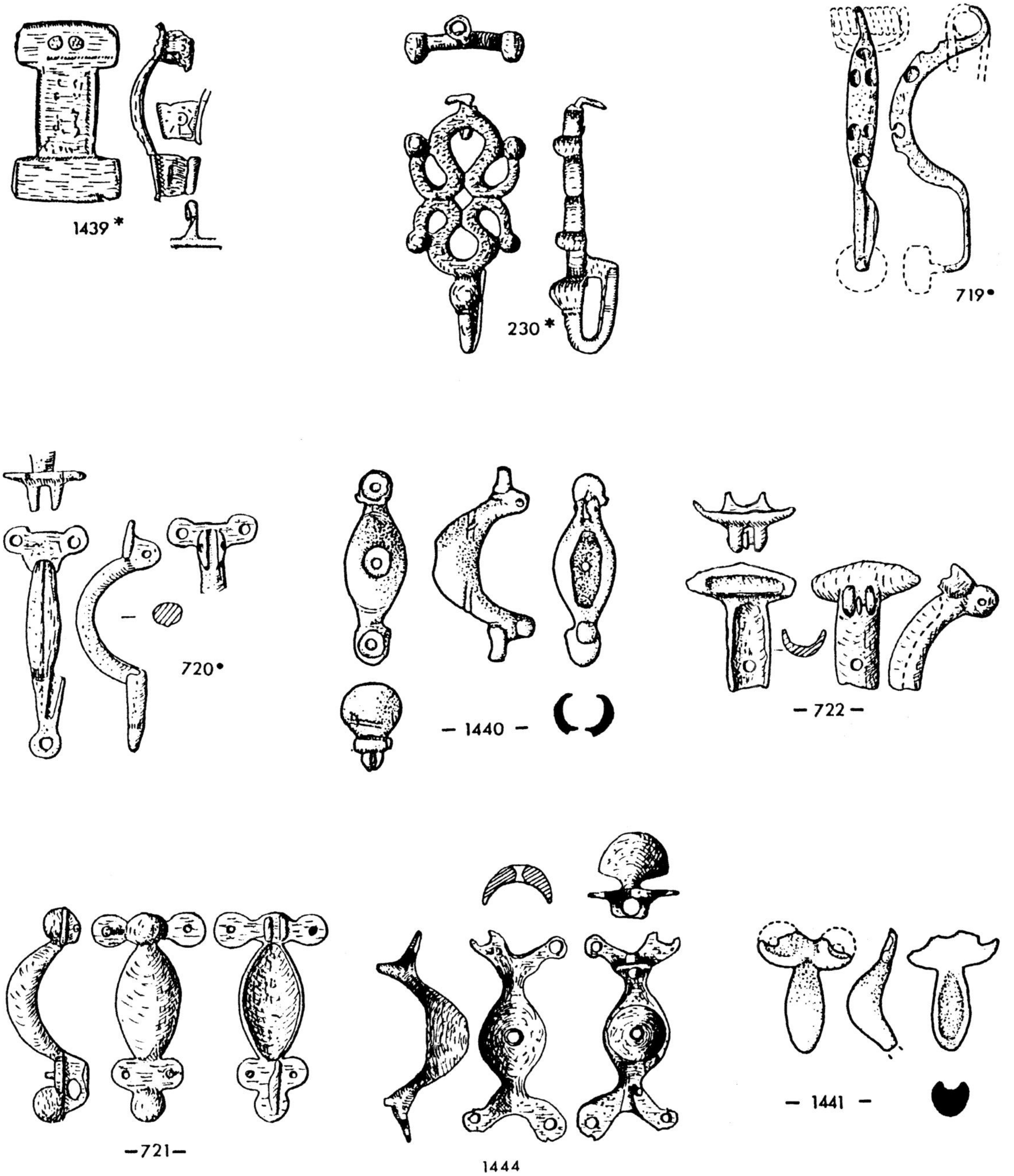

1–212 in ARBB
213–718 in IARB
719–1441 in BoA
1442–1729 in ABOA

Fig. 146 British Iron Age brooches, 6th–3rd century BC.

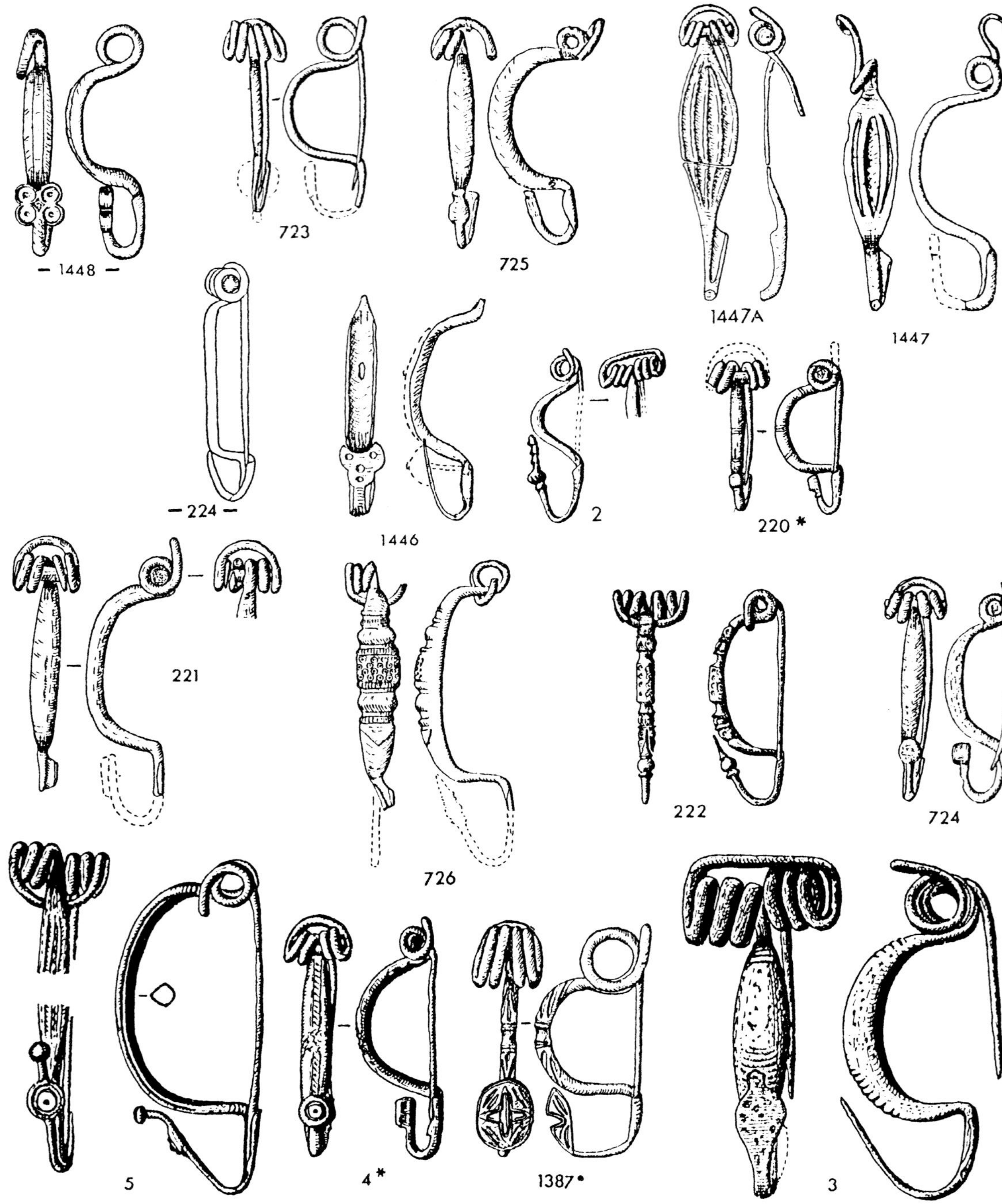

1–212 in ARBB
213–718 in IARB
719–1441 in BoA
1442–1729 in ABOA

Fig. 147 La Tène I type brooches. 4th–3rd century BC.

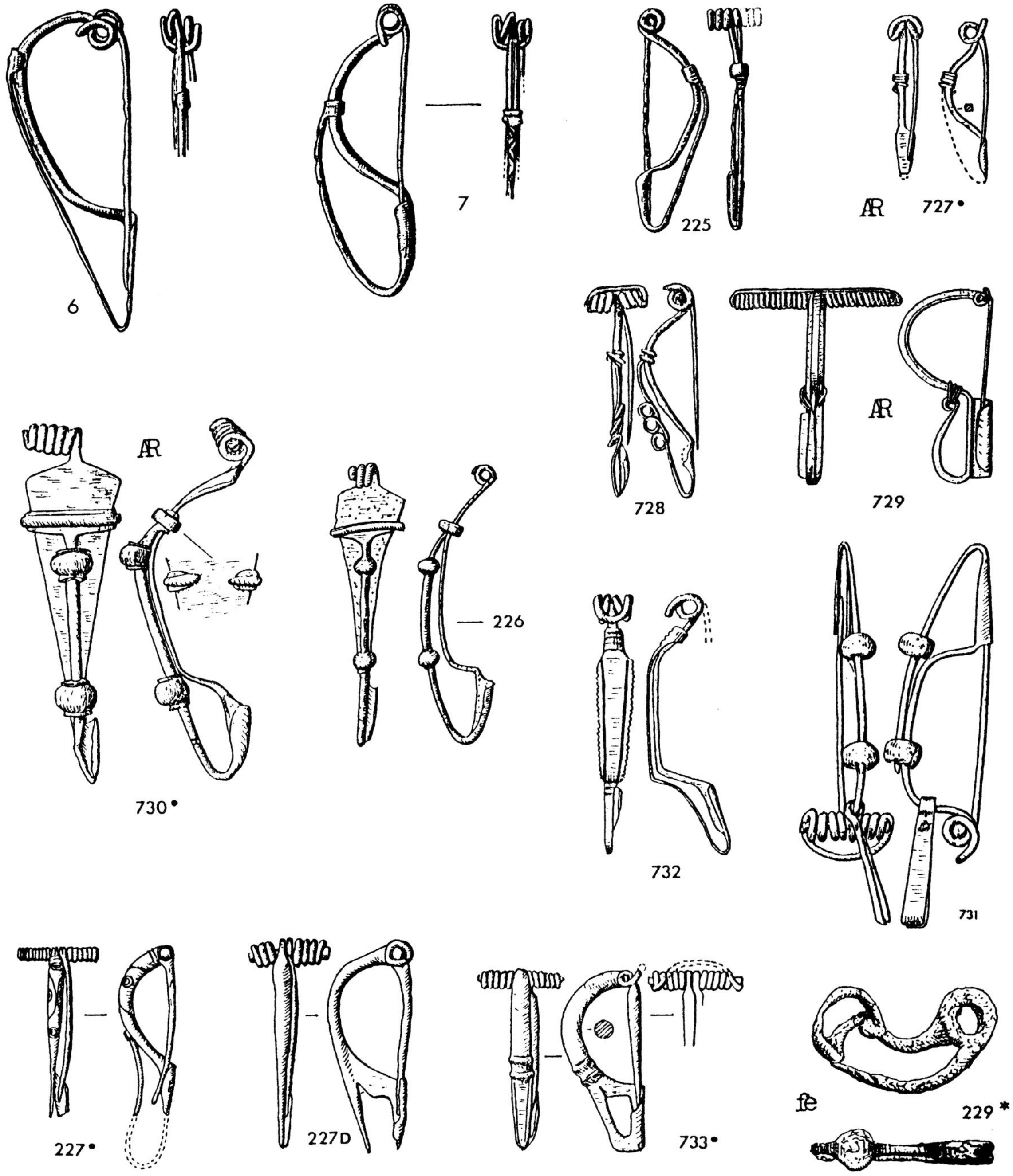

Fig. 148 La Tène II type brooches. 2nd–1st century BC. Below: 227, a variant; 227D and 733, Glastonbury type; 229, Involute type.

1–212 in **ARBB**
213–718 in **IARB**
719–1441 in **BoA**
1442–1729 in **ABOA**

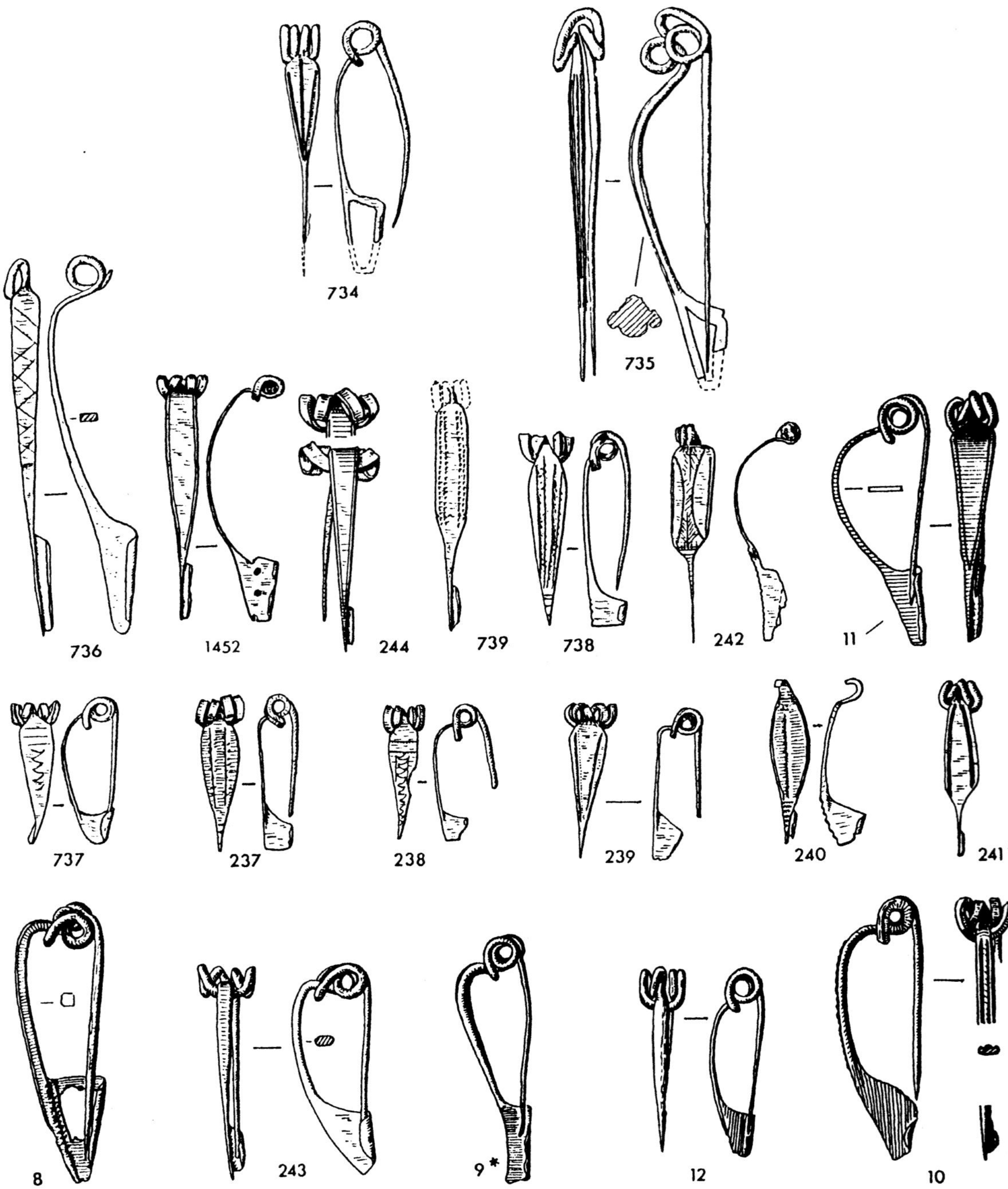

Fig. 149 La Tène III type brooches. 1st century BC/AD. 734–735, Nauheim type progenitors.

1–212 in **ARBB**
213–718 in **IARB**
719–1441 in **BoA**
1442–1729 in **ABOA**

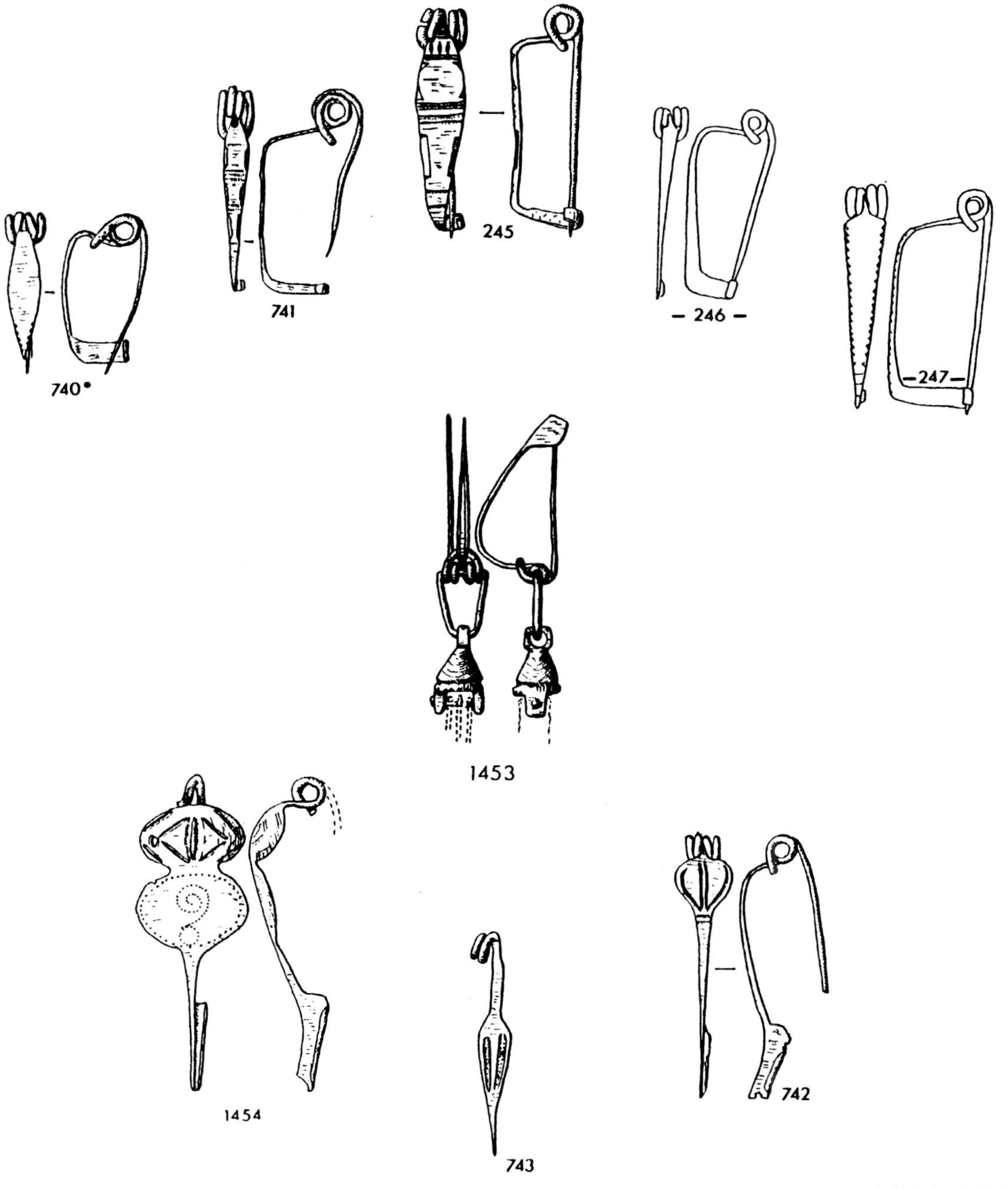

1–212 in ARBB
213–718 in IARB
719–1441 in BoA
1442–1729 in ABOA

Fig. 150 La Tène III brooches. Above, Winchester type; below, oddities.

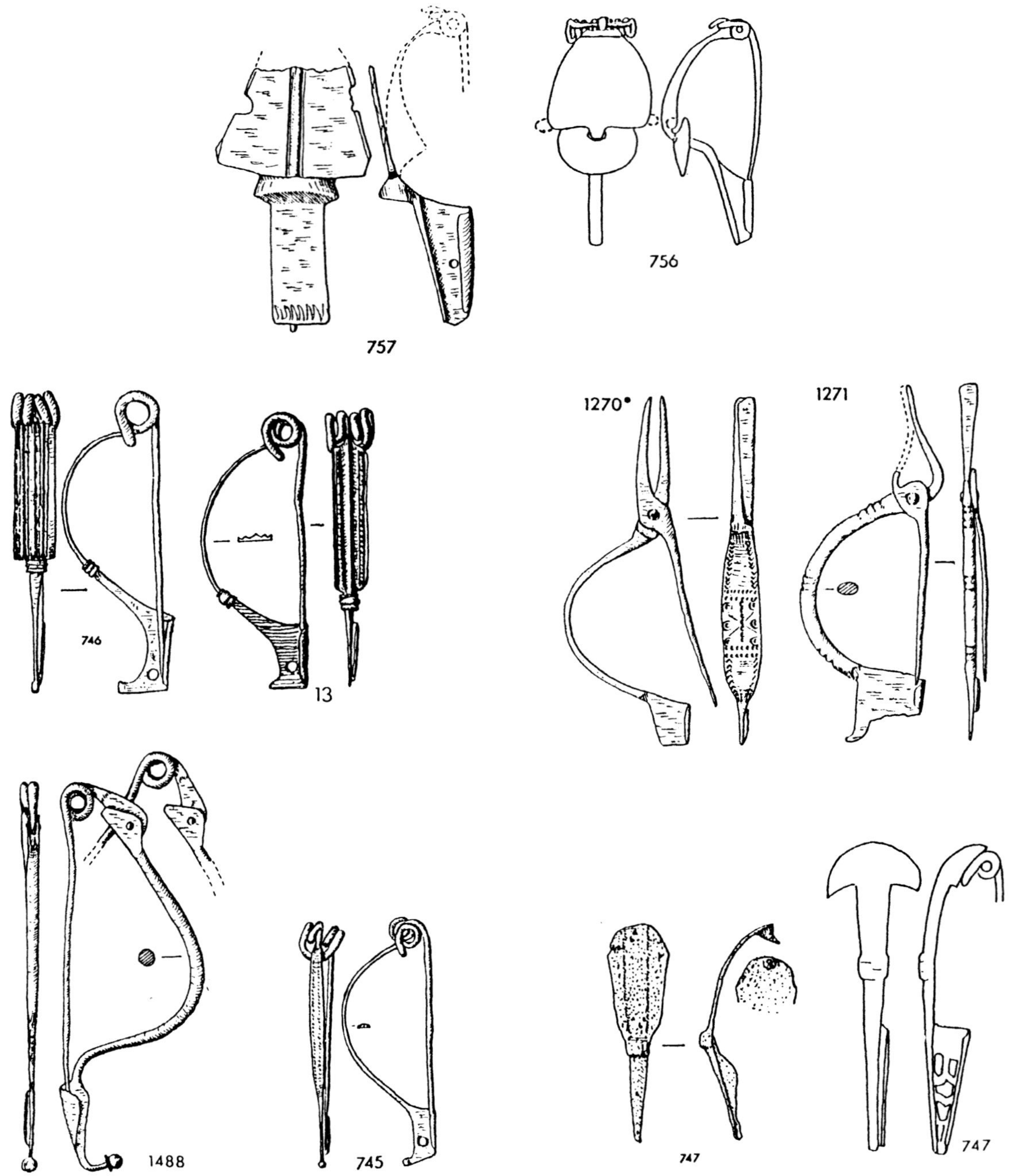

1–212 in ARBB
213–718 in IARB
719–1441 in BoA
1442–1729 in ABOA

Fig. 151 European brooches of the 1st century BC/AD. Above, Kragenfibeln; centre, Jezerine and Pincer types; below Gorica type and Schüsselfibel.

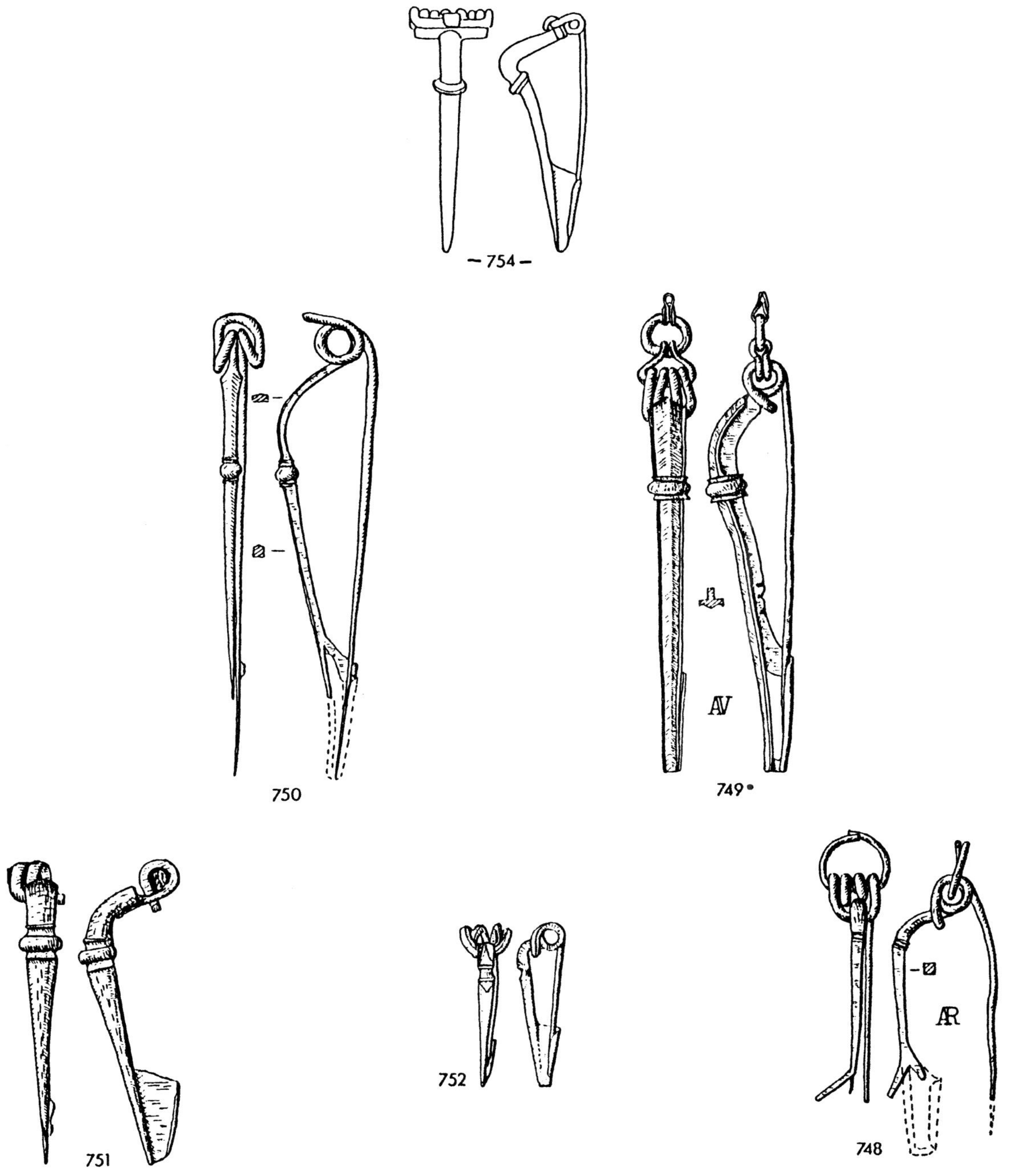

Fig. 152 European brooches of the 1st century BC/AD. 754, Knickfibel; remainder Knotenfibeln.

1–212 in **ARBB**
213–718 in **IARB**
719–1441 in **BoA**
1442–1729 in **ABOA**

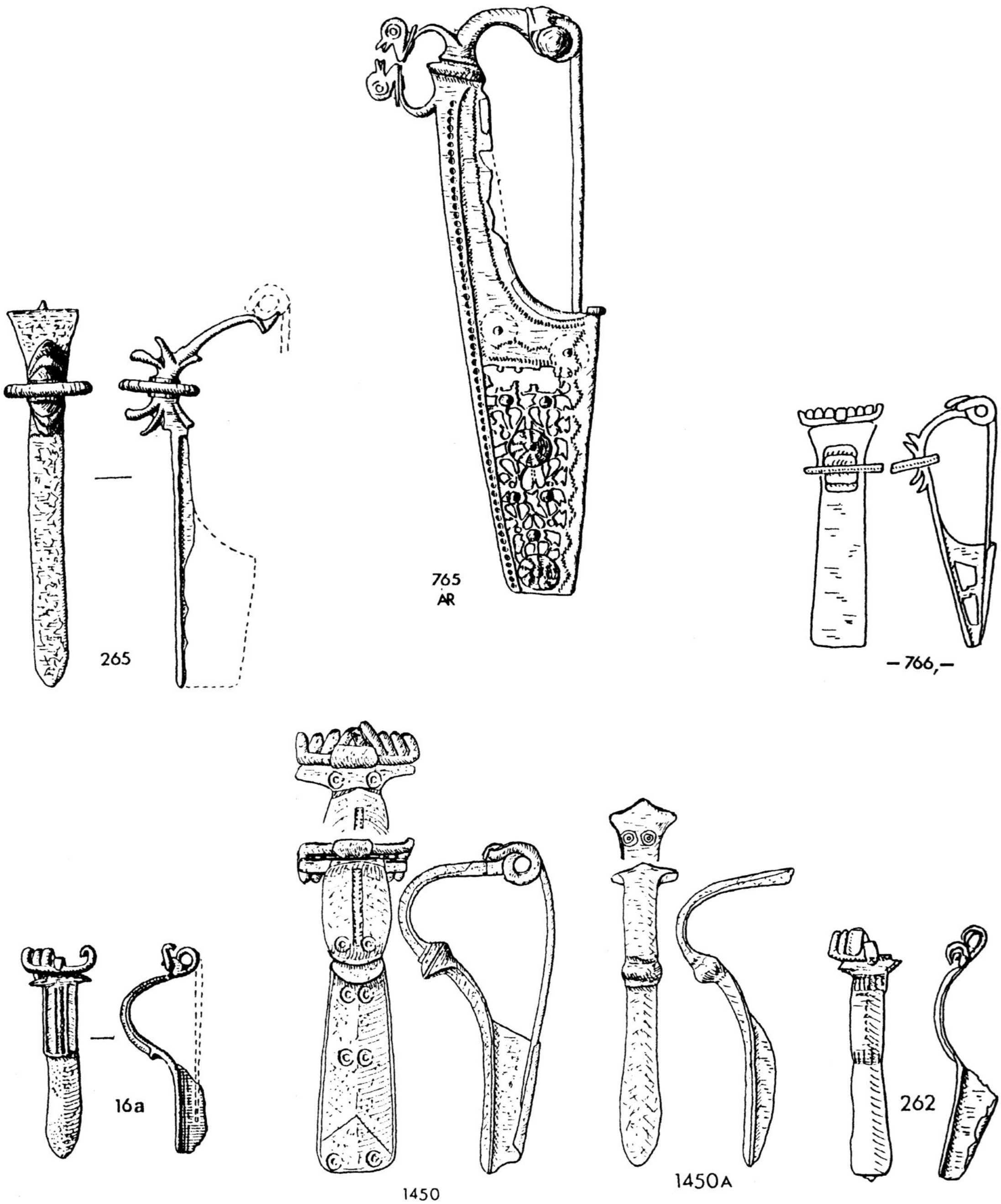

Fig. 153 European brooches of the 1st century AD. Above, Flugelfibel; centre, fibules à ailettes; below, Eye type.

1–212 in **ARBB**
213–718 in **IARB**
719–1441 in **BoA**
1442–1729 in **ABOA**

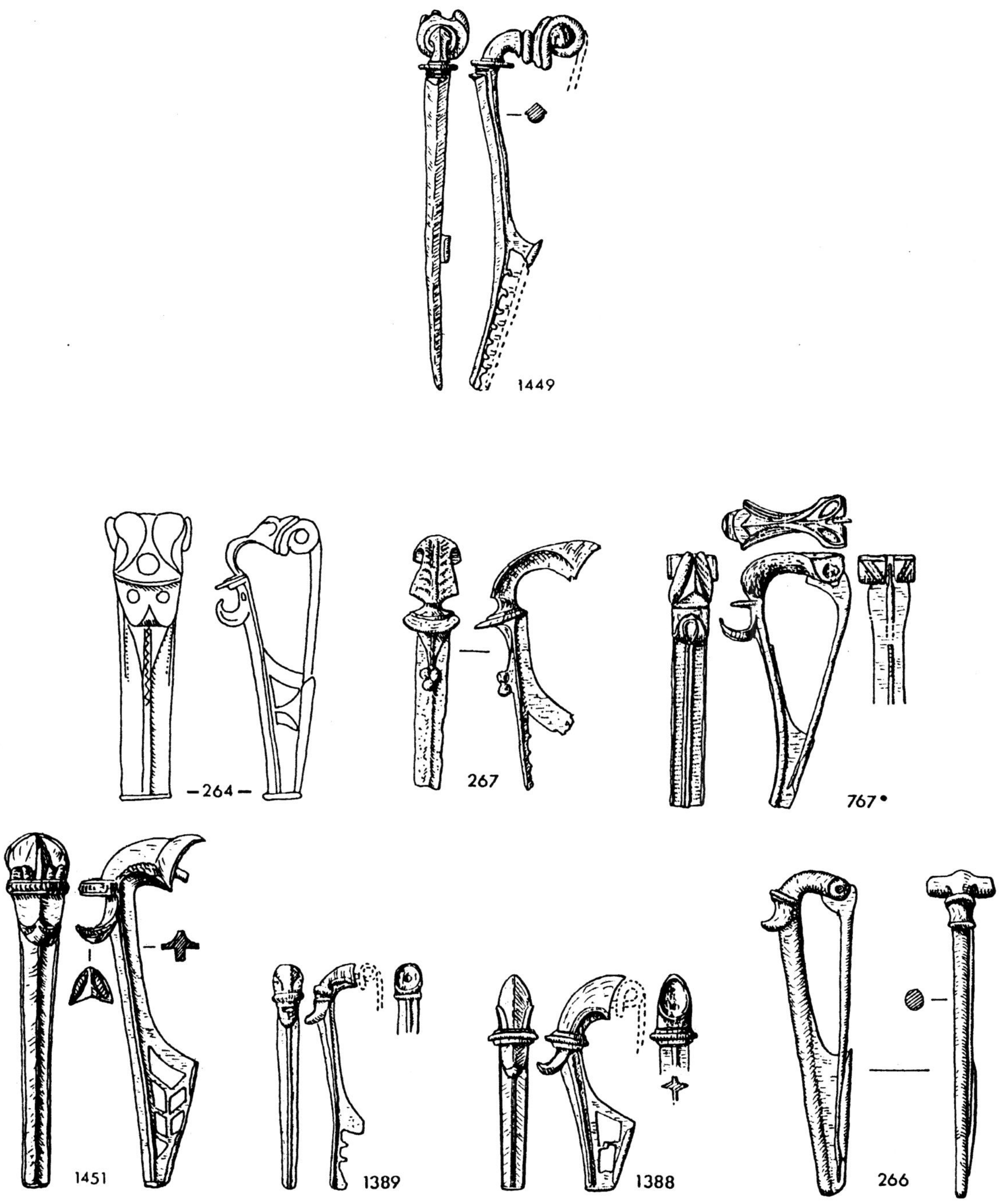

1–212 in ARBB
213–718 in IARB
719–1441 in BoA
1442–1729 in ABOA

Fig. 154 British bow brooches of the 1st century AD. 1449, Aylesford type; below, Birdlip type.

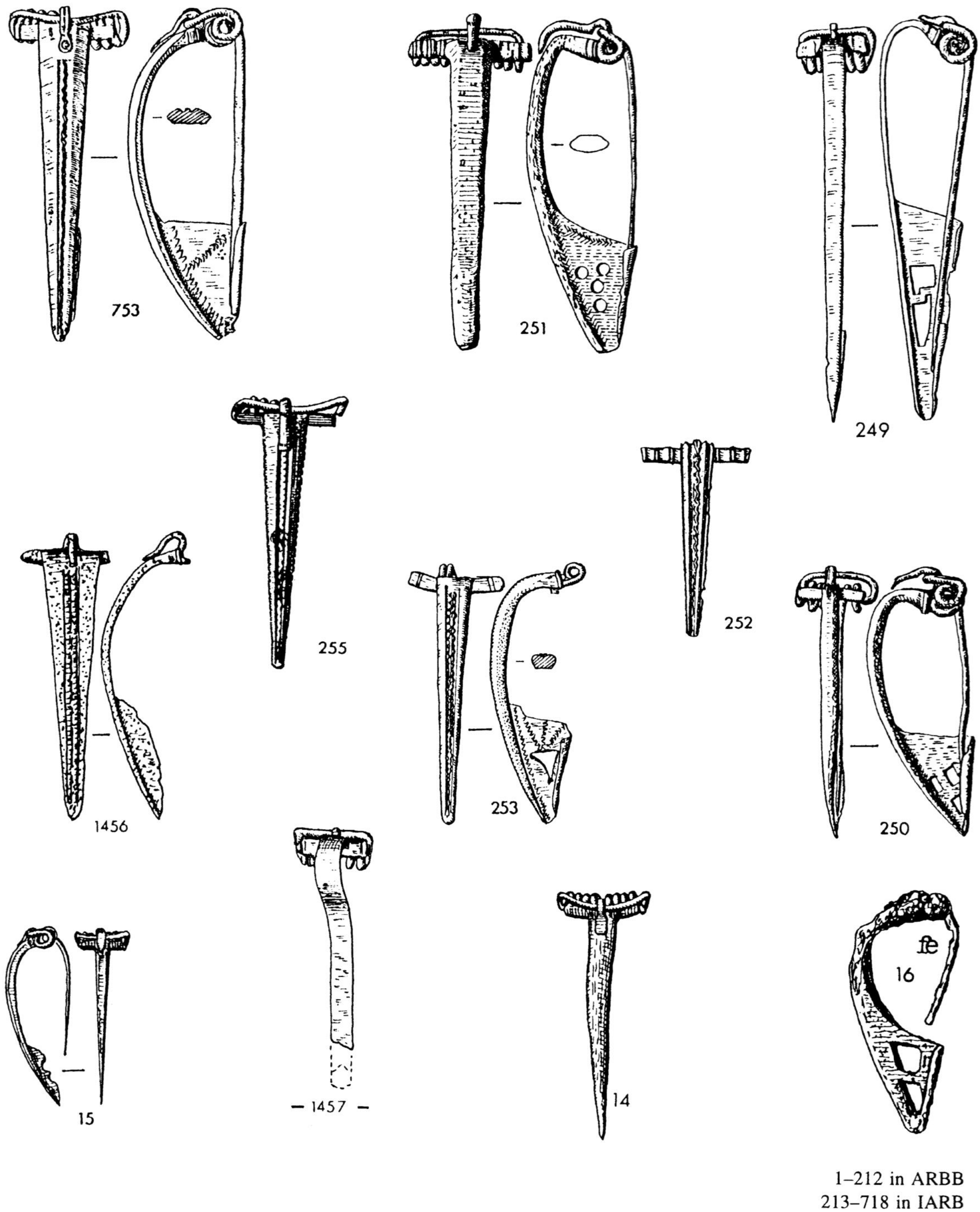

1–212 in ARBB
213–718 in IARB
719–1441 in BoA
1442–1729 in ABOA

Fig. 155 Colchester type one-piece brooches. 1st century AD.

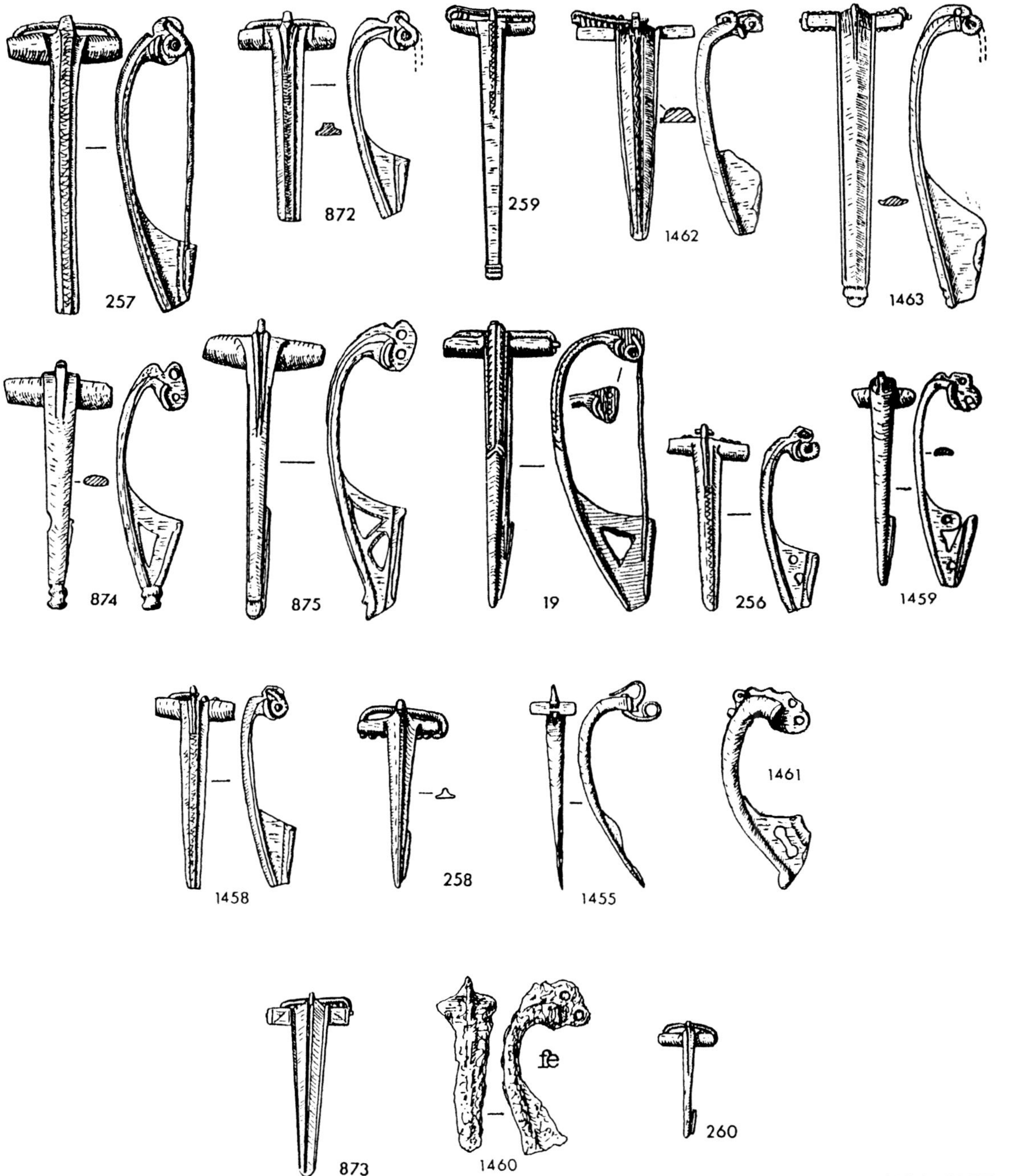

1–212 in **ARBB**
213–718 in **IARB**
719–1441 in **BoA**
1442–1729 in **ABOA**

Fig. 156 Colchester type two-piece brooches. 1st century AD.

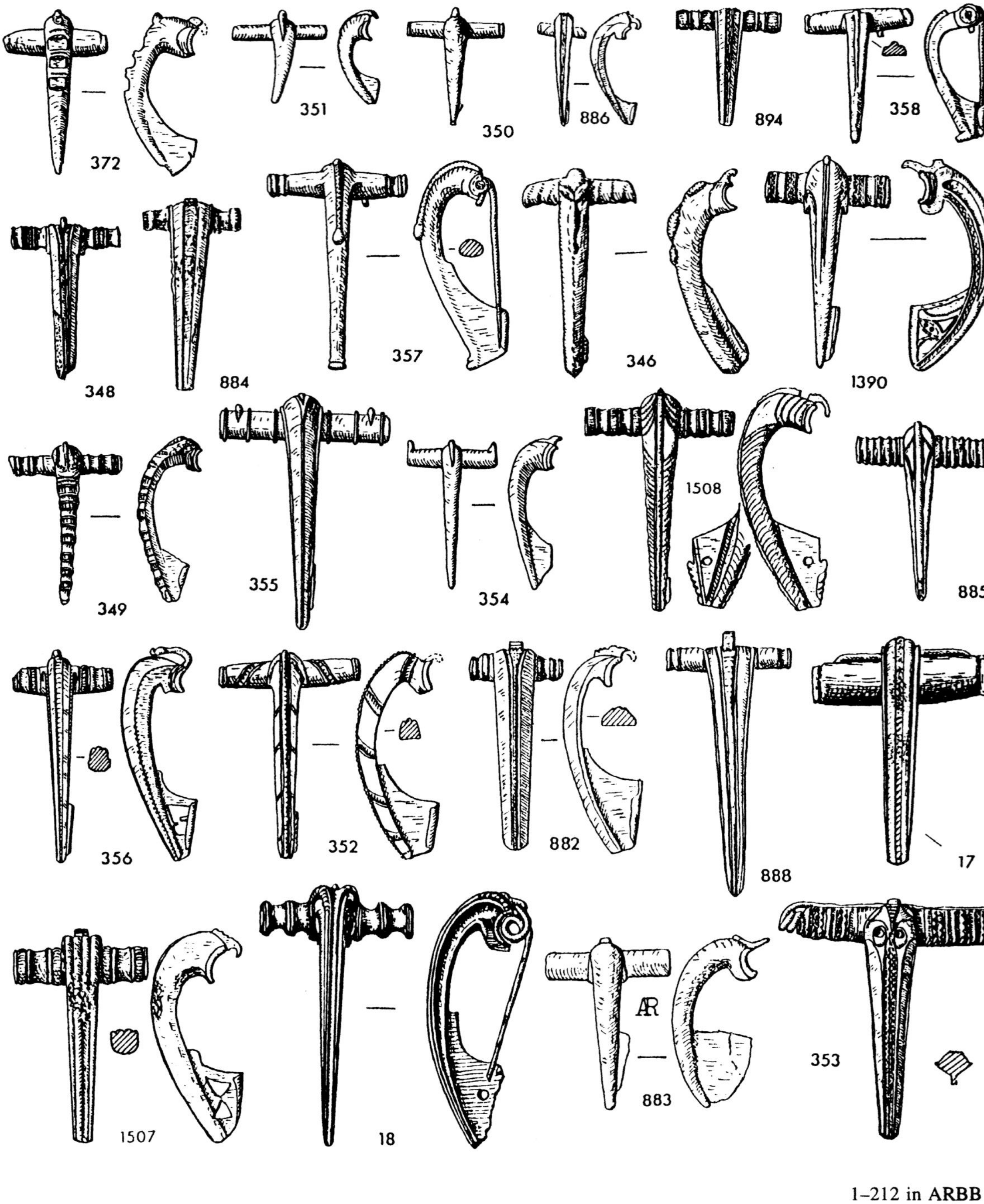

1–212 in ARBB
213–718 in IARB
719–1441 in BoA
1442–1729 in ABOA

Fig. 157 Dolphin type brooches with spring mechanism, 1st century AD.

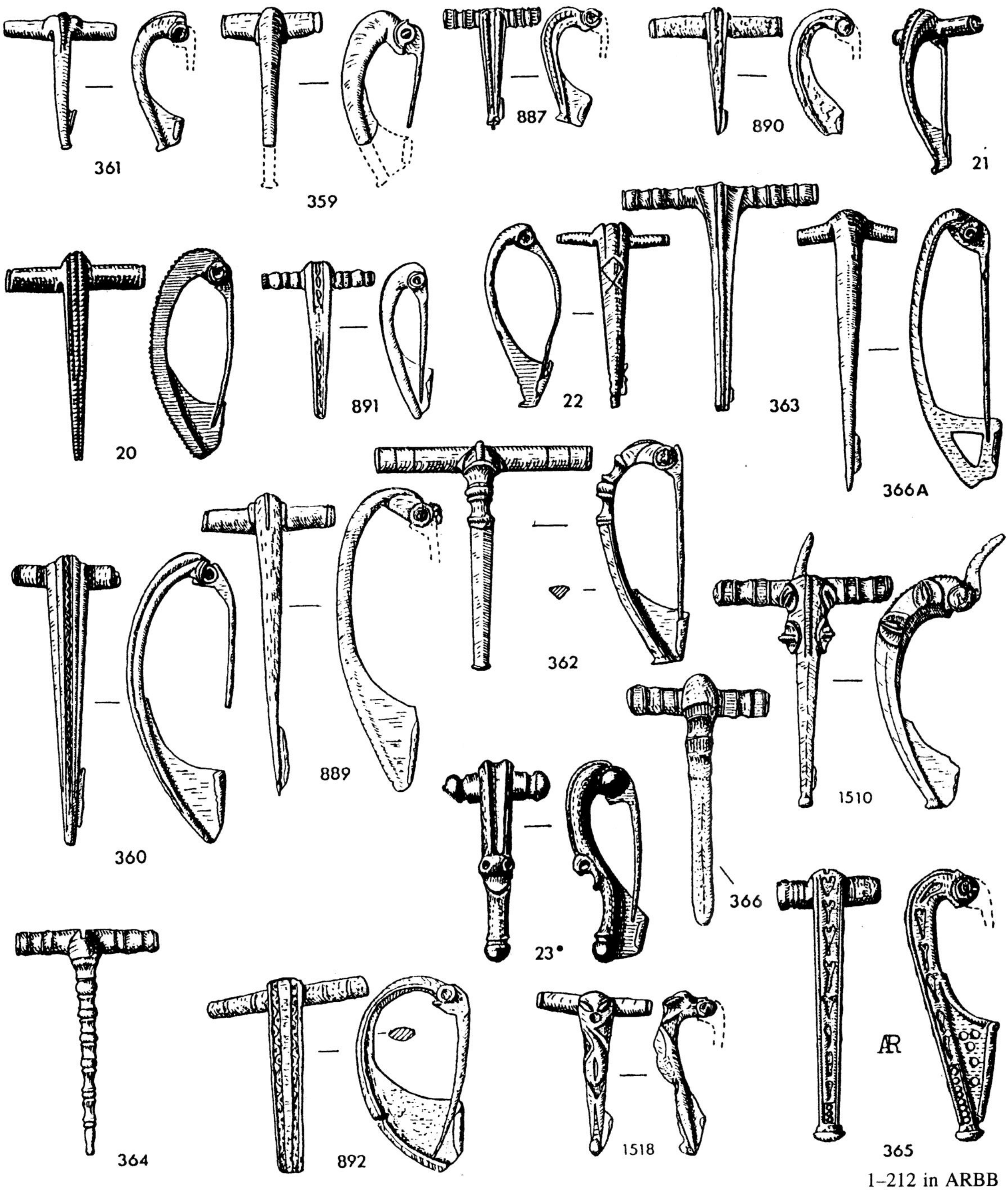

1–212 in ARBB
213–718 in IARB
719–1441 in BoA
1442–1729 in ABOA

Fig. 158 Dolphin type brooches with hinge mechanism, 1st century AD.

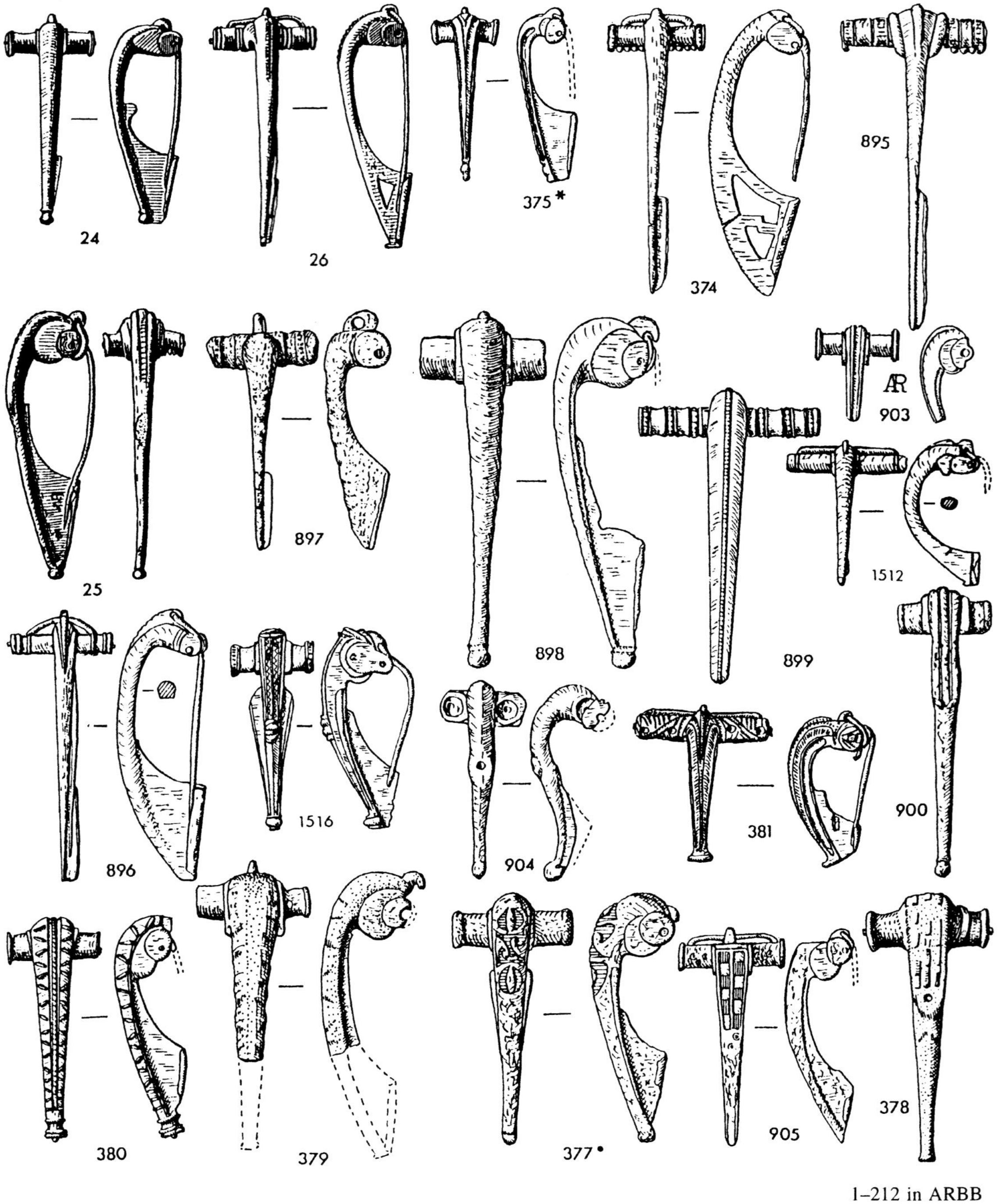

1–212 in ARBB
213–718 in IARB
719–1441 in BoA
1442–1729 in ABOA

Fig. 159 Polden Hill type brooches, 1st century AD.

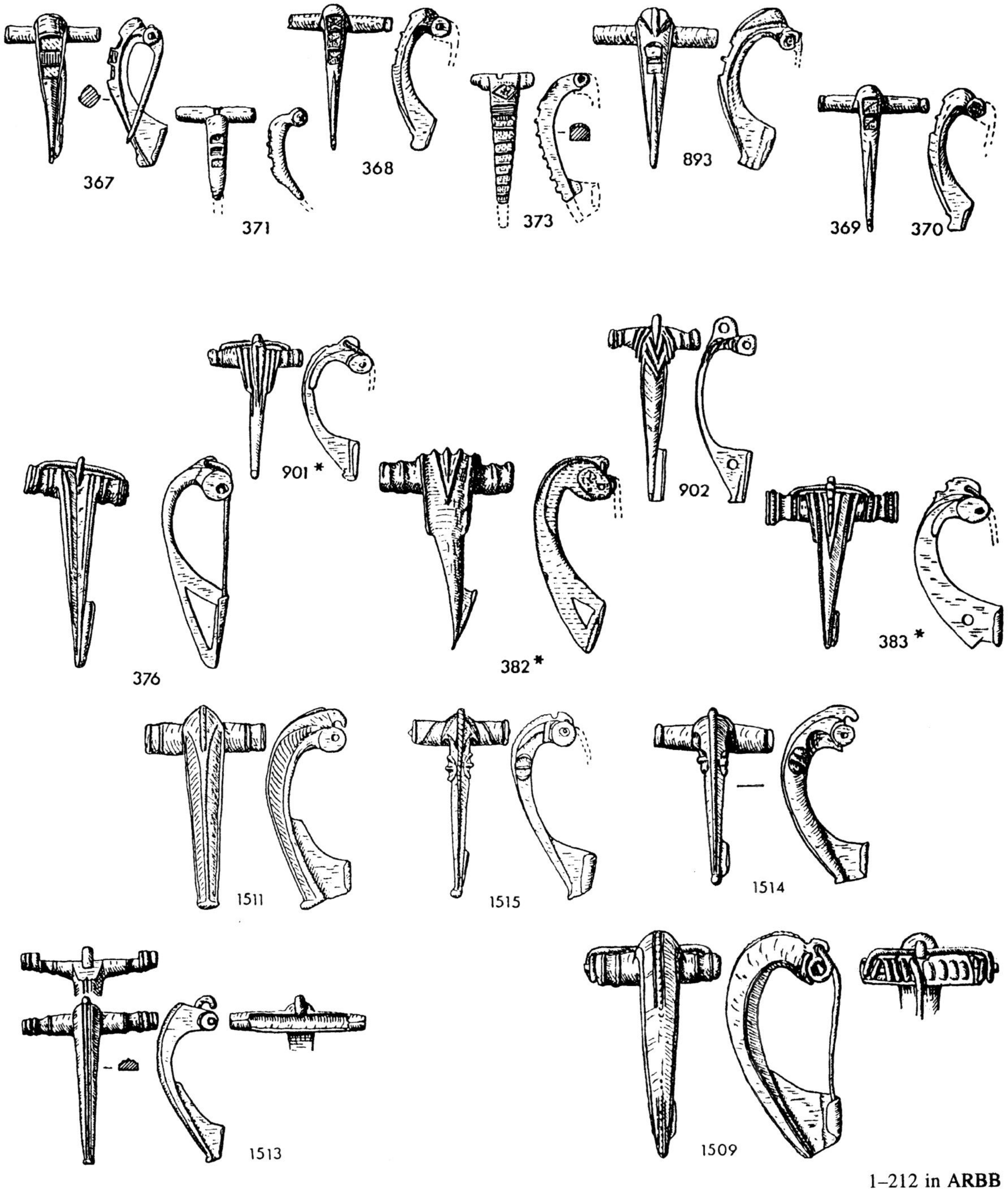

Fig. 160 Dolphin and Polden Hill variants, 1st century AD. Above, Dolphin hinged variants with slotted enamel; centre, Polden Hills with varied appendages; below, odd mouldings and mechanisms.

1–212 in **ARBB**
213–718 in **IARB**
719–1441 in **BoA**
1442–1729 in **ABOA**

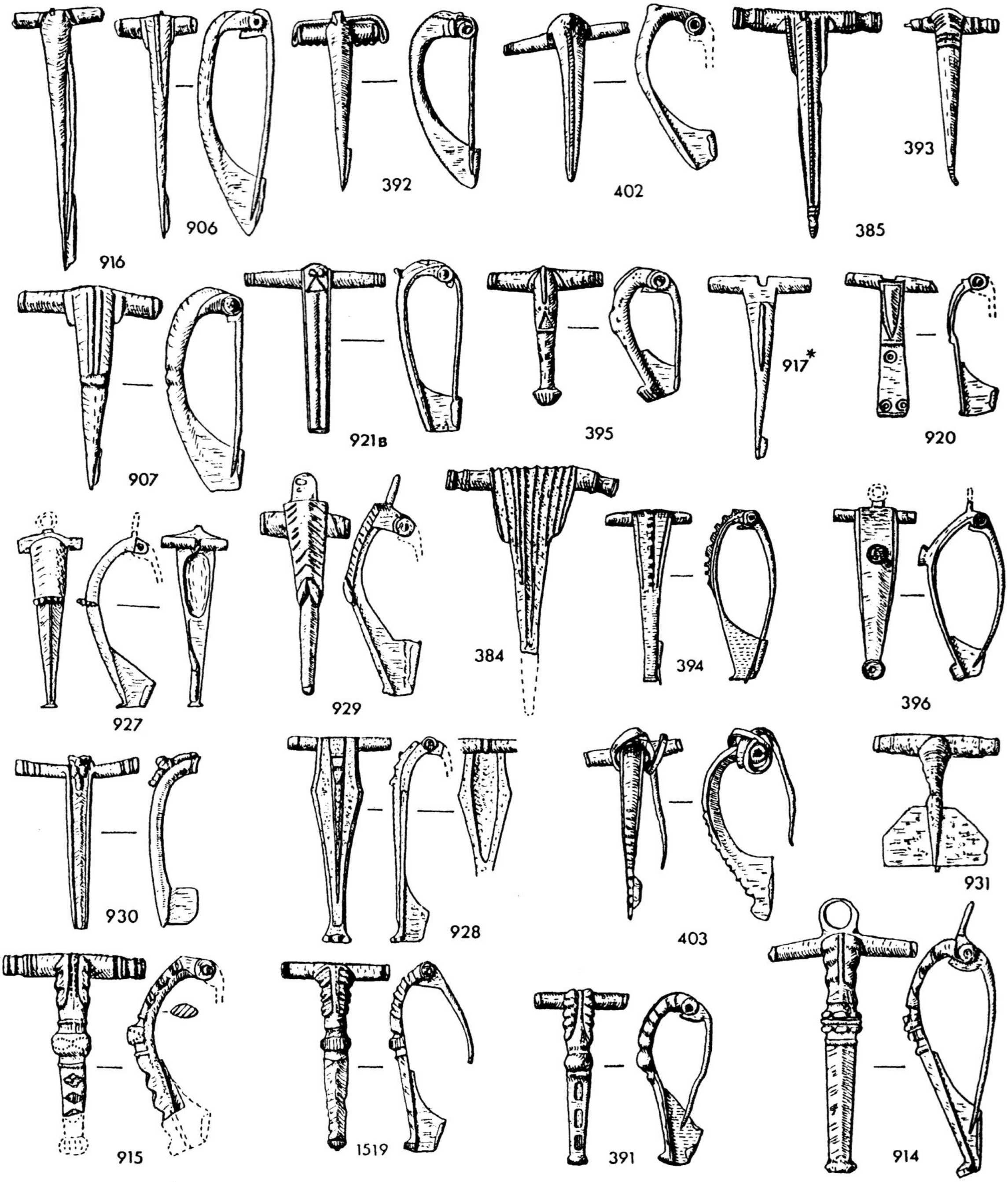

1–212 in **ARBB**
213–718 in **IARB**
719–1441 in **BoA**
1442–1729 in **ABOA**

Fig. 161 T-shape brooches, 1st–2nd century AD. Various forms. Bottom row, Wilsford type.

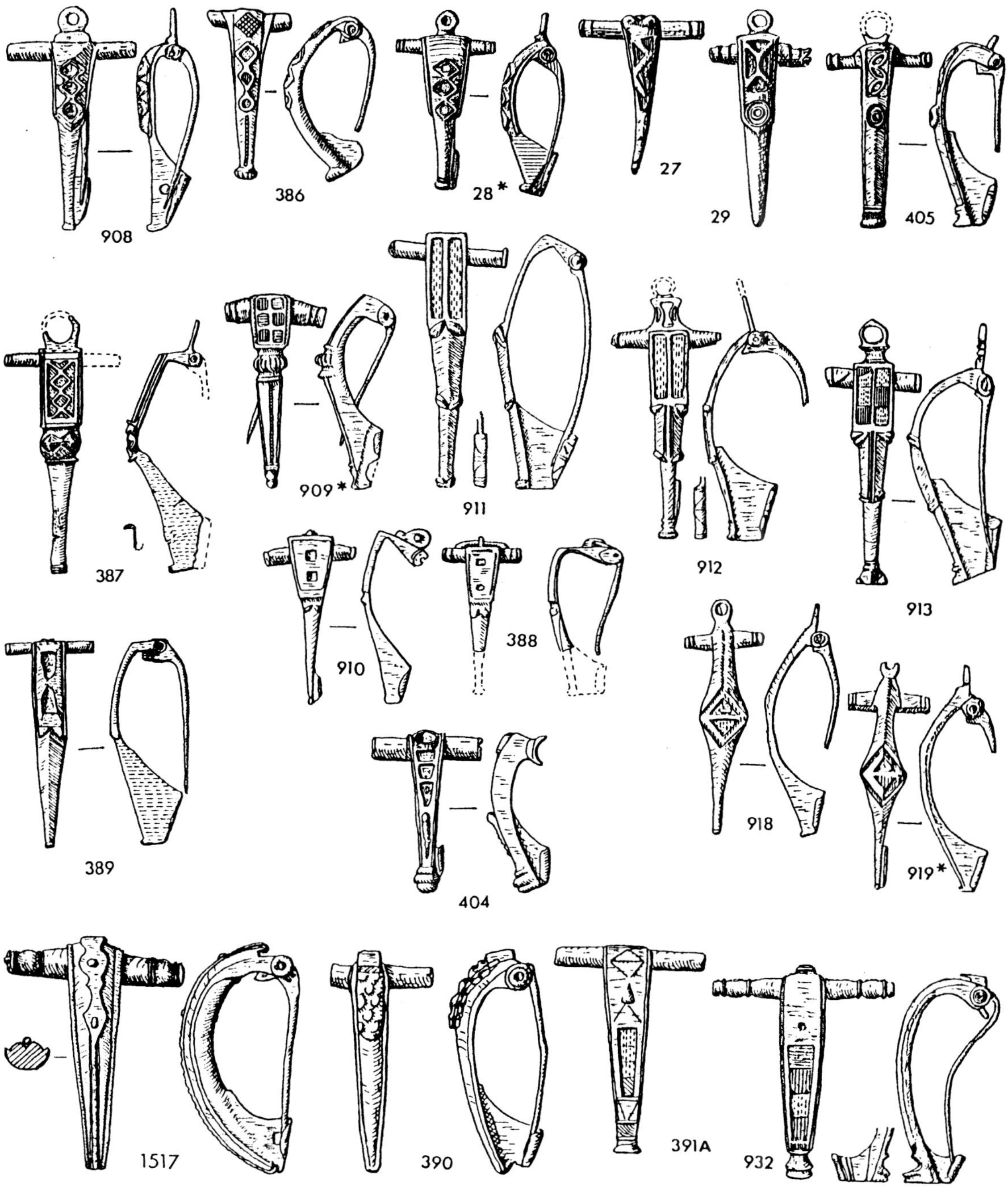

Fig. 162 T-shape brooches, 1st–2nd century AD. Enamelled types, and (bottom left) with applied hook.

1–212 in ARBB
213–718 in IARB
719–1441 in BoA
1442–1729 in ABOA

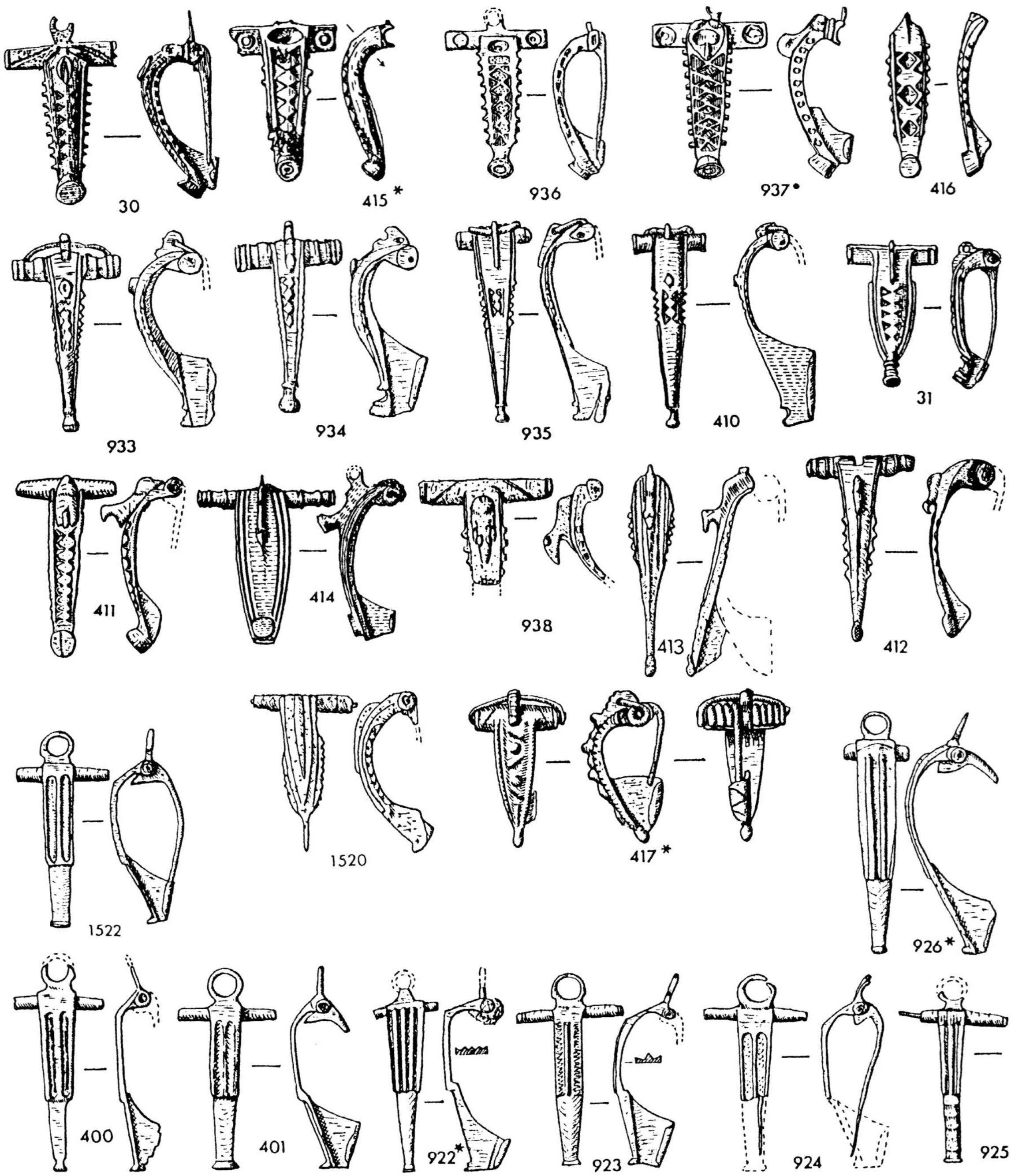

1–212 in ARBB
213–718 in IARB
719–1441 in BoA
1442–1729 in ABOA

Fig. 163 T-shape brooches, 1st–2nd century AD. Above, Sawfish and allied types; below, Dorset type.

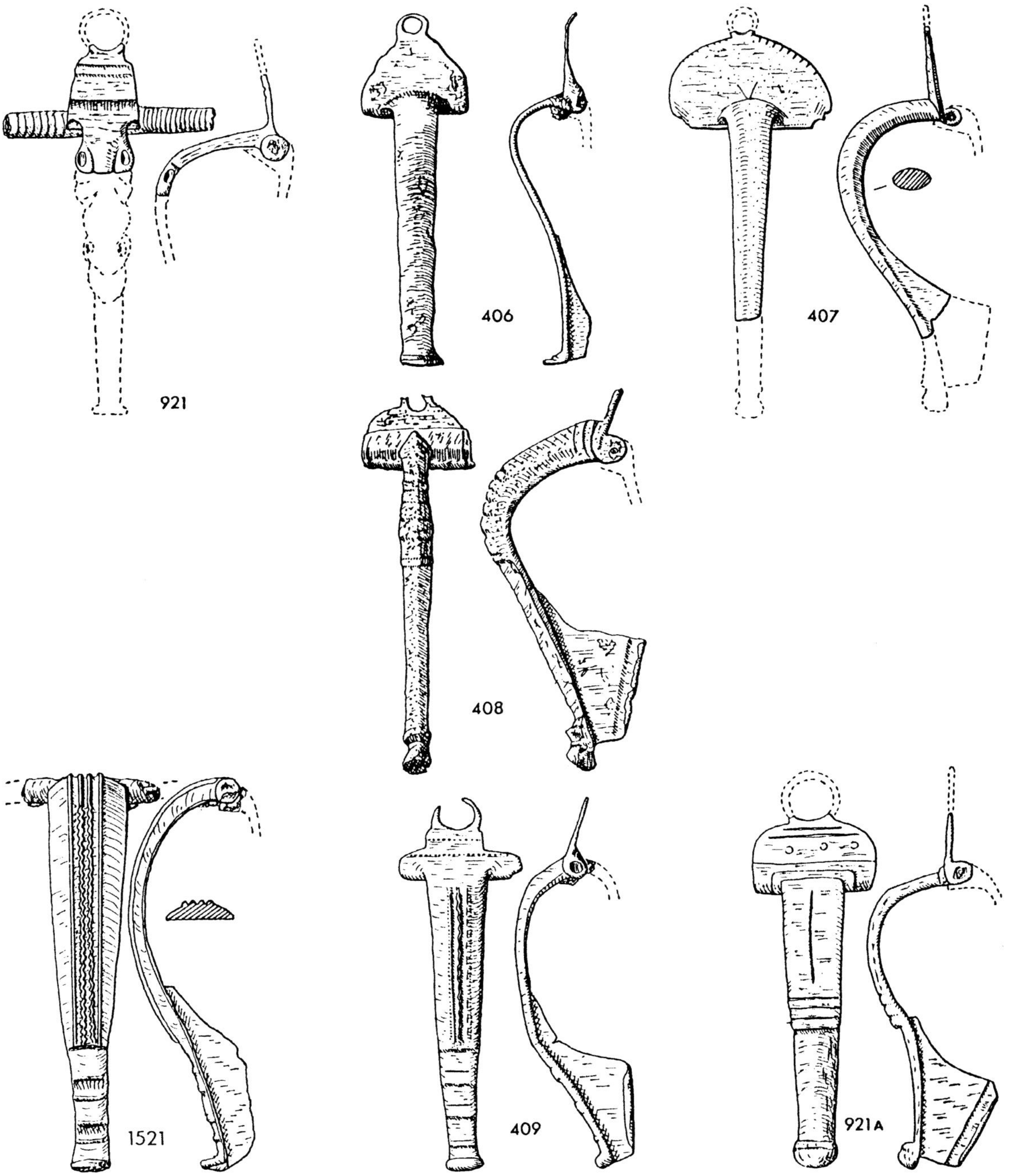

1–212 in **ARBB**
213–718 in **IARB**
719–1441 in **BoA**
1442–1729 in **ABOA**

Fig. 164 T-Shape brooches, plate-headed. Probably 2nd century AD.

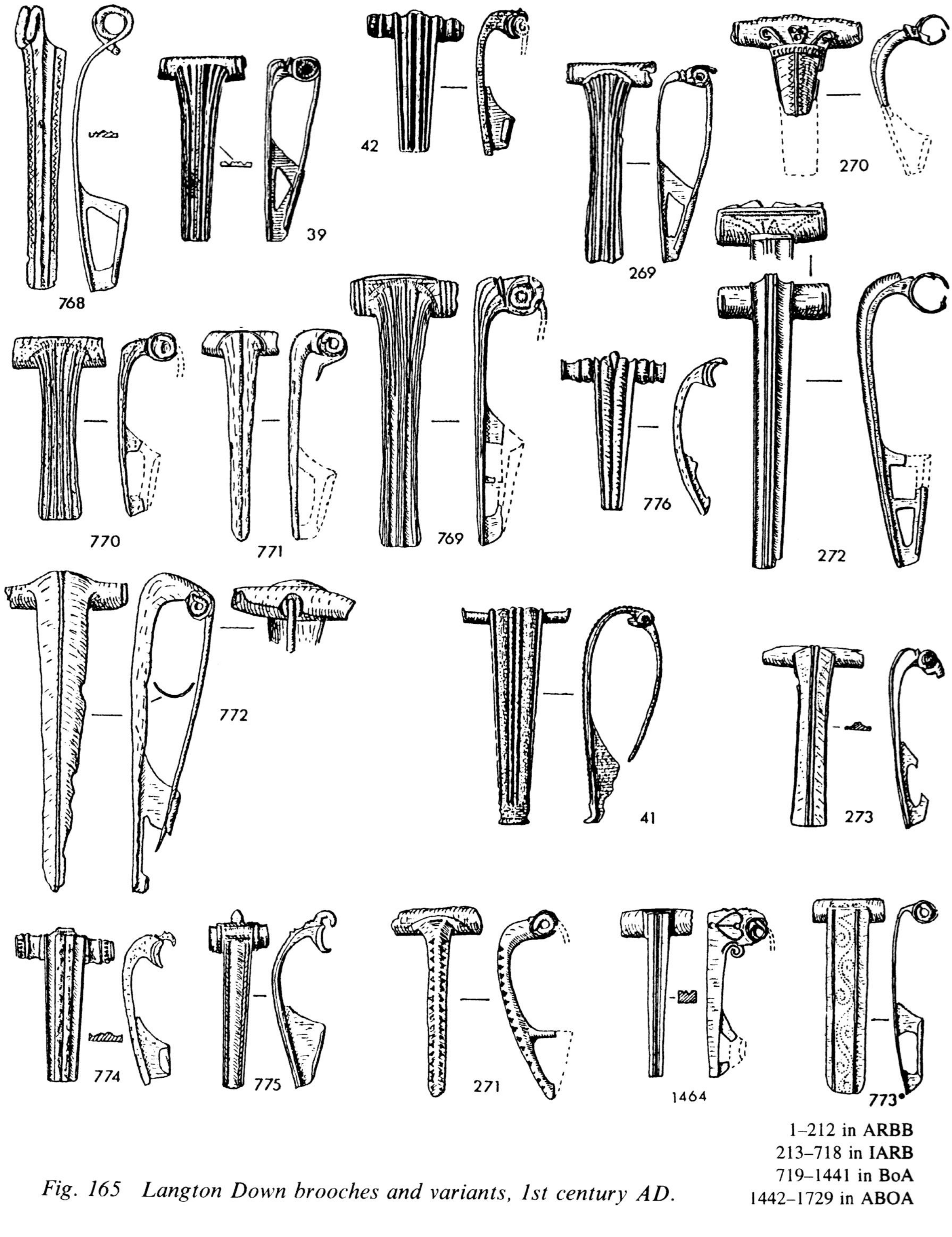

Fig. 165 Langton Down brooches and variants, 1st century AD.

1–212 in ARBB
213–718 in IARB
719–1441 in BoA
1442–1729 in ABOA

1–212 in ARBB
213–718 in IARB
719–1441 in BoA
1442–1729 in ABOA

Fig. 166 Lion bow brooches and derivatives. 1st century AD.

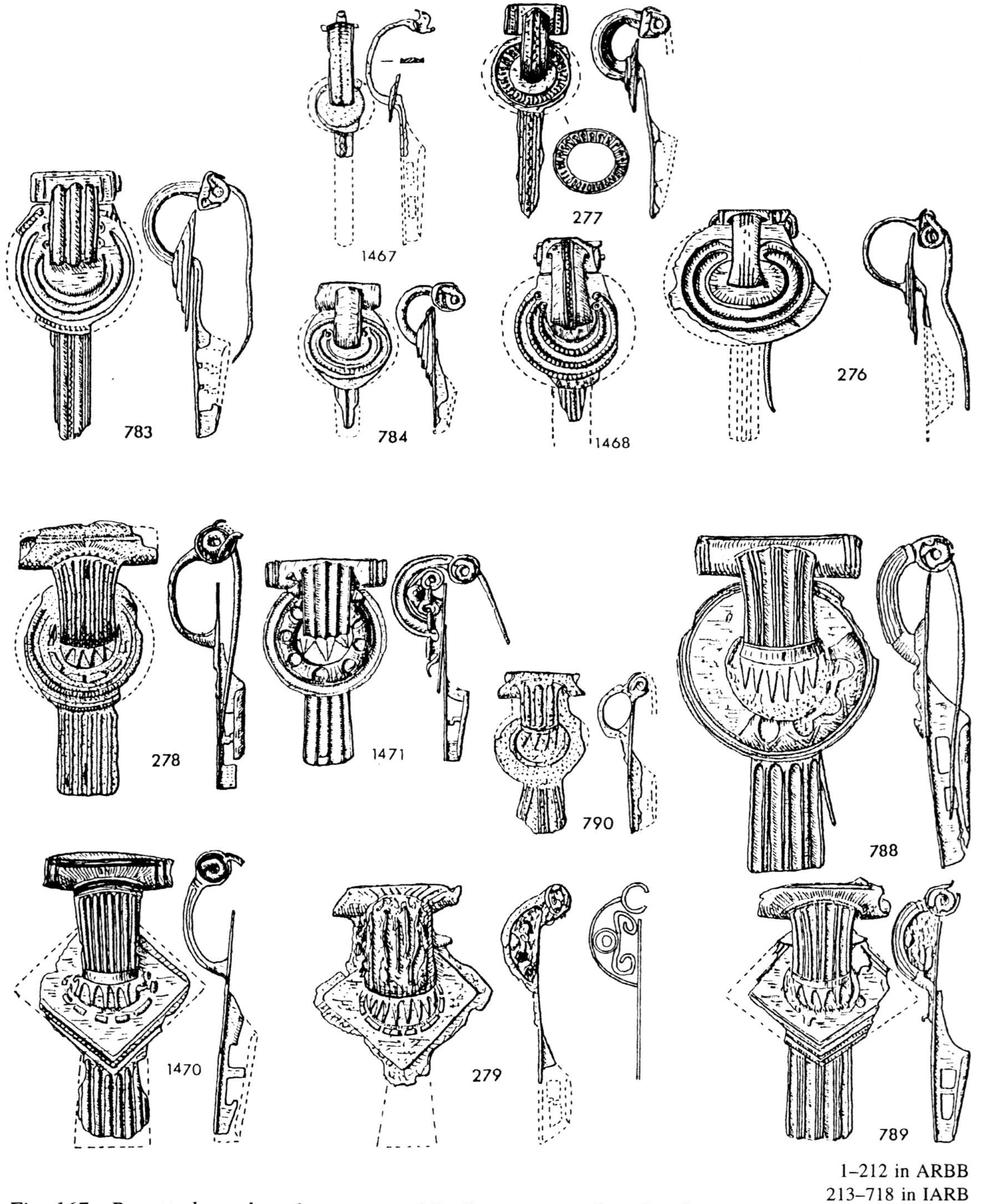

Fig. 167 Rosette brooches, 1st century AD. Prototype and earlier forms above.

1–212 in ARBB
213–718 in IARB
719–1441 in BoA
1442–1729 in ABOA

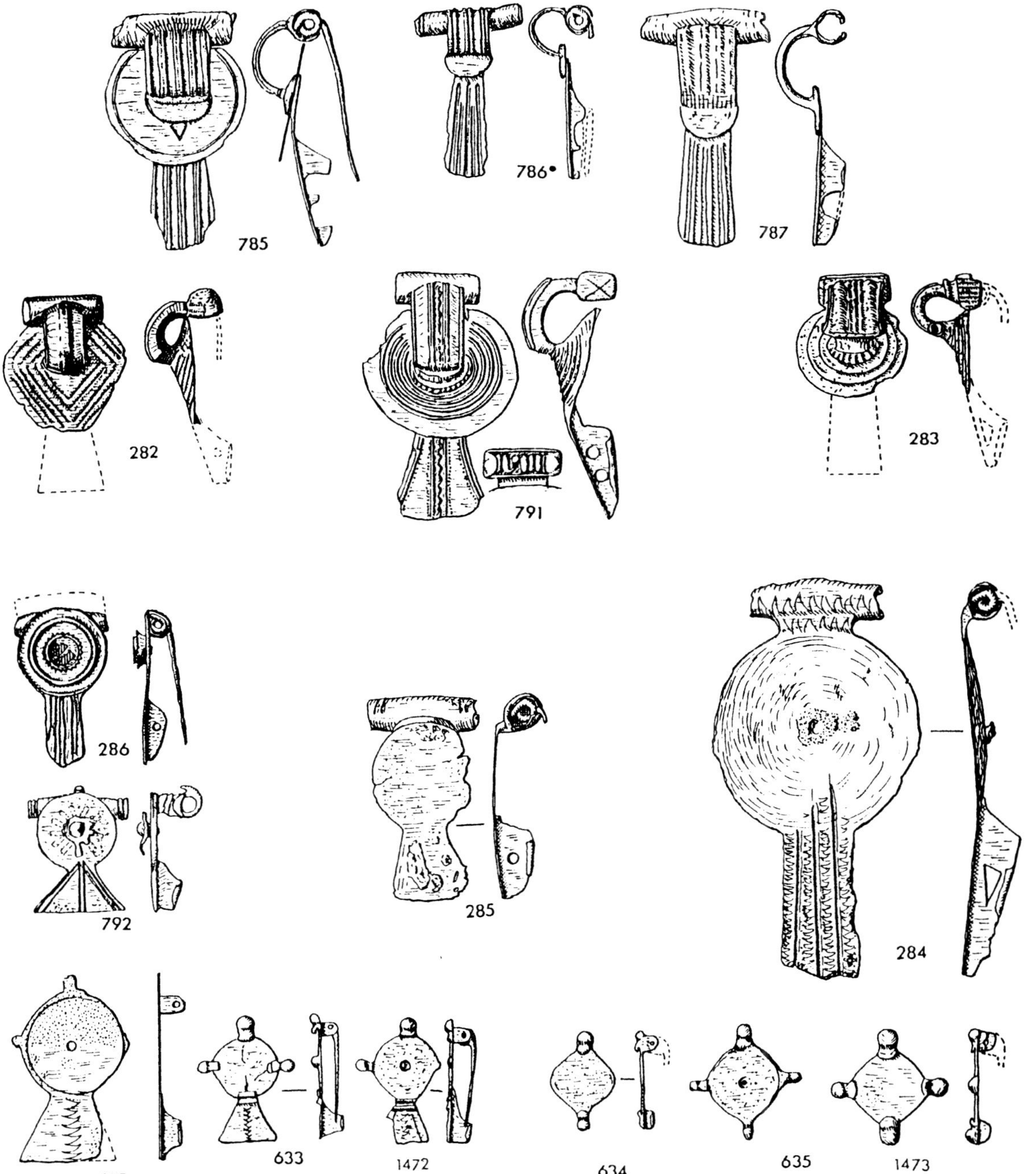

1–212 in ARBB
213–718 in IARB
719–1441 in BoA
1442–1729 in ABOA

Fig. 168 Rosette brooches, 1st century AD. Various forms. 'Keyhole' type below. Bottom line, hinged variants and Sub-keyhole type.

1–212 in **ARBB**
213–718 in **IARB**
719–1441 in **BoA**
1442–1729 in **ABOA**

Fig. 169 Aesica type brooches, 1st century AD.

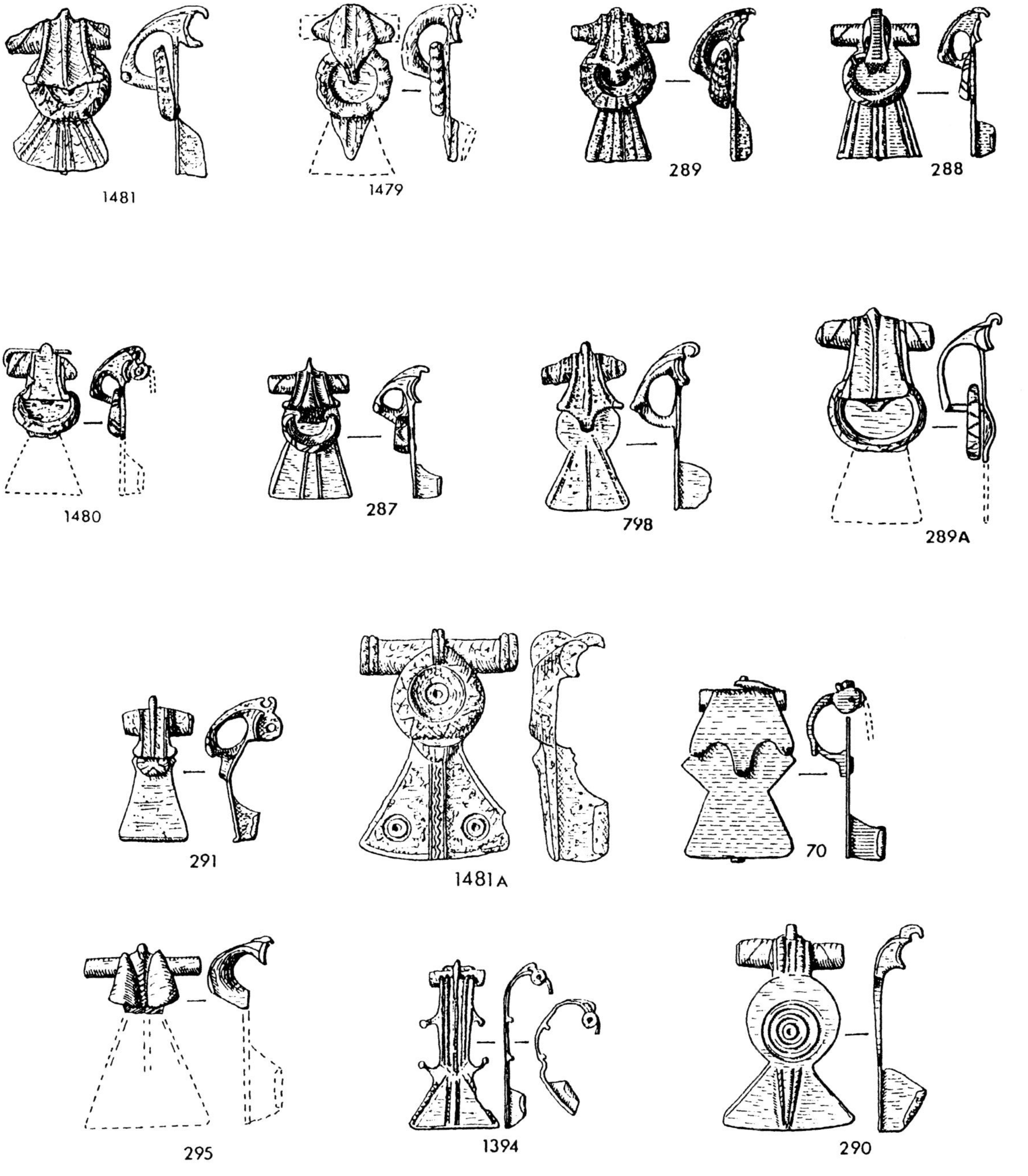

1–212 in ARBB
213–718 in IARB
719–1441 in BoA
1442–1729 in ABOA

Fig. 170 Crescent type Aesica brooches, and oddities below. 1st century AD.

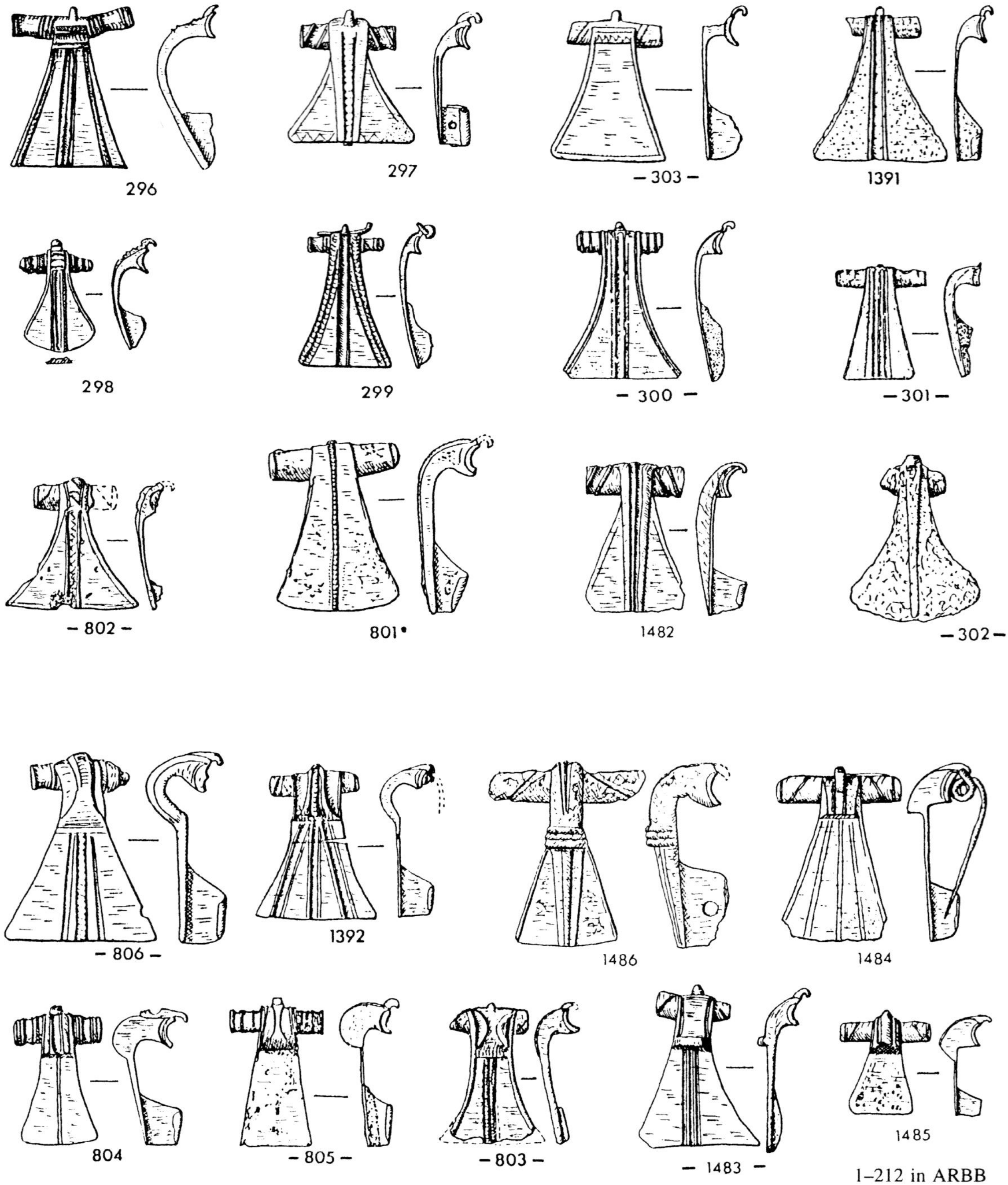

1–212 in ARBB
213–718 in IARB
719–1441 in BoA
1442–1729 in ABOA

Fig. 171 Wing-and-fanbow brooches. Below, Humped type. 1st century AD.

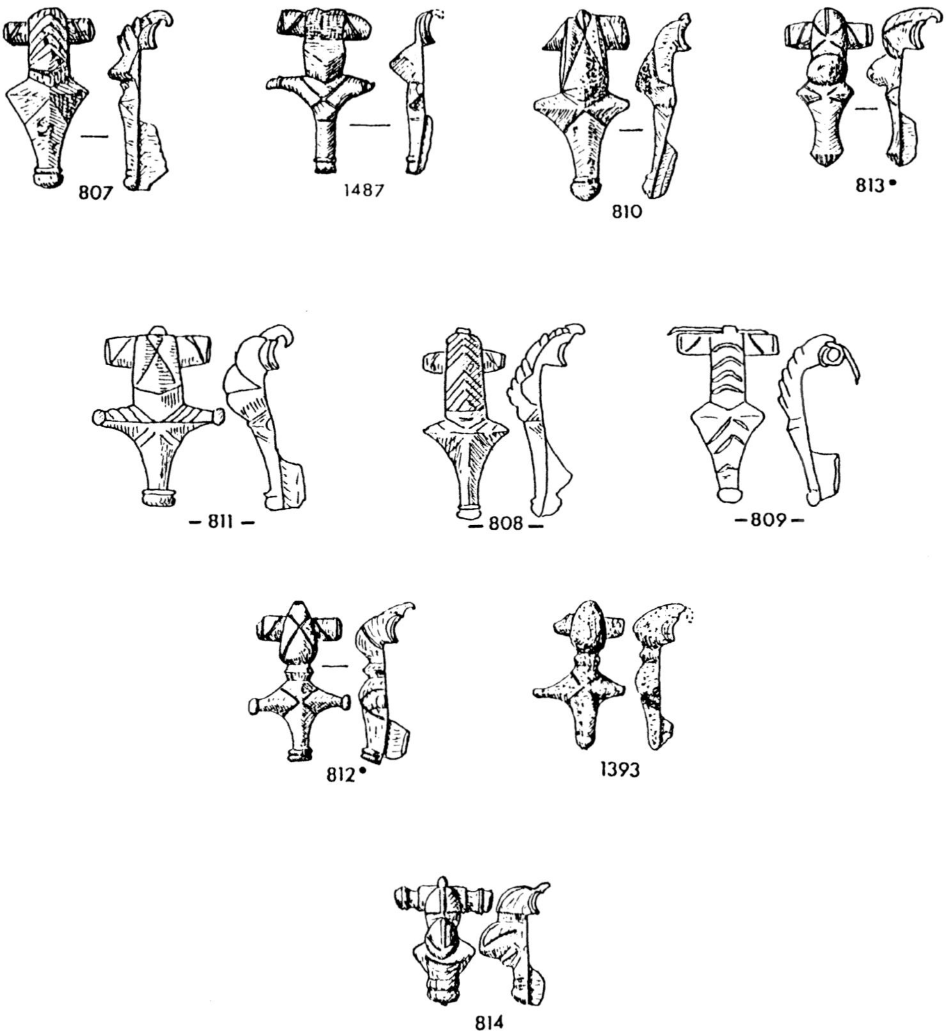

1–212 in ARBB
213–718 in IARB
719–1441 in BoA
1442–1729 in ABOA

Fig. 172 Reversed fantail brooches. 1st century AD.

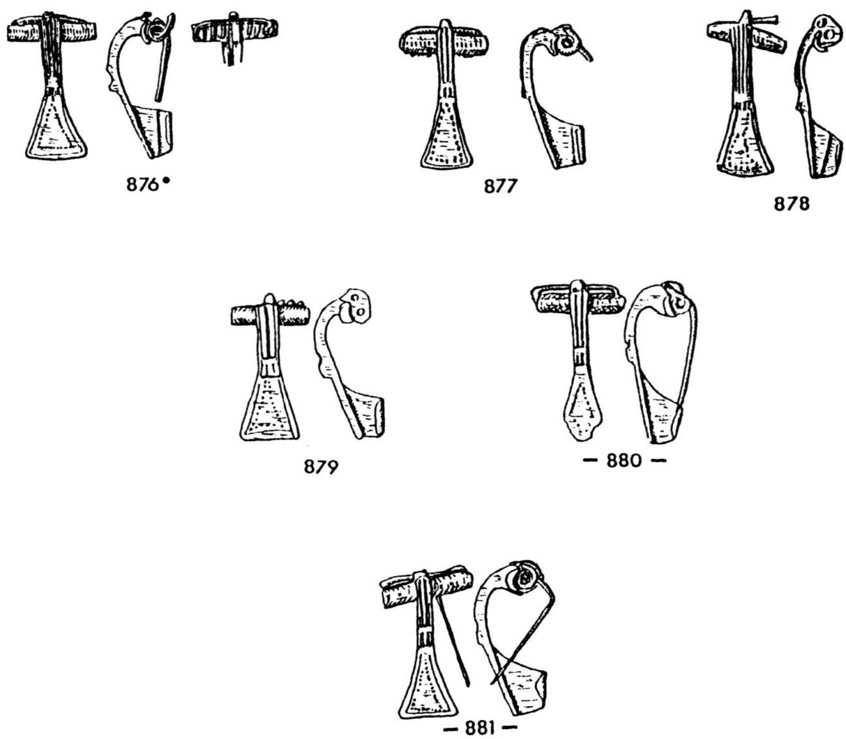

1–212 in ARBB
213–718 in IARB
719–1441 in BoA
1442–1729 in ABOA

Fig. 173 Maxey type Bow-and-fantail brooches. Late 1st century AD.

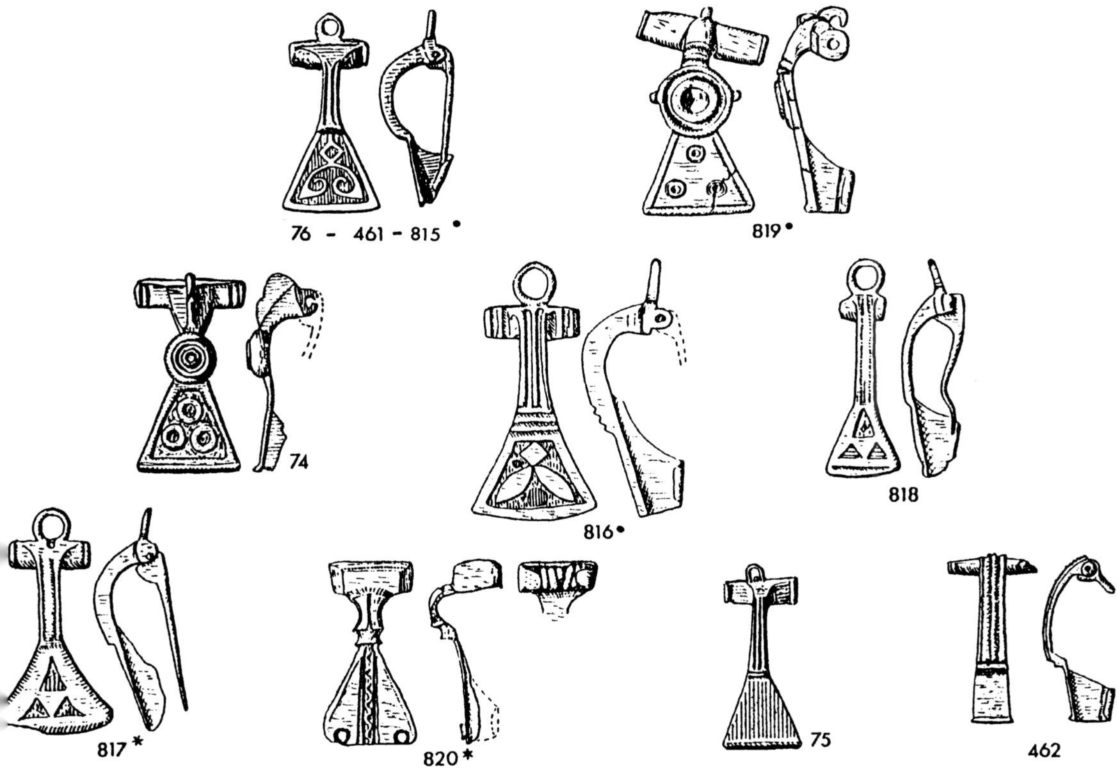

1–212 in ARBB
213–718 in IARB
719–1441 in BoA
1442–1729 in ABOA

Fig. 174 Bow-and-fantail brooches. 1st–2nd century AD.

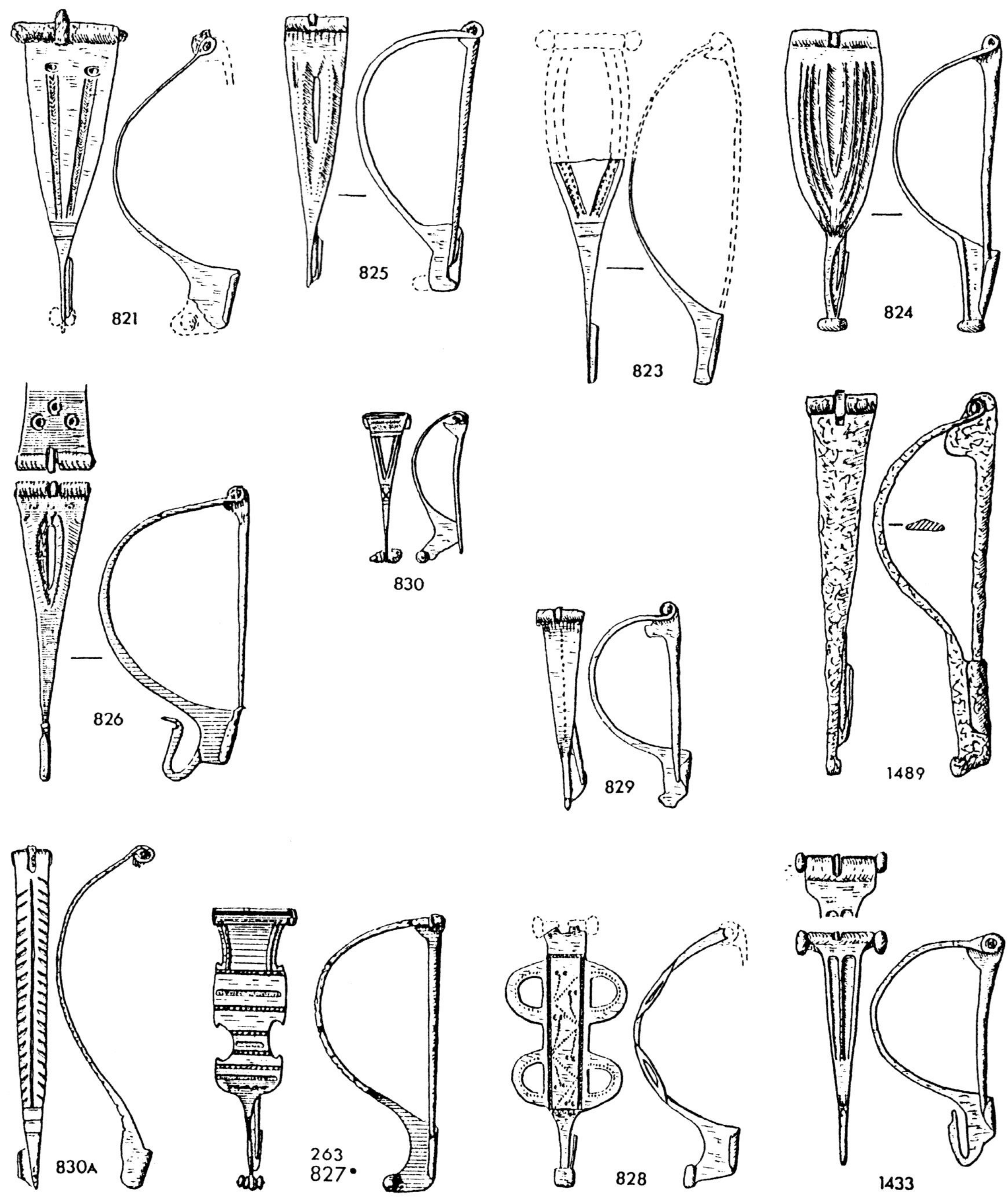

1–212 in ARBB
213–718 in IARB
719–1441 in BoA
1442–1729 in ABOA

Fig. 175 Alesia type brooches. Continental, late 1st century BC.

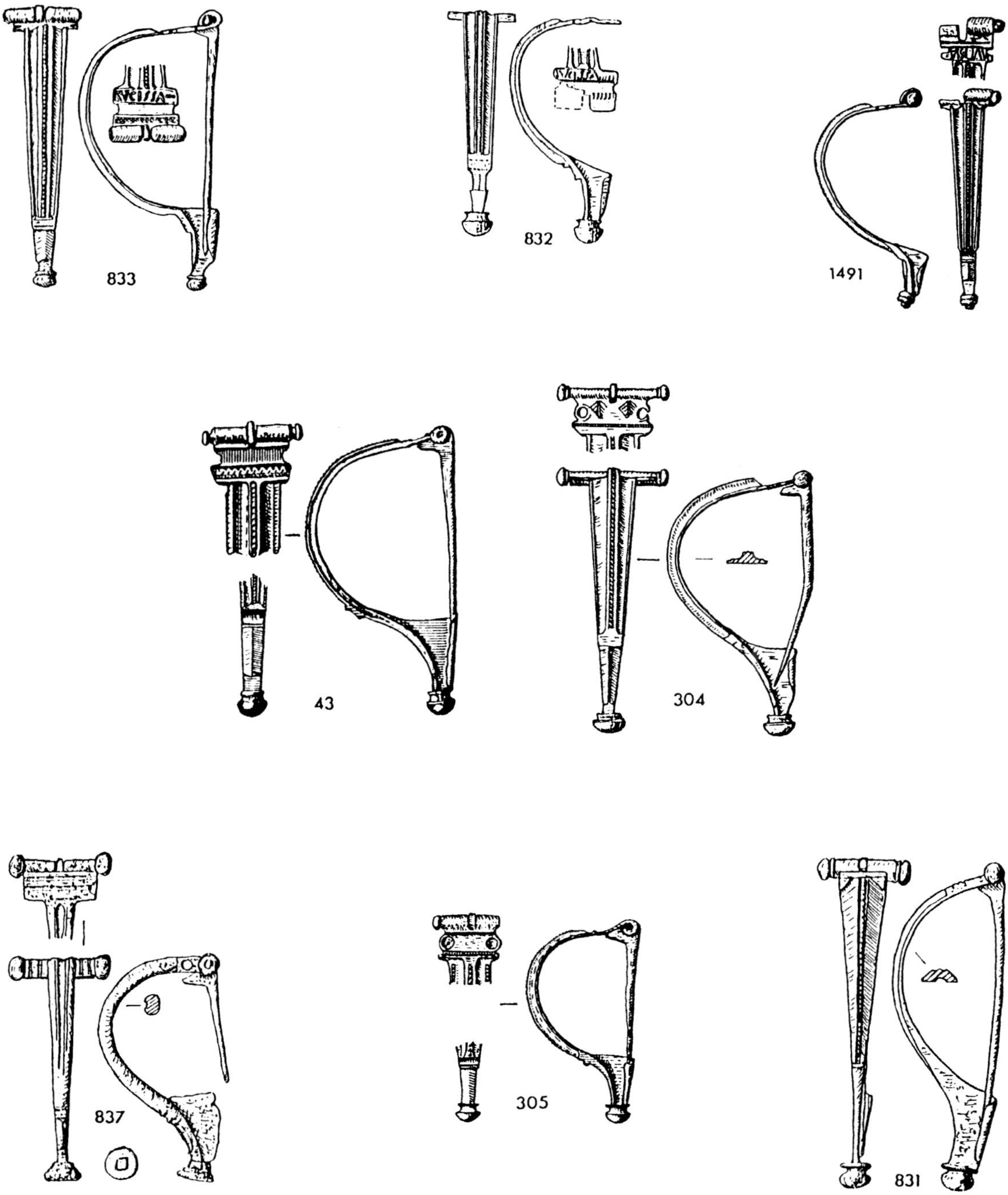

Fig. 176 Aucissa brooches. 1st century AD. (Variants overleaf)

1–212 in **ARBB**
213–718 in **IARB**
719–1441 in **BoA**
1442–1729 in **ABOA**

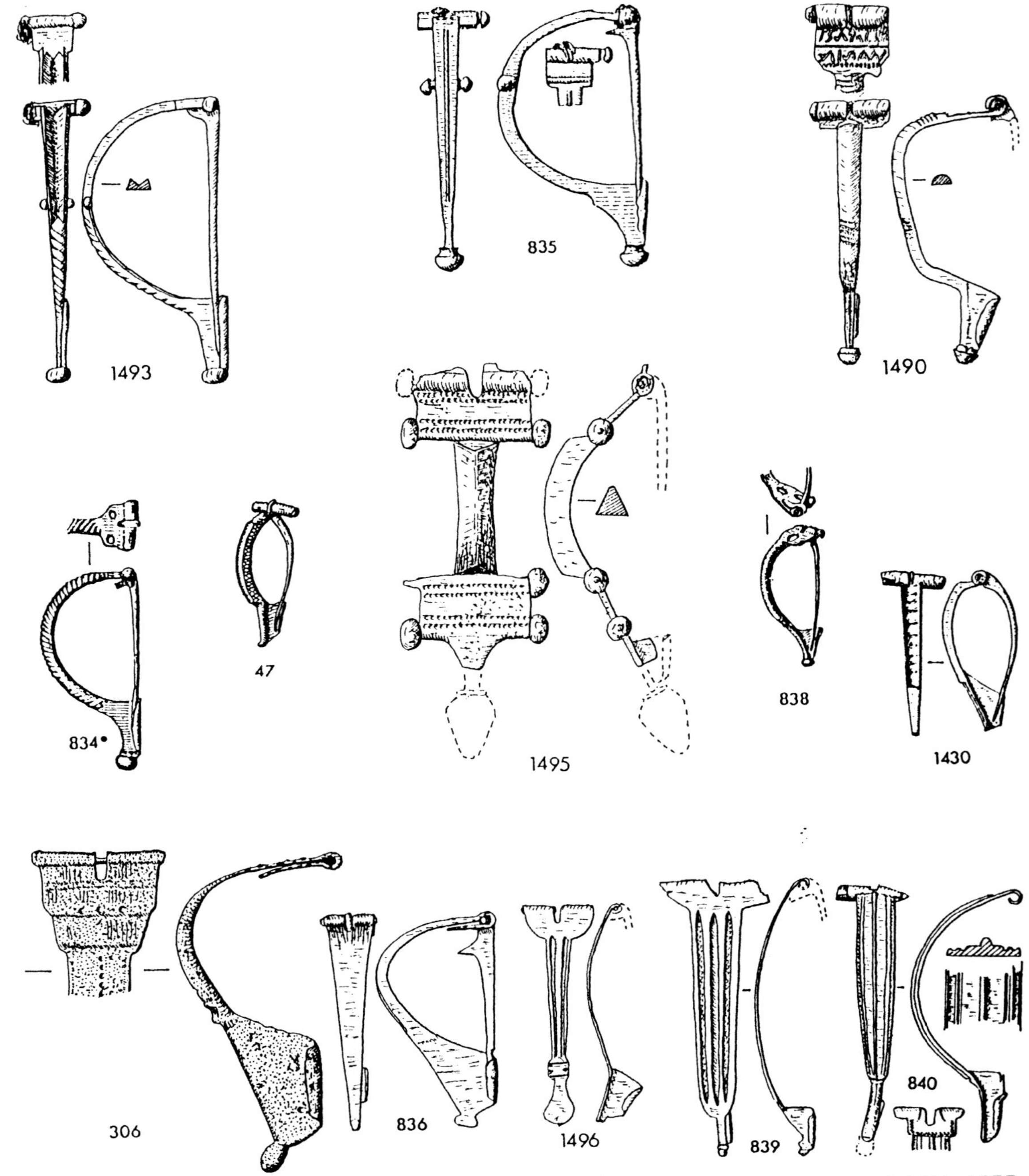

1–212 in **ARBB**
213–718 in **IARB**
719–1441 in **BoA**
1442–1729 in **ABOA**

Fig. 177 Aucissa variant brooches. 1st century AD. 1496–840, native British copies.

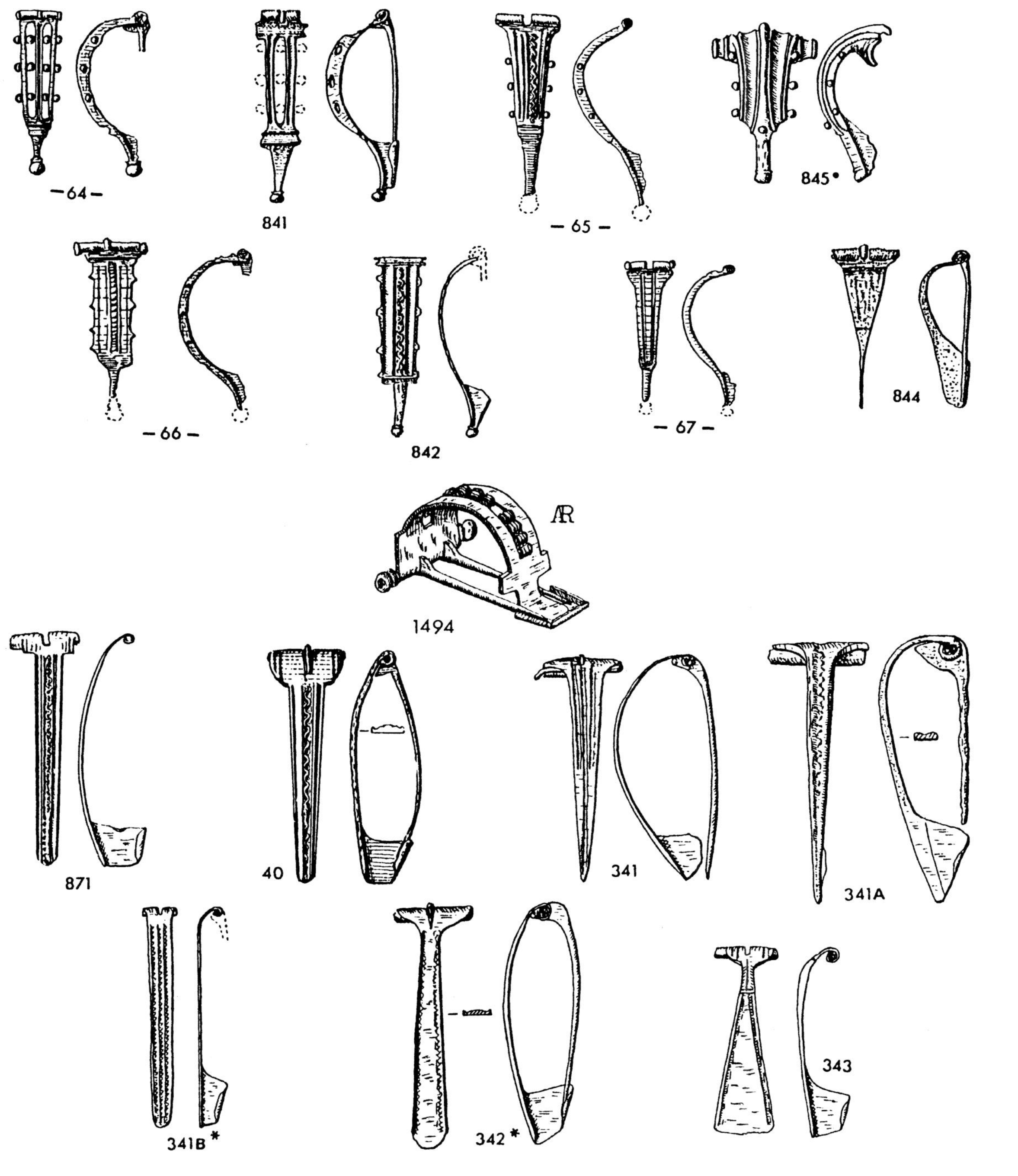

Fig. 178 Aucissa derivative brooches, 1st century AD. Above, Bagendon type; centre, a continental silver dual pinned brooch; below, Strip bow brooches.

1–212 in ARBB
213–718 in IARB
719–1441 in BoA
1442–1729 in ABOA

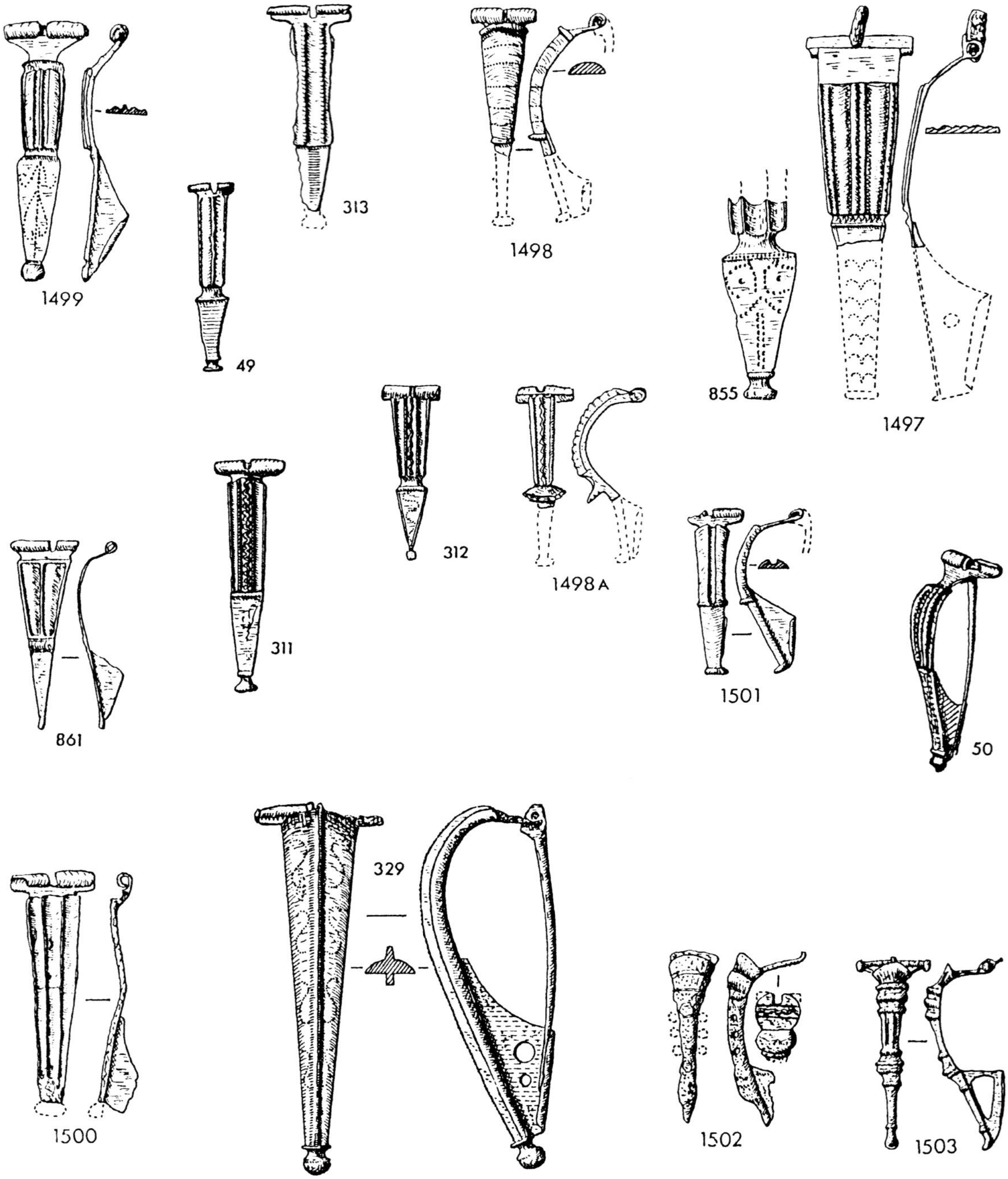

Fig. 179 Hod Hill type brooches, 1st century AD. Various forms without side lugs.

1–212 in ARBB
213–718 in IARB
719–1441 in BoA
1442–1729 in ABOA

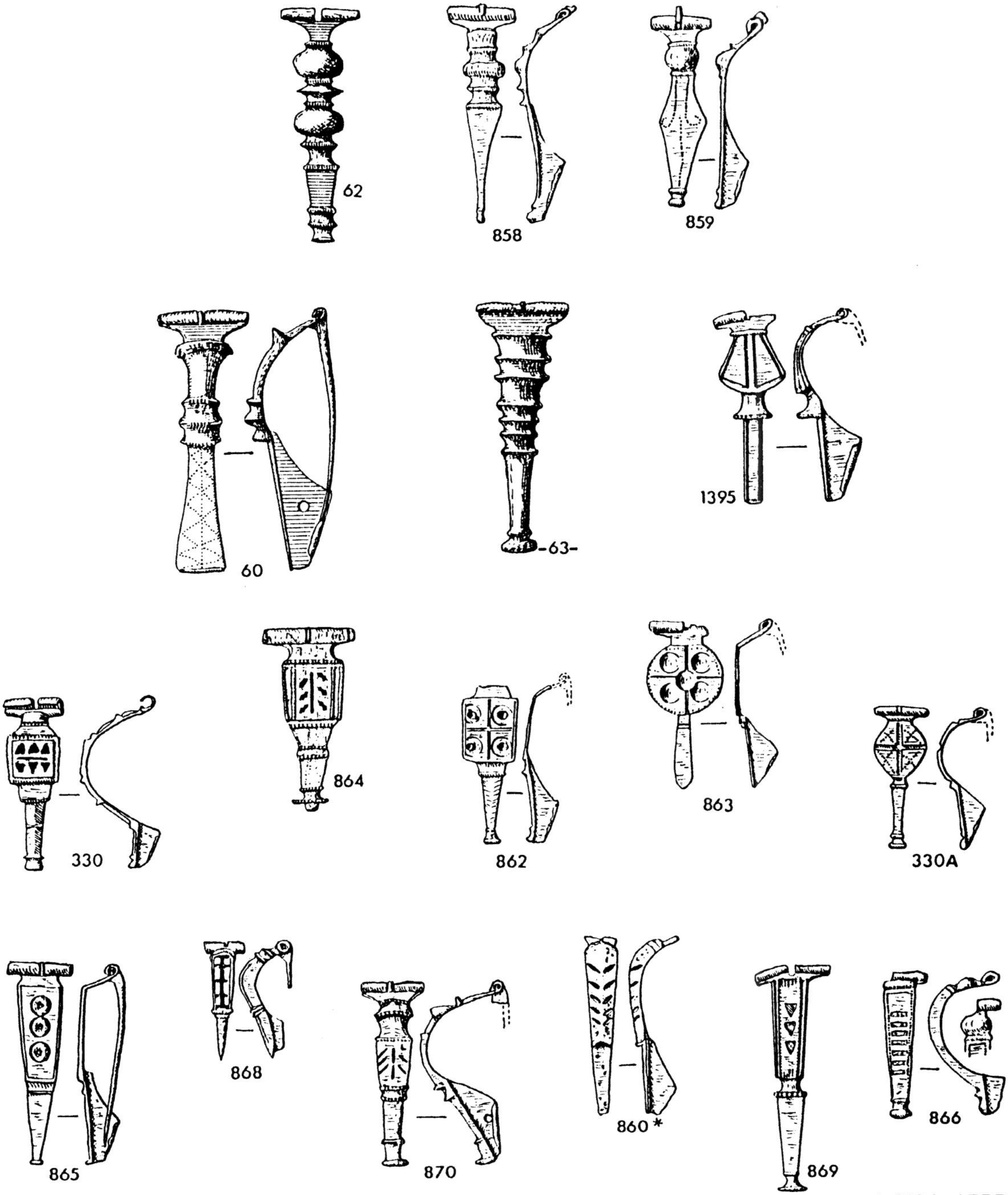

1–212 in **ARBB**
213–718 in **IARB**
719–1441 in **BoA**
1442–1729 in **ABOA**

Fig. 180 Hod hill type brooches. 1st century AD. Various forms without side-lugs.

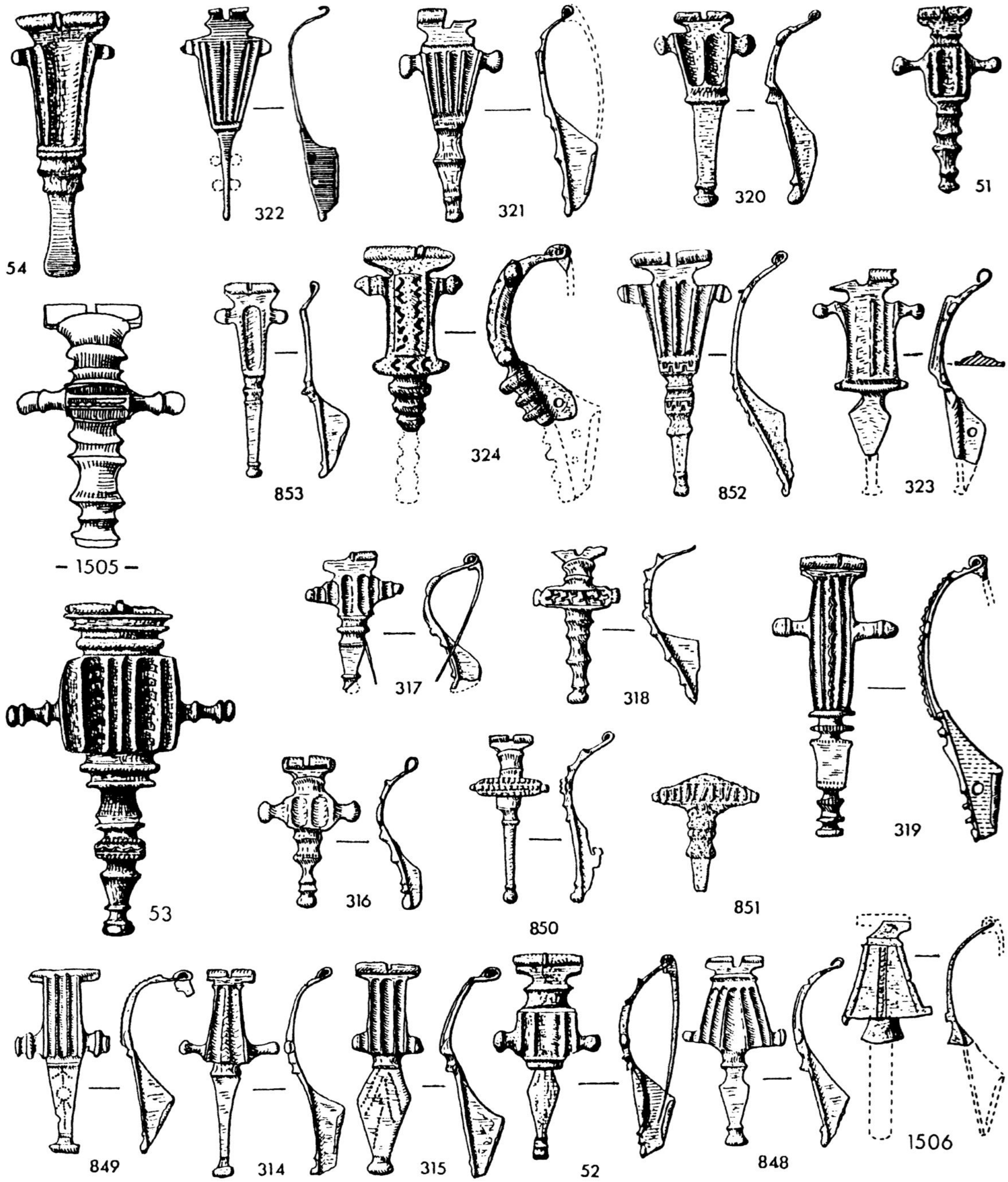

Fig. 181 Hod Hill brooches with side lugs, upper, middle and lower. 1st century AD.

1–212 in **ARBB**
213–718 in **IARB**
719–1441 in **BoA**
1442–1729 in **ABOA**

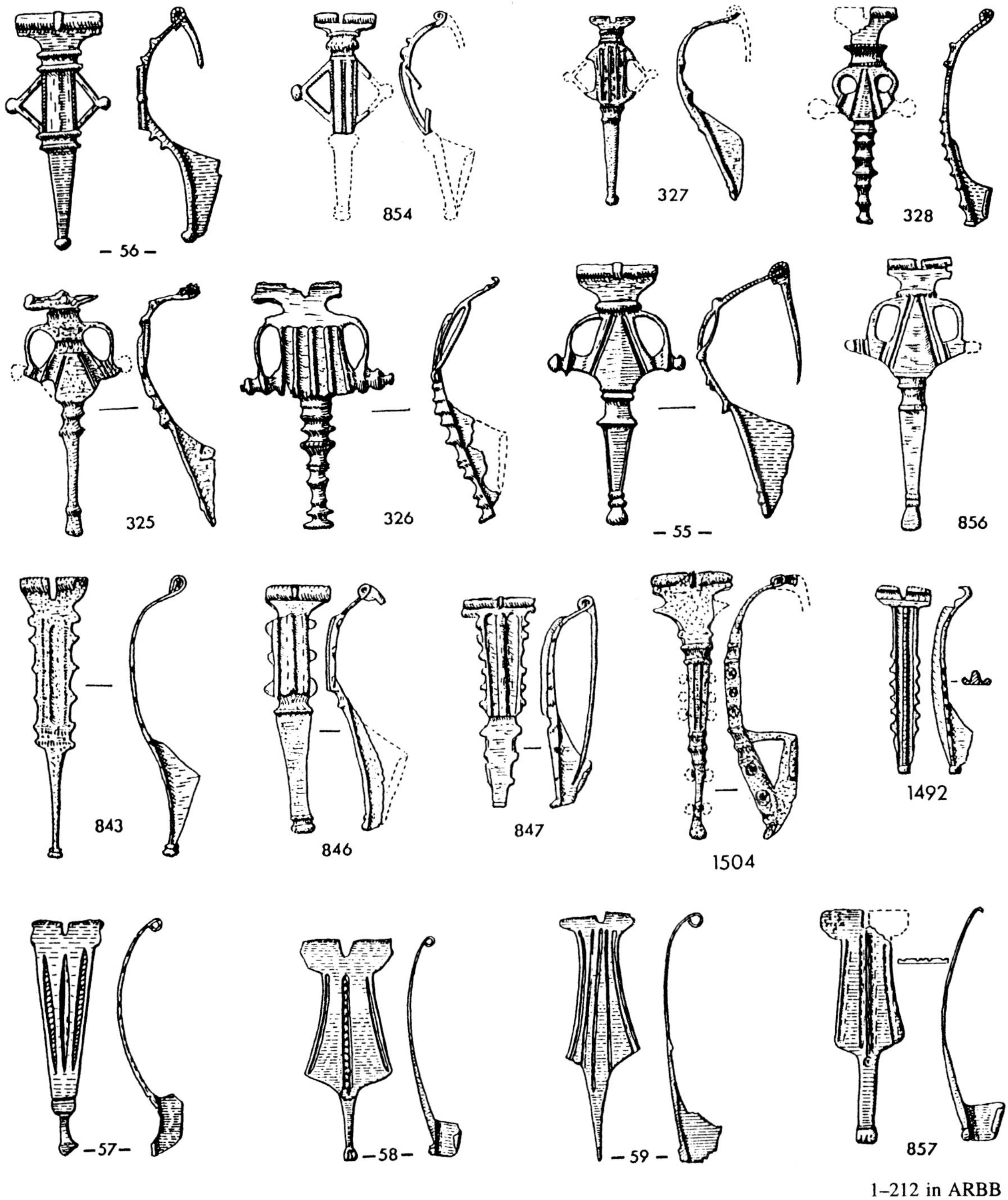

1–212 in ARBB
213–718 in IARB
719–1441 in BoA
1442–1729 in ABOA

Fig. 182 Hod Hill brooches, 1st century AD. Above, openwork type; centre, Bagendon influenced; below, 'Fiddle' type.

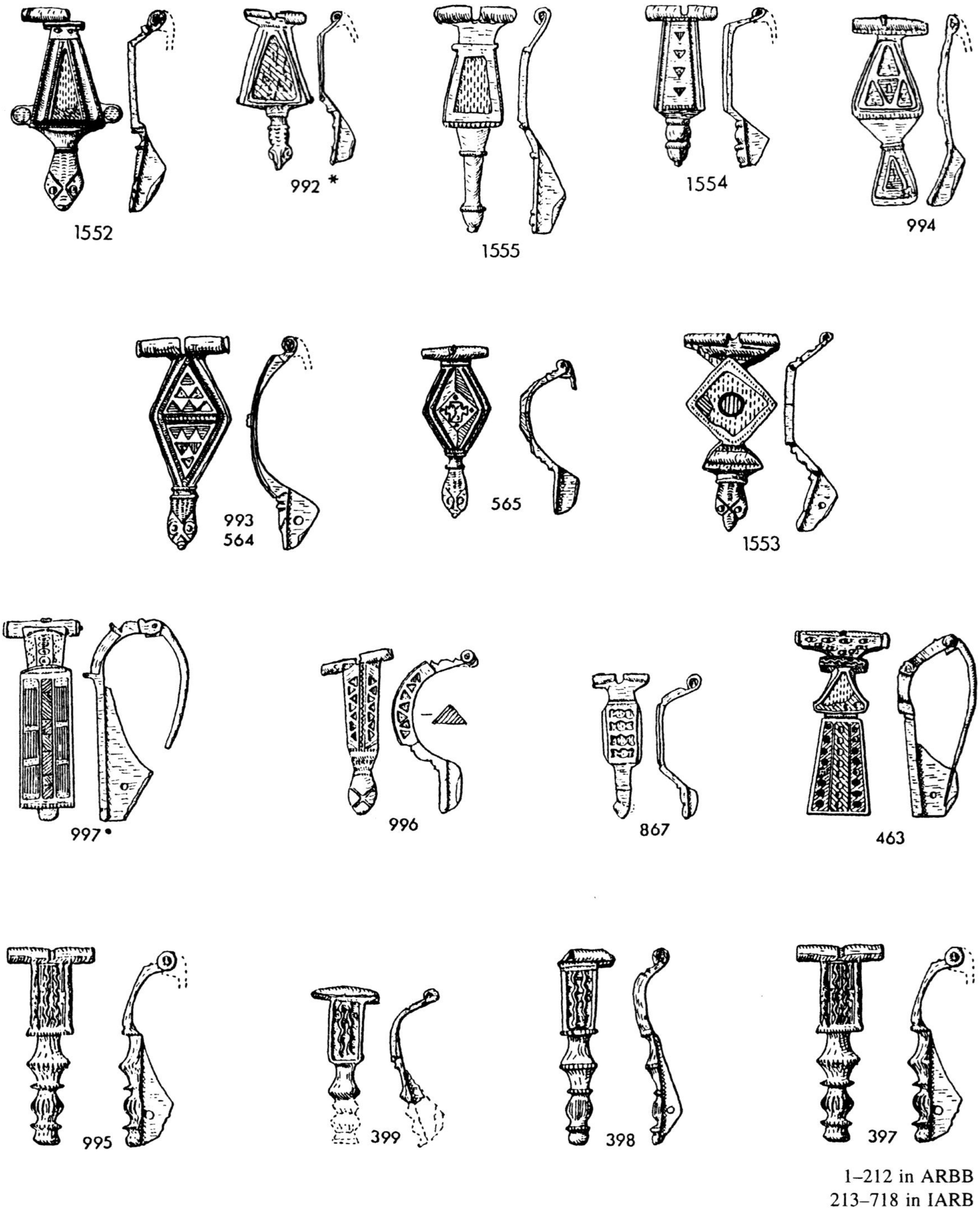

1–212 in ARBB
213–718 in IARB
719–1441 in BoA
1442–1729 in ABOA

Fig. 183 Hinge-headed enamelled brooches, 1st–2nd century AD.

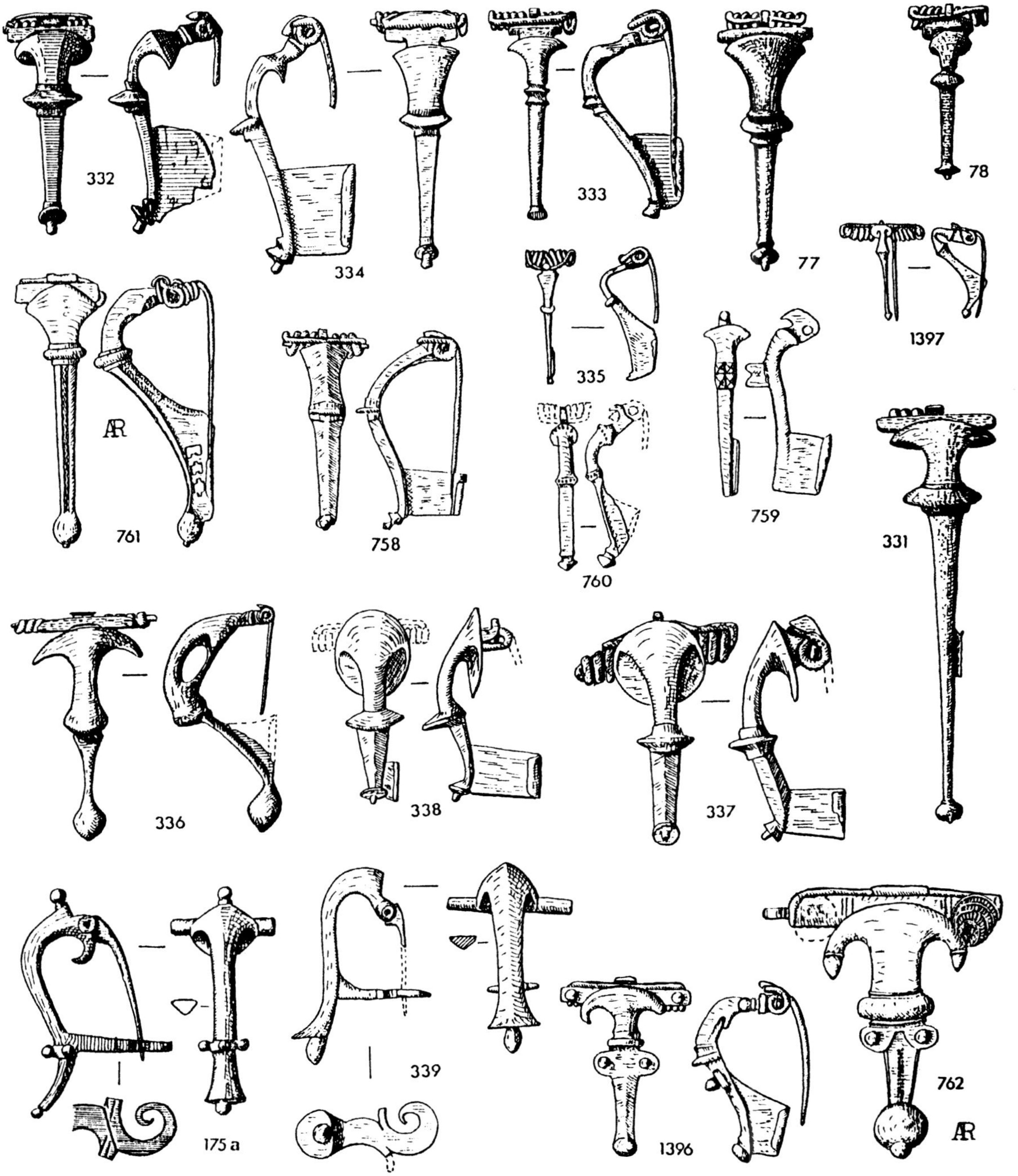

1–212 in **ARBB**
213–718 in **IARB**
719–1441 in **BoA**
1442–1729 in **ABOA**

Fig. 184 Kräftig profilierte type, 1st century AD. European.

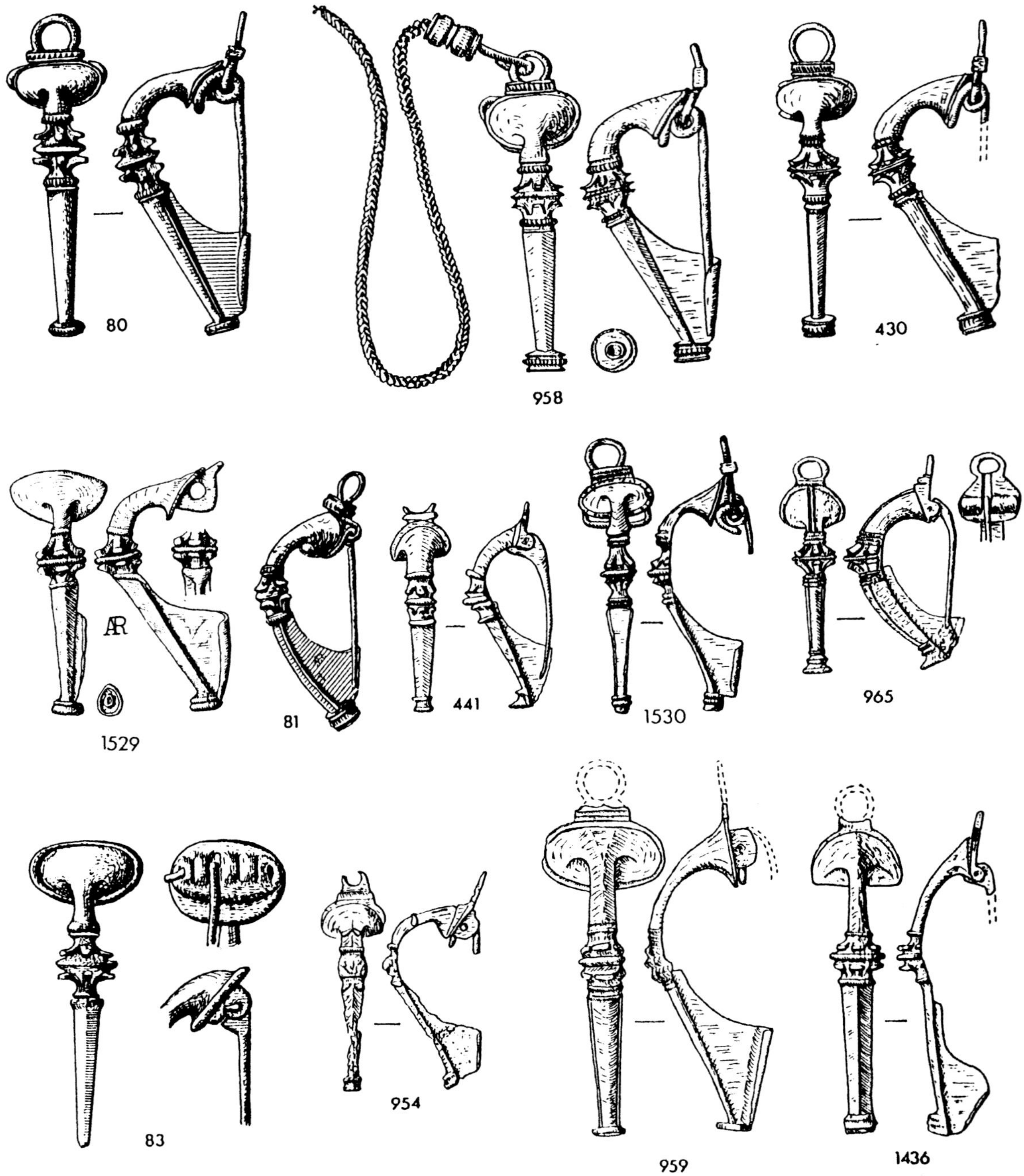

1–212 in **ARBB**
213–718 in **IARB**
719–1441 in **BoA**
1442–1729 in **ABOA**

Fig. 185 Trumpet brooches, 1st–2nd century AD. Non-enamelled with full acanthus.

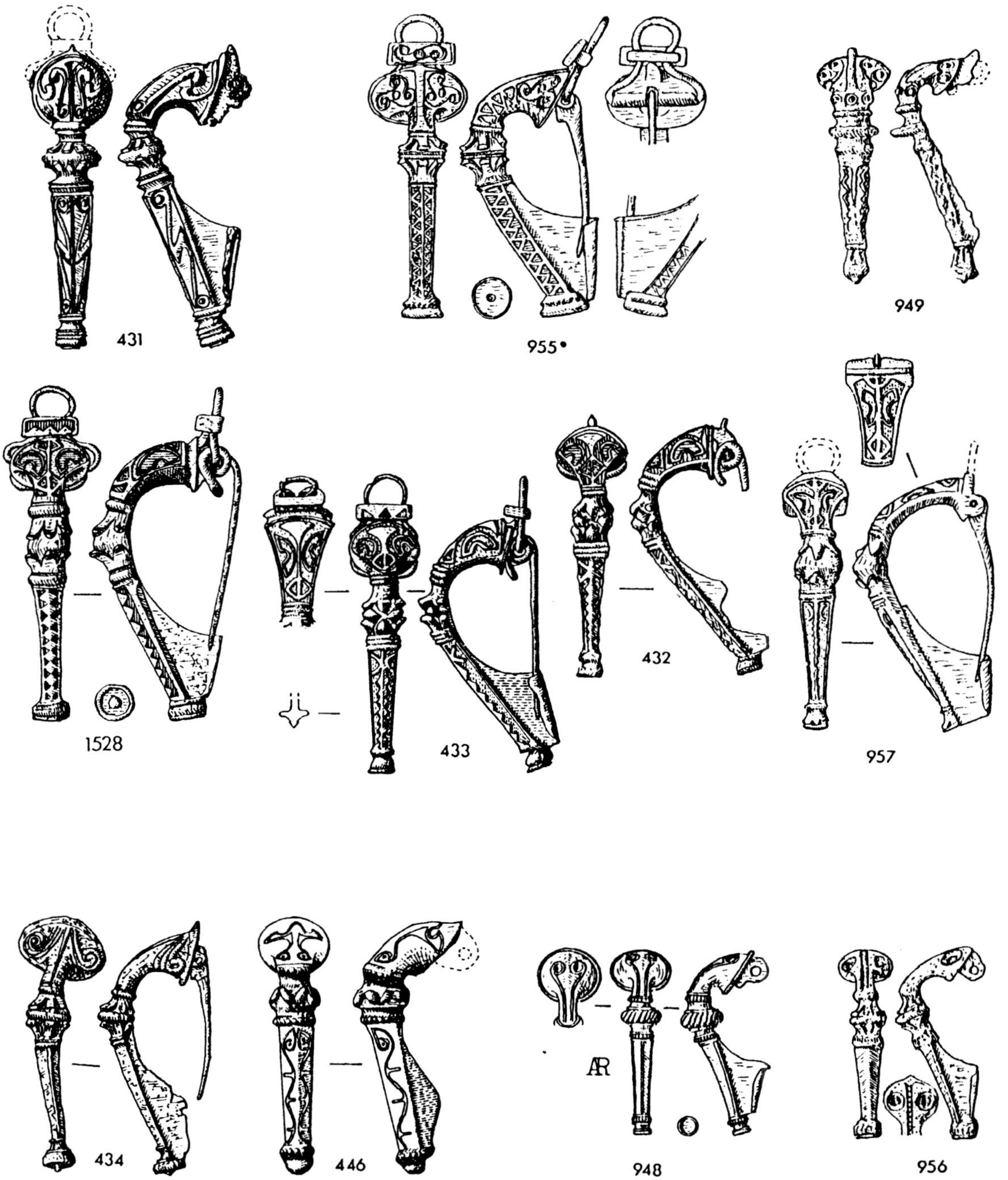

Fig. 186 Trumpet brooches, 1st–2nd century AD. Above, enamelled decoration; below, moulded or inlaid decoration.

1–212 in ARBB
213–718 in IARB
719–1441 in BoA
1442–1729 in ABOA

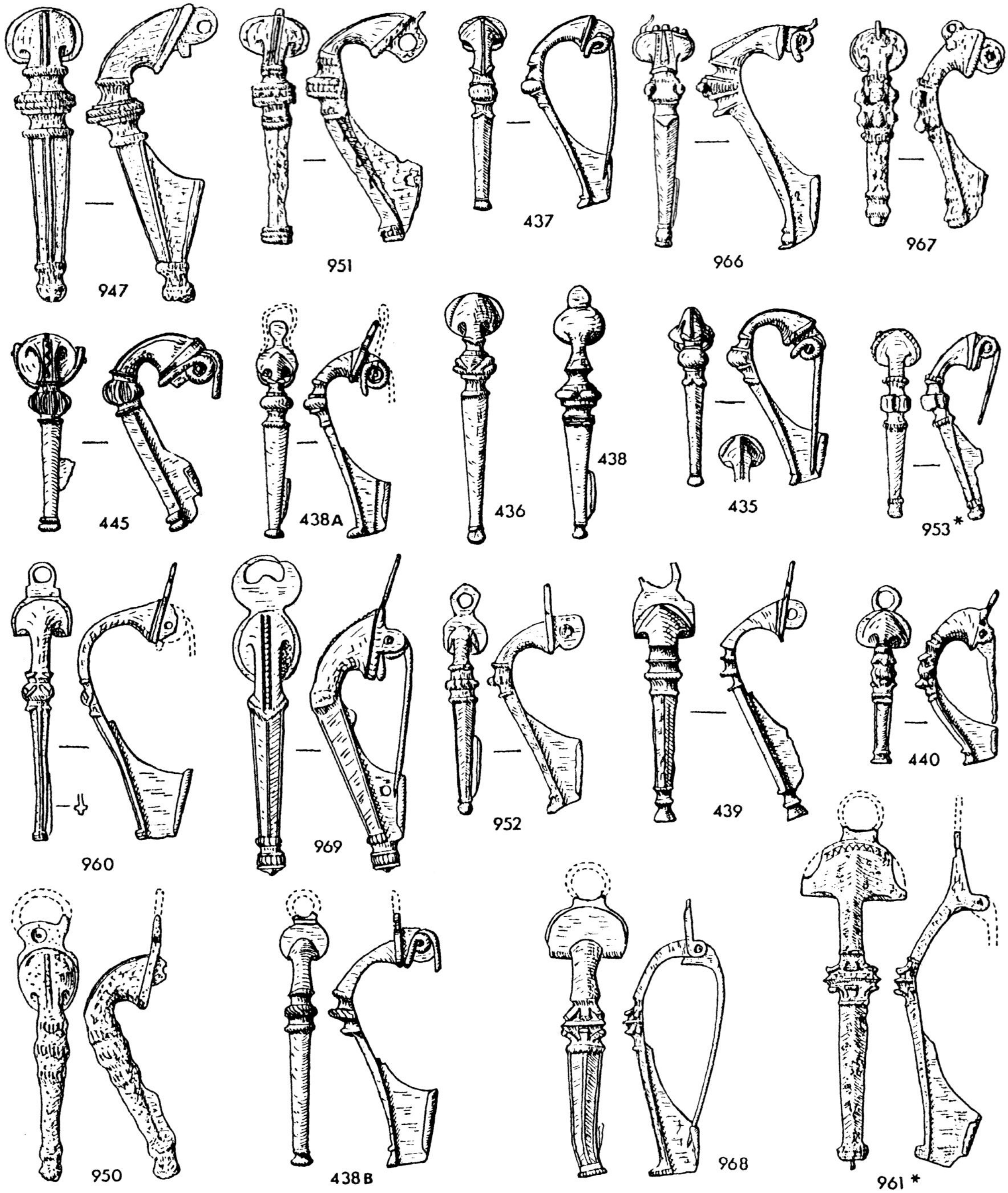

1–212 in ARBB
213–718 in IARB
719–1441 in BoA
1442–1729 in ABOA

Fig. 187 Trumpet brooches, 1st–2nd century AD. Above, with variant buttons; below, with variant heads.

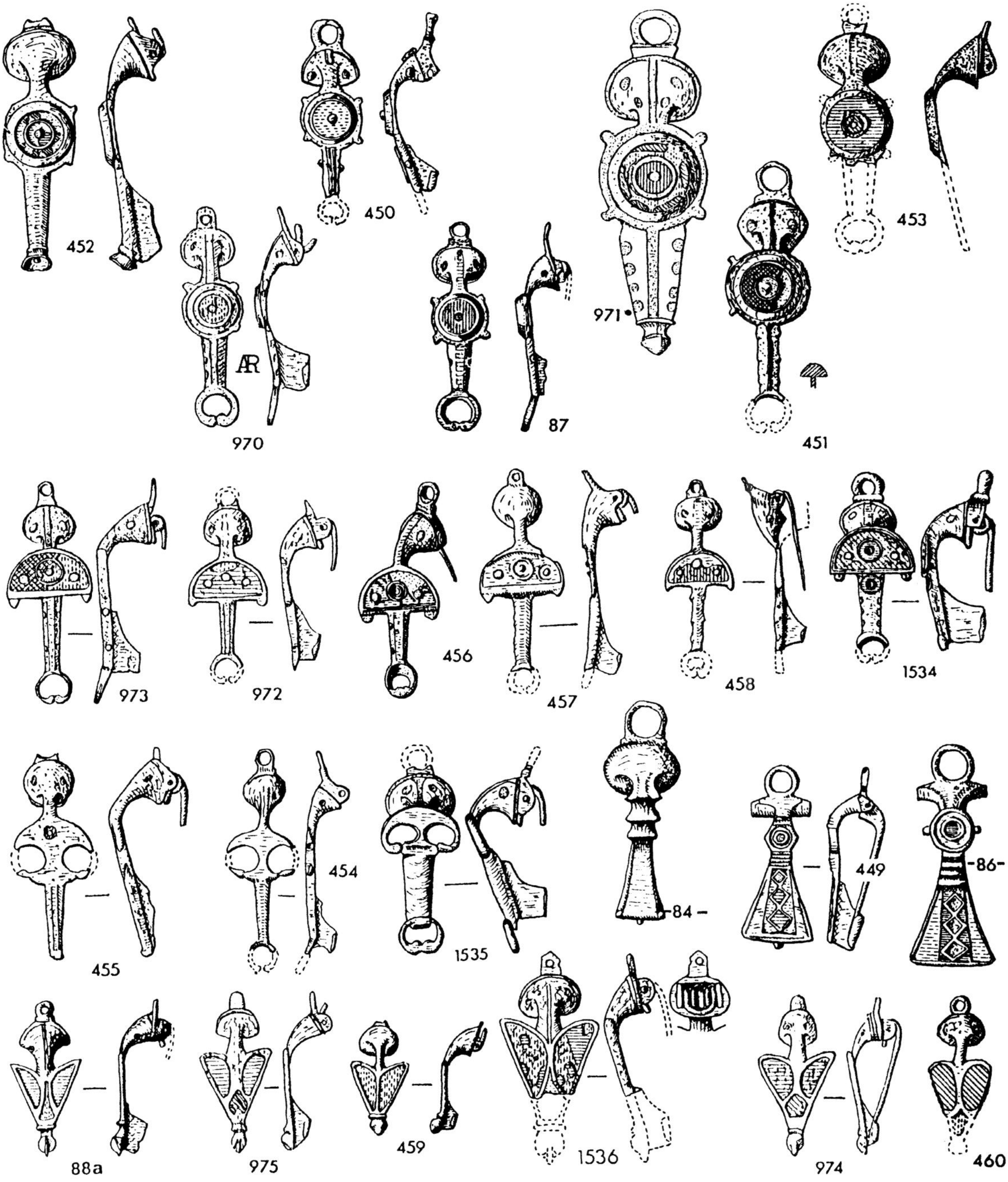

Fig. 188 Trumpet headed brooches, 2nd century AD. Various forms.

1–212 in **ARBB**
213–718 in **IARB**
719–1441 in **BoA**
1442–1729 in **ABOA**

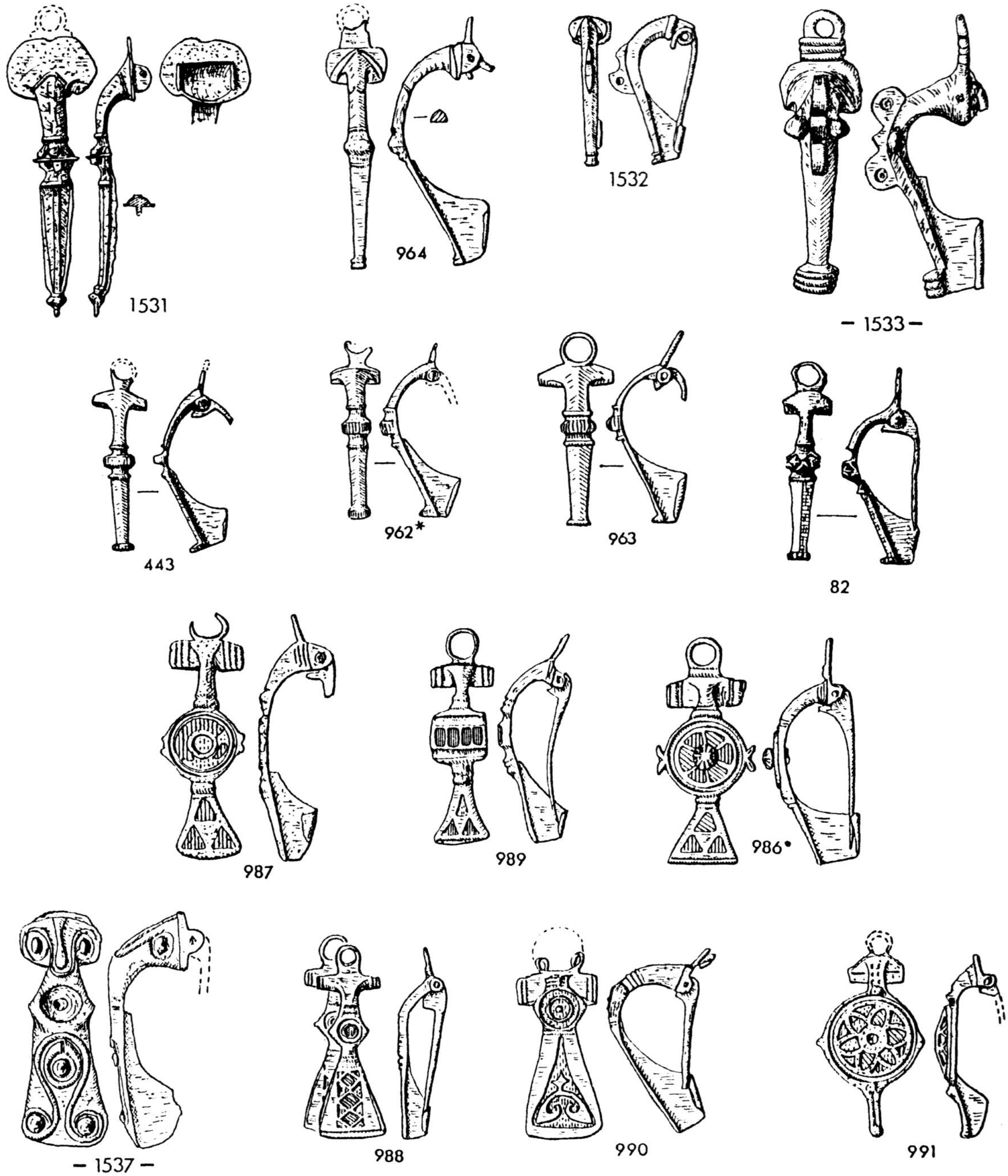

1–212 in **ARBB**
213–718 in **IARB**
719–1441 in **BoA**
1442–1729 in **ABOA**

Fig. 189 Trumpet derivative brooches, 1st–2nd century AD.

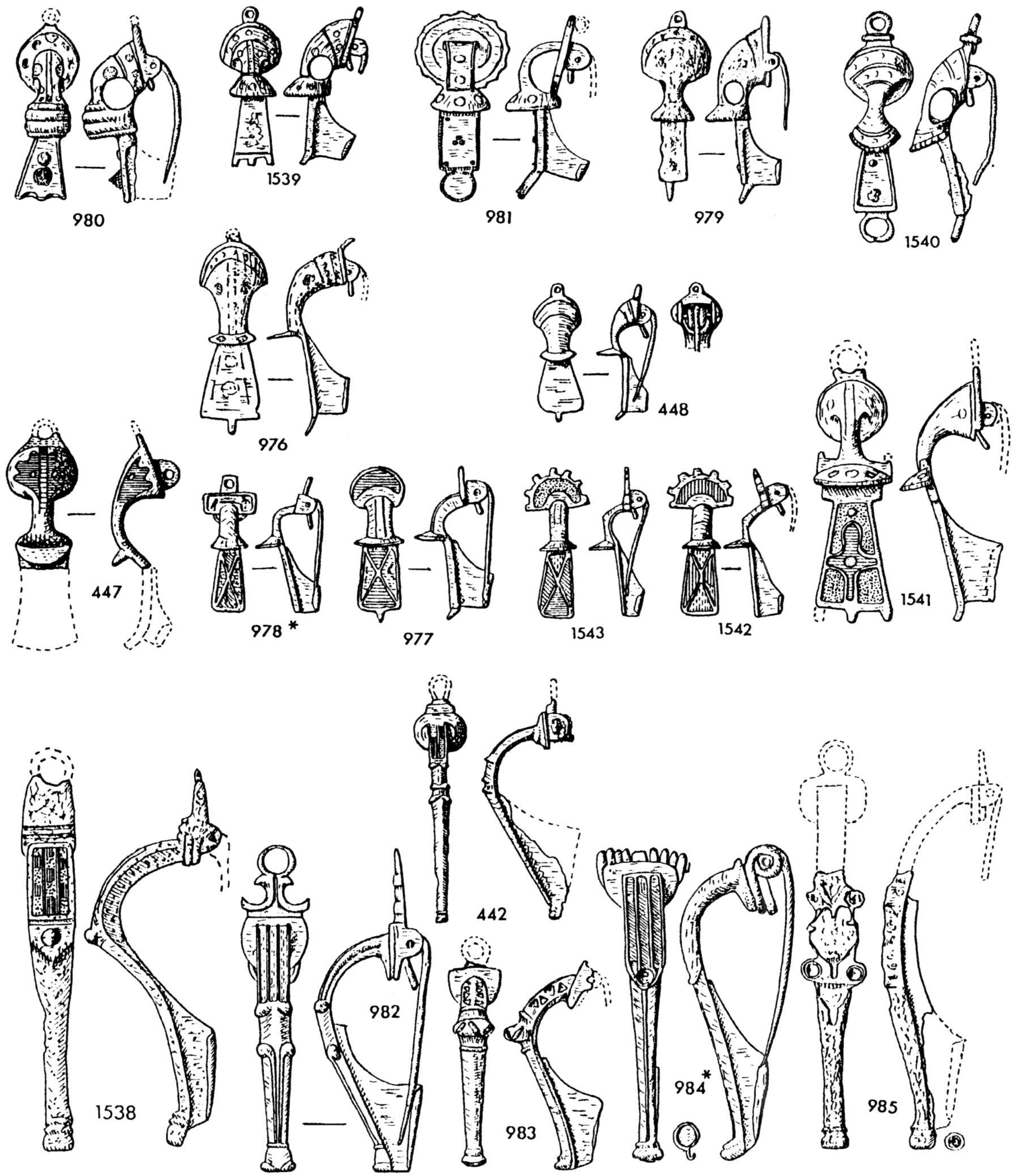

Fig. 190 Trumpet derivative brooches, 1st–2nd century AD. Above, Alcester type; below, Wroxeter type.

1–212 in ARBB
213–718 in IARB
719–1441 in BoA
1442–1729 in ABOA

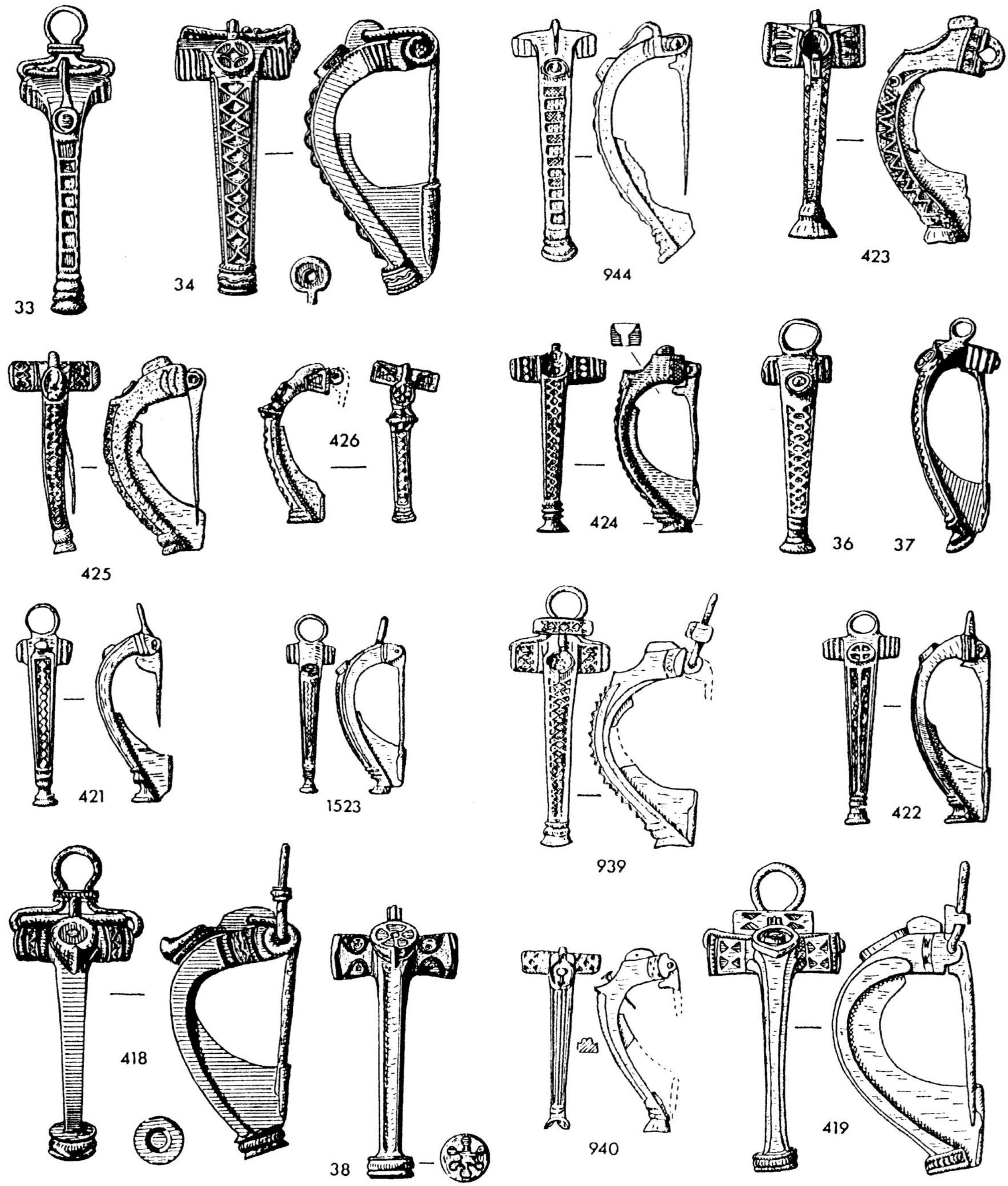

1–212 in ARBB
213–718 in IARB
719–1441 in BoA
1442–1729 in ABOA

Fig. 191 Headstud brooches, enamelled, 2nd century AD.

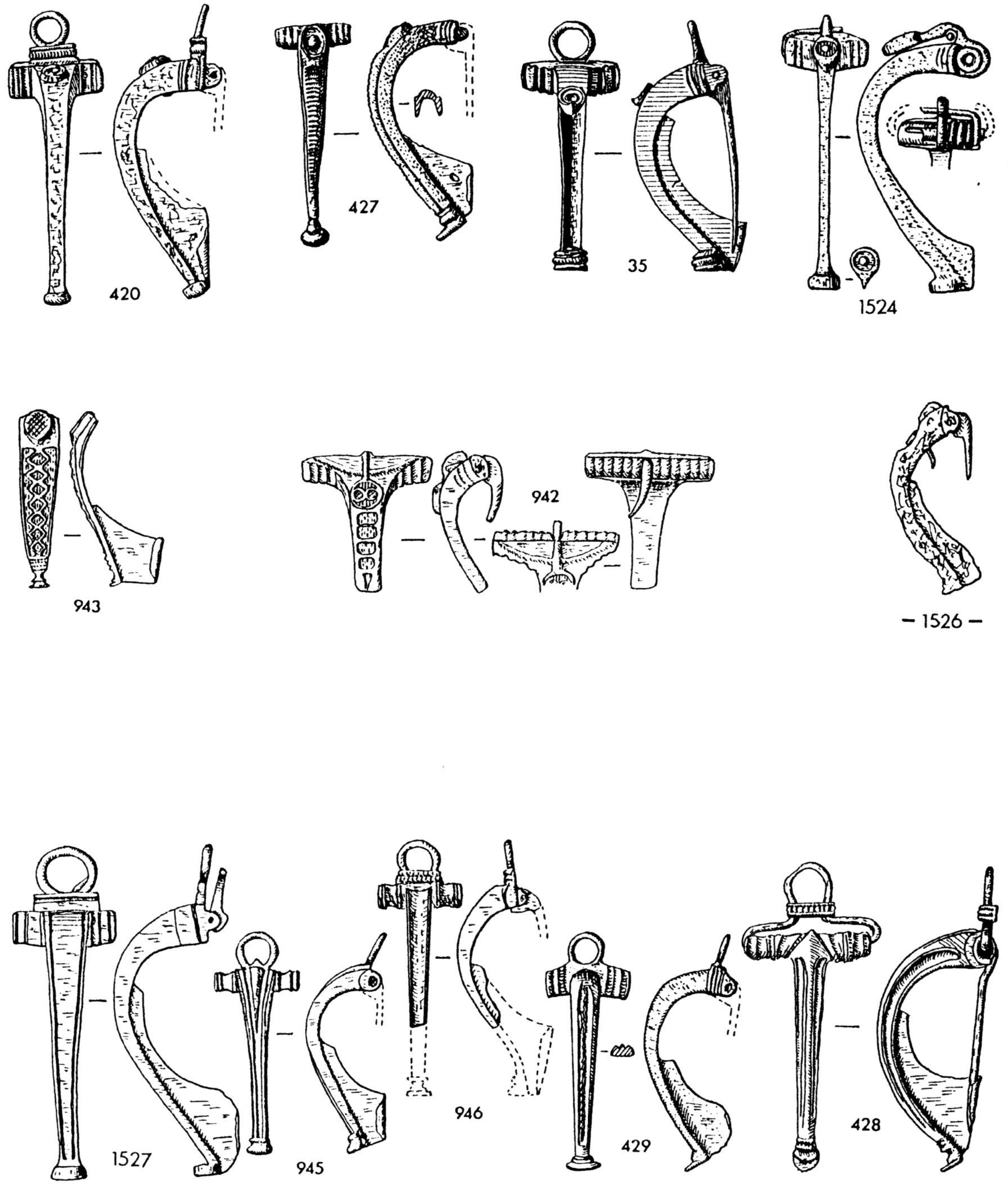

1–212 in **ARBB**
213–718 in **IARB**
719–1441 in **BoA**
1442–1729 in **ABOA**

Fig. 192 Headstud variant brooches, 2nd century AD. Thealby type below.

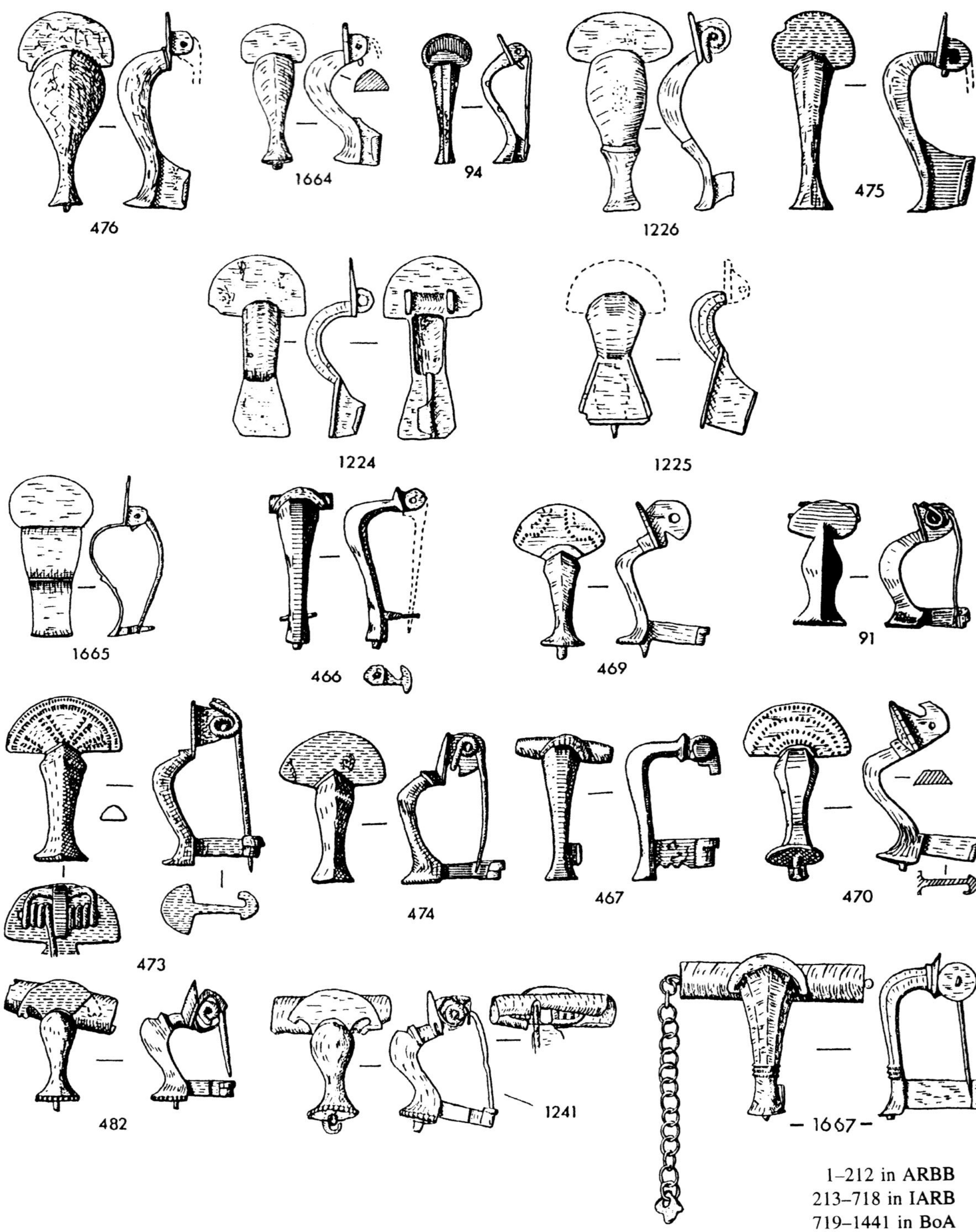

1–212 in ARBB
213–718 in IARB
719–1441 in BoA
1442–1729 in ABOA

Fig. 193 Knee brooches, 2nd century AD. Semicircular headed types. Above, with vertical catch; below, with horizontal catch, some with hooded springs.

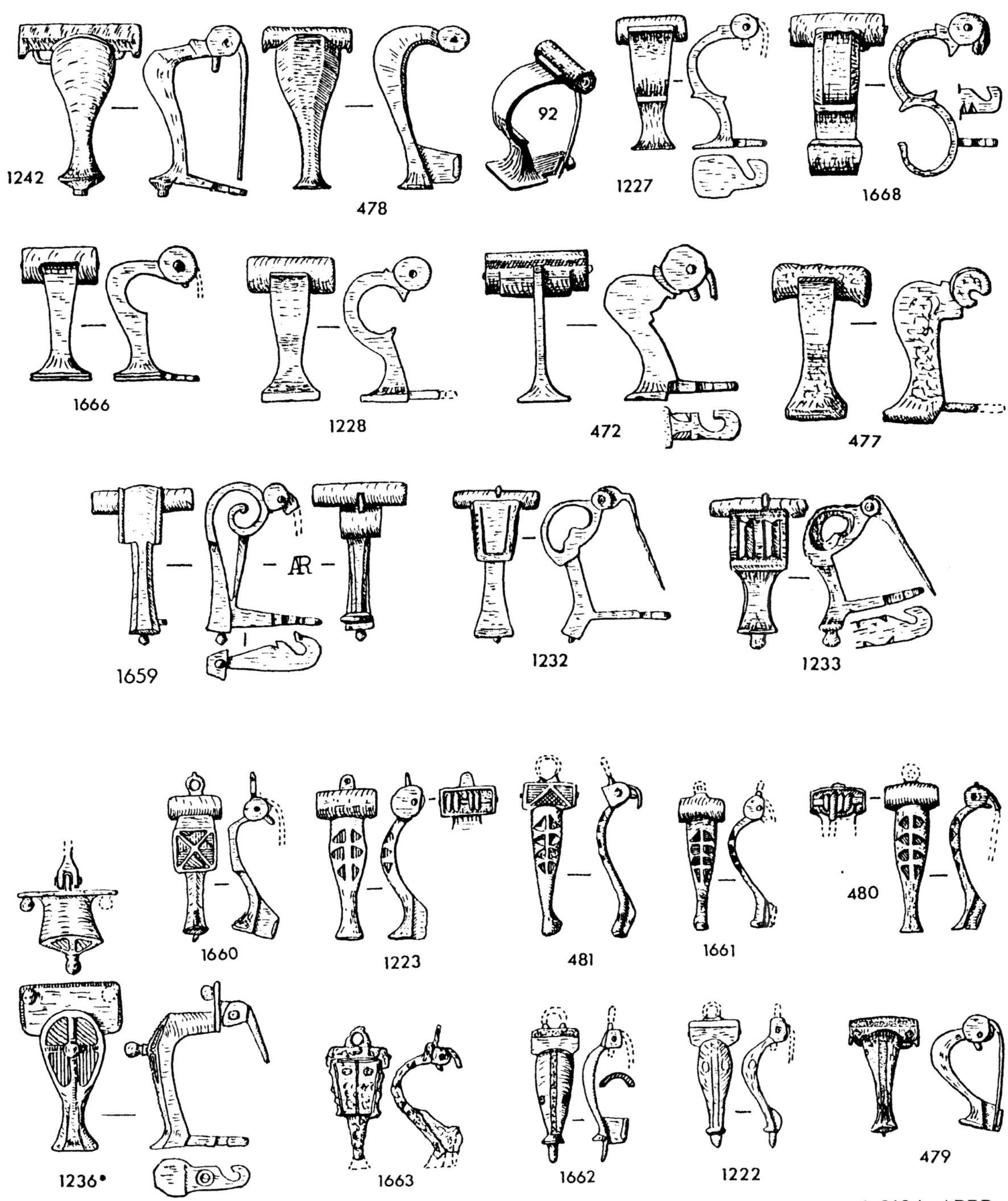

Fig. 194 Knee brooches, 2nd century AD. Above, tubular headed. Below, enamelled and silver inlaid.

1–212 in ARBB
213–718 in IARB
719–1441 in BoA
1442–1729 in ABOA

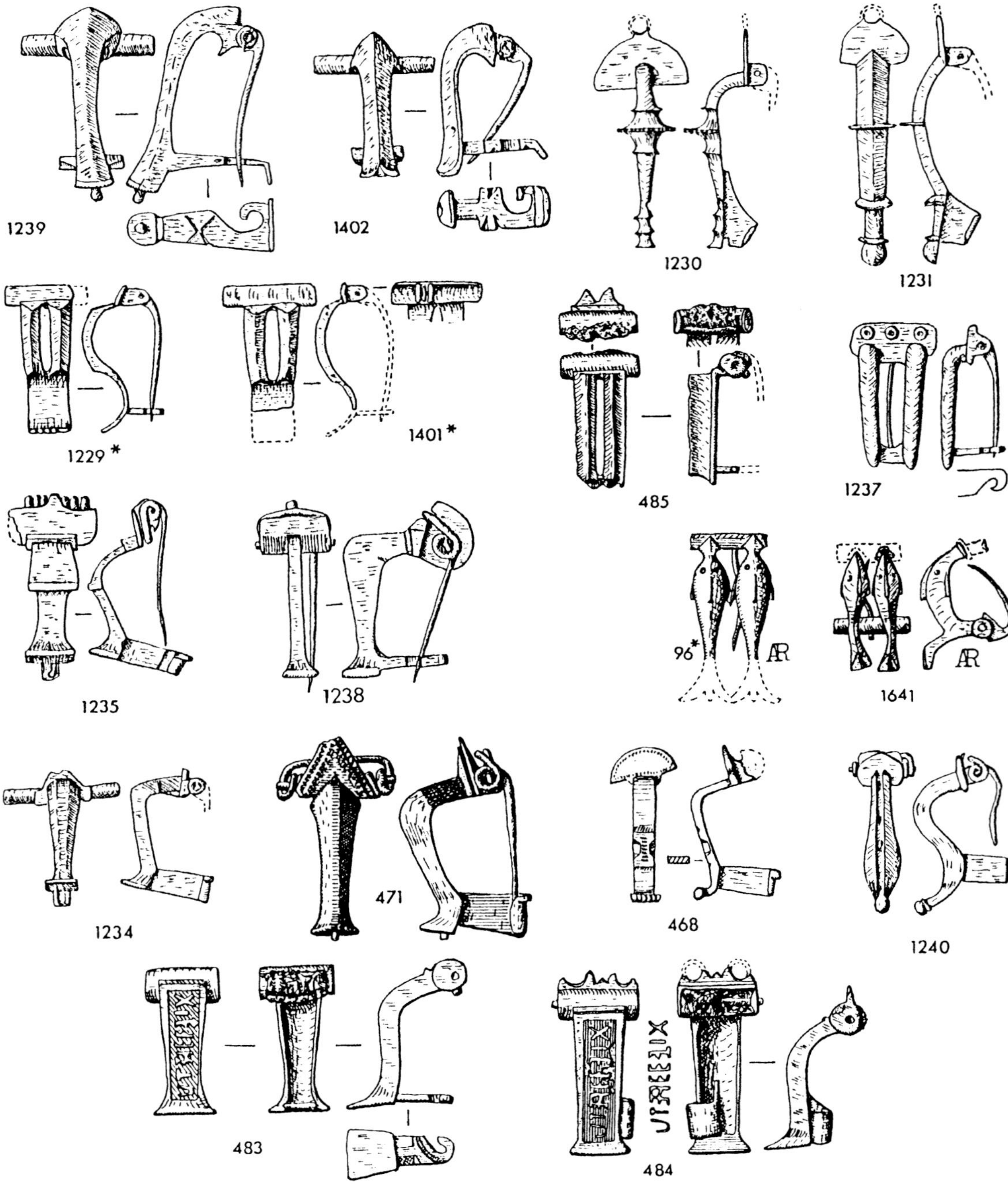

Fig. 195 Knee brooch variants, 2nd century AD. 483–4, inscribed and enamelled.

1–212 in ARBB
213–718 in IARB
719–1441 in BoA
1442–1729 in ABOA

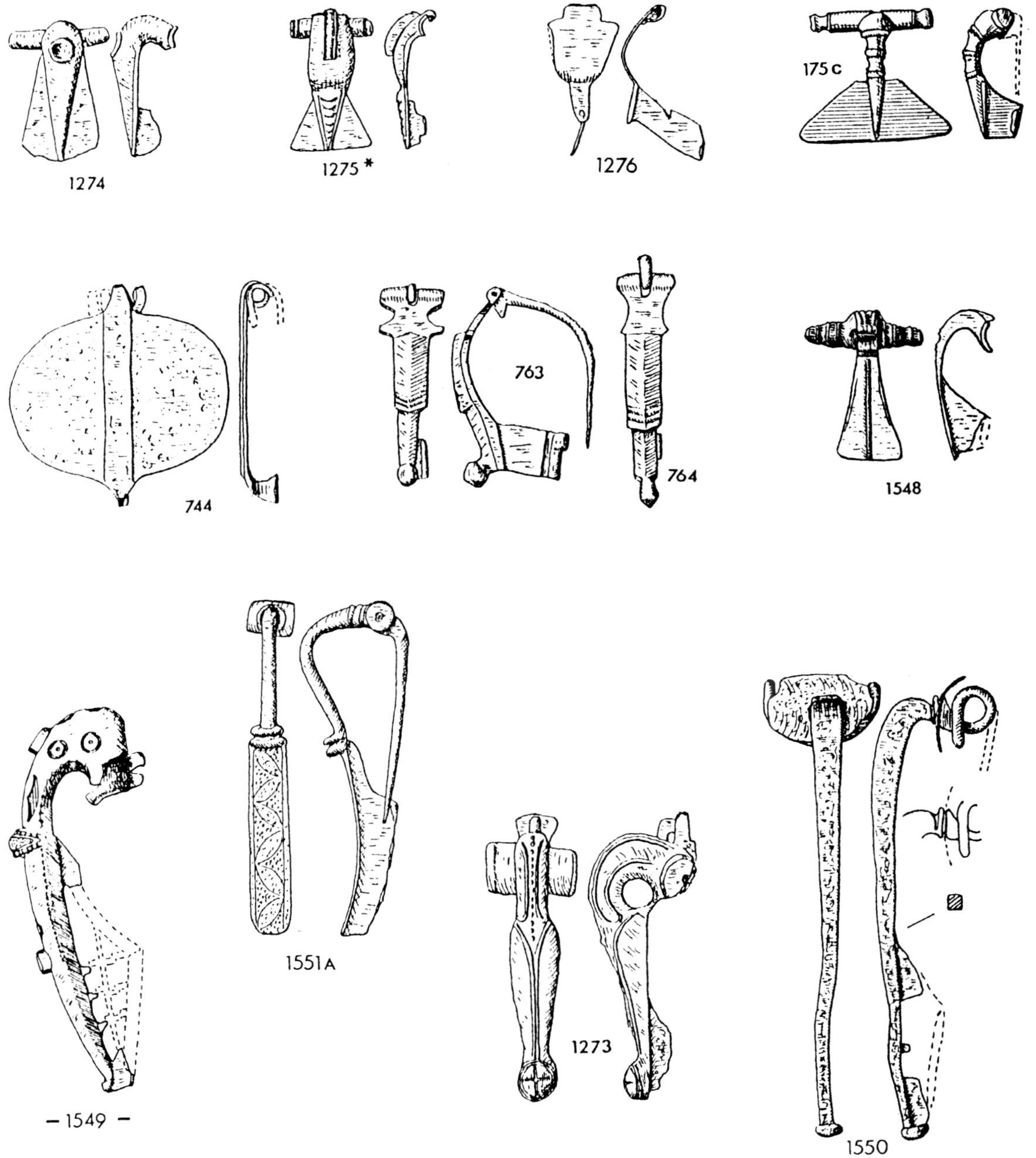

Fig. 196 Unclassified Bow brooches. c. 1st century BC/AD.

1–212 in **ARBB**
213–718 in **IARB**
719–1441 in **BoA**
1442–1729 in **ABOA**

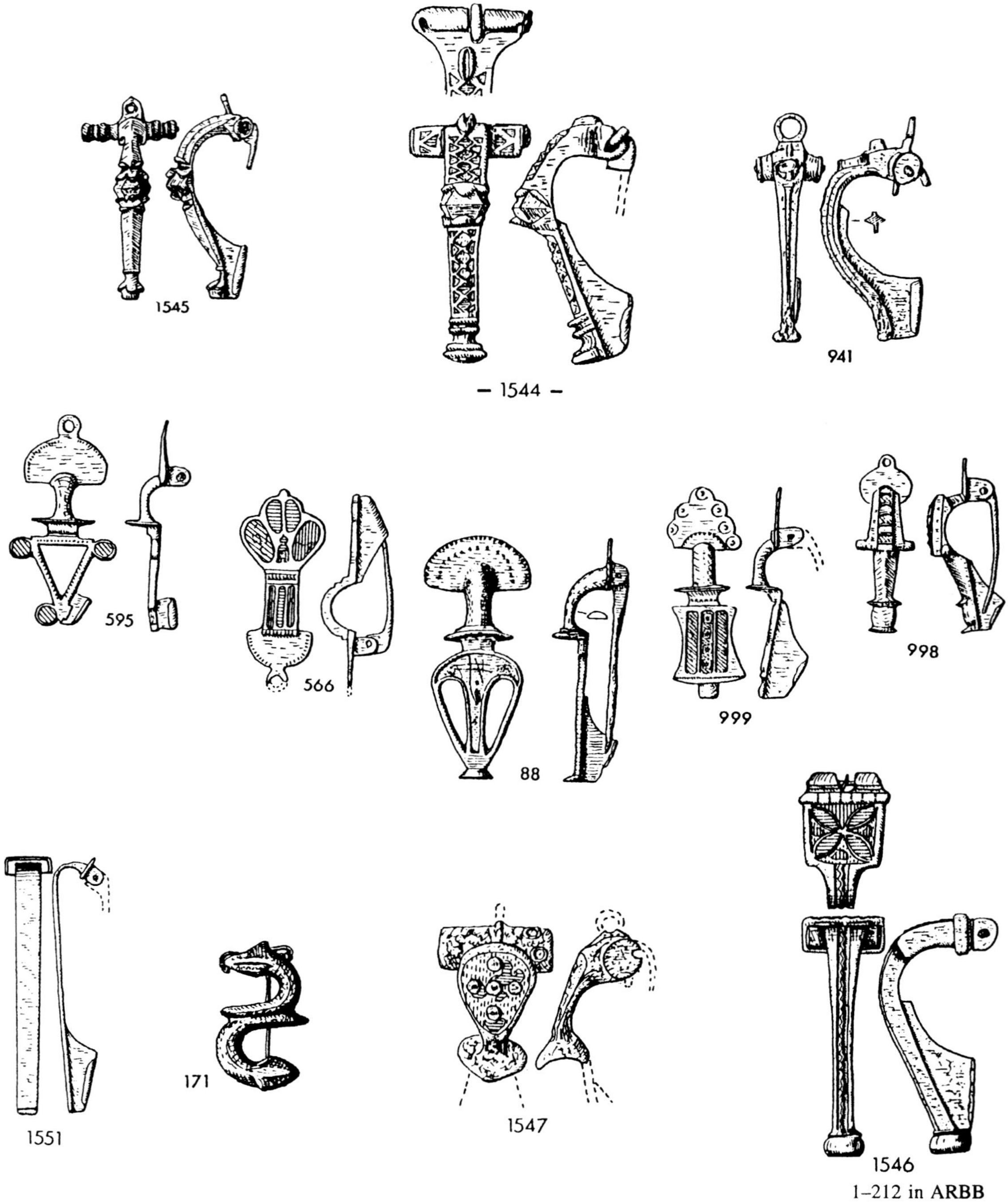

1–212 in ARBB
213–718 in IARB
719–1441 in BoA
1442–1729 in ABOA

Fig. 197 Unclassified Bow brooches. c. 2nd century AD.

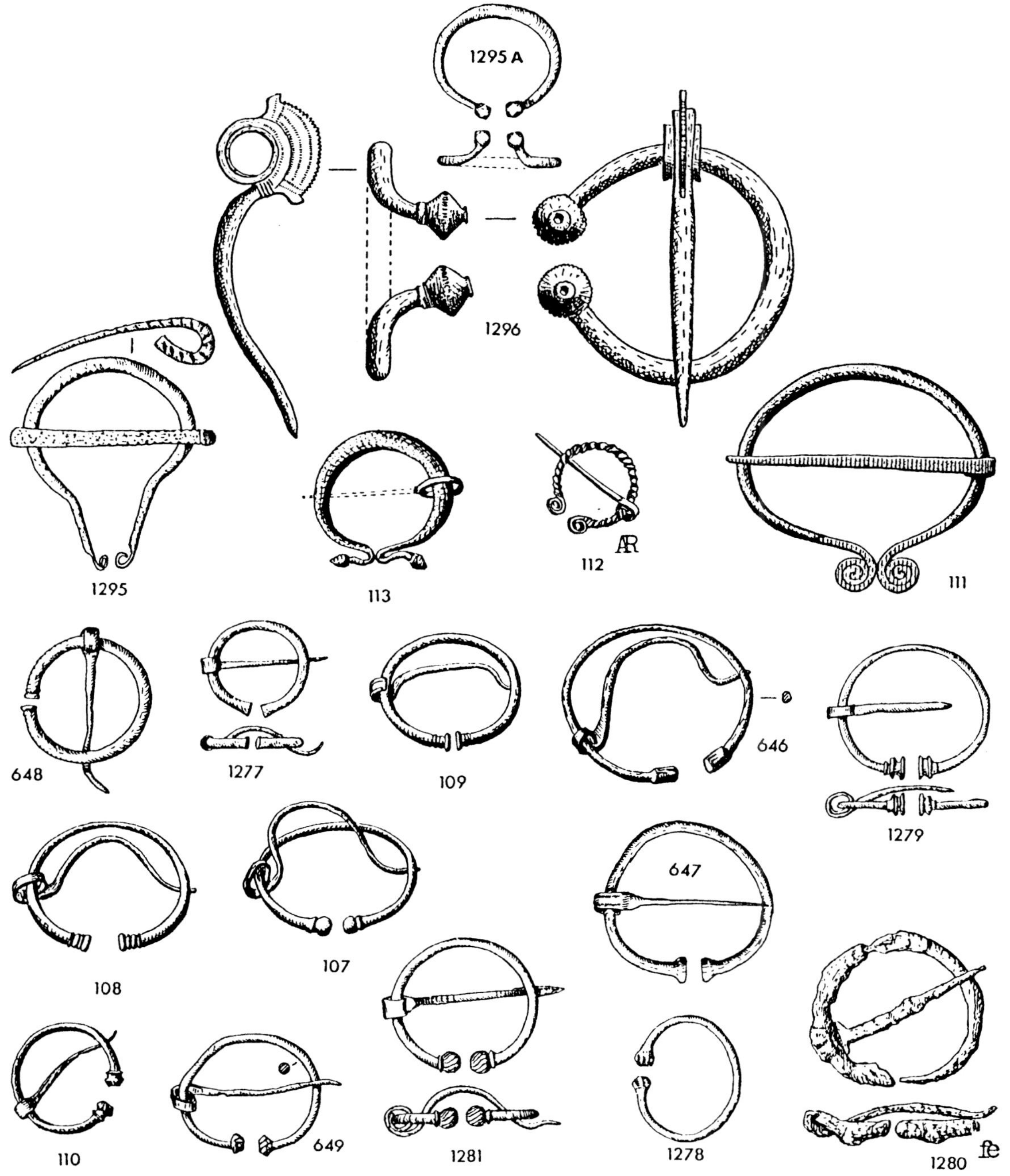

Fig. 198 Penannular brooches. Above, Germanic, late century BC; second row, types B and B1, 1st century BC/AD; remainder, types A1–4, Roman period.

1–212 in ARBB
213–718 in IARB
719–1441 in BoA
1442–1729 in ABOA

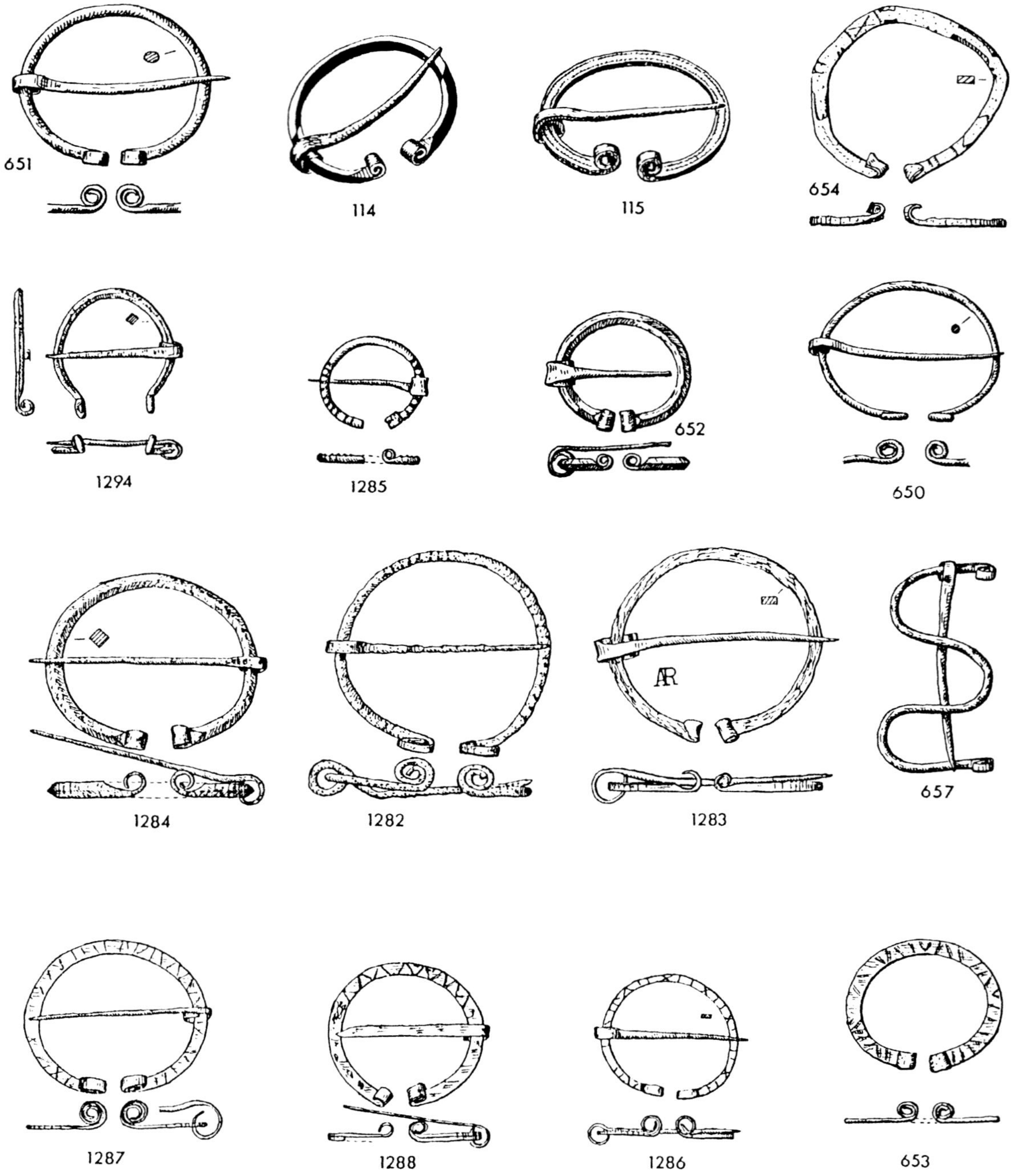

Fig. 199 Penannular brooches. Type C. Above, 1st century BC/AD; bottom row, incised flat ring type, up to 4th century AD.

1–212 in ARBB
213–718 in IARB
719–1441 in BoA
1442–1729 in ABOA

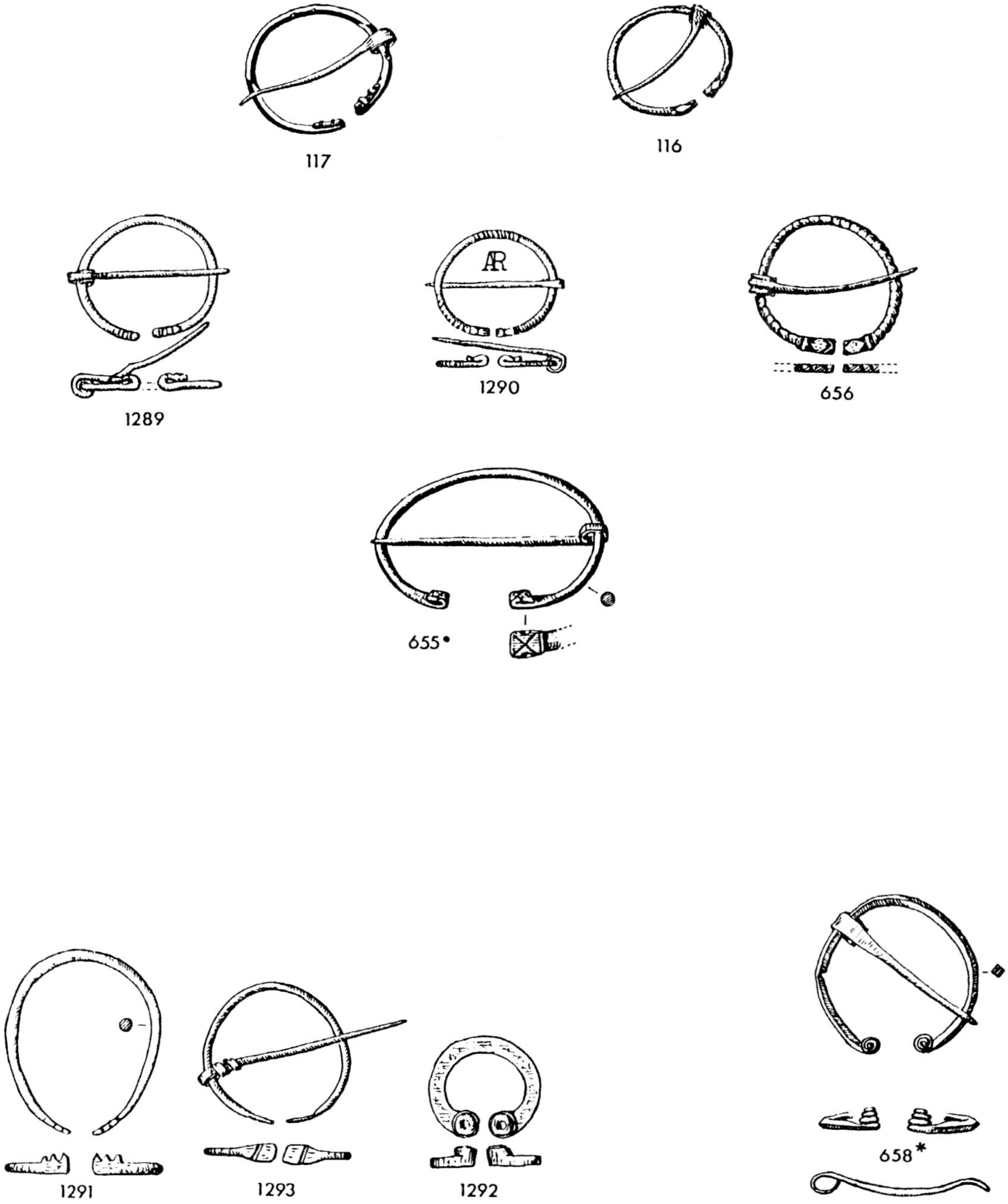

Fig. 200 Penannular brooches. Above, types D–D5, Roman period; below, types D7 and H3, 5th century AD; 658 unclassified beehive terminals.

1–212 in **ARBB**
213–718 in **IARB**
719–1441 in **BoA**
1442–1729 in **ABOA**

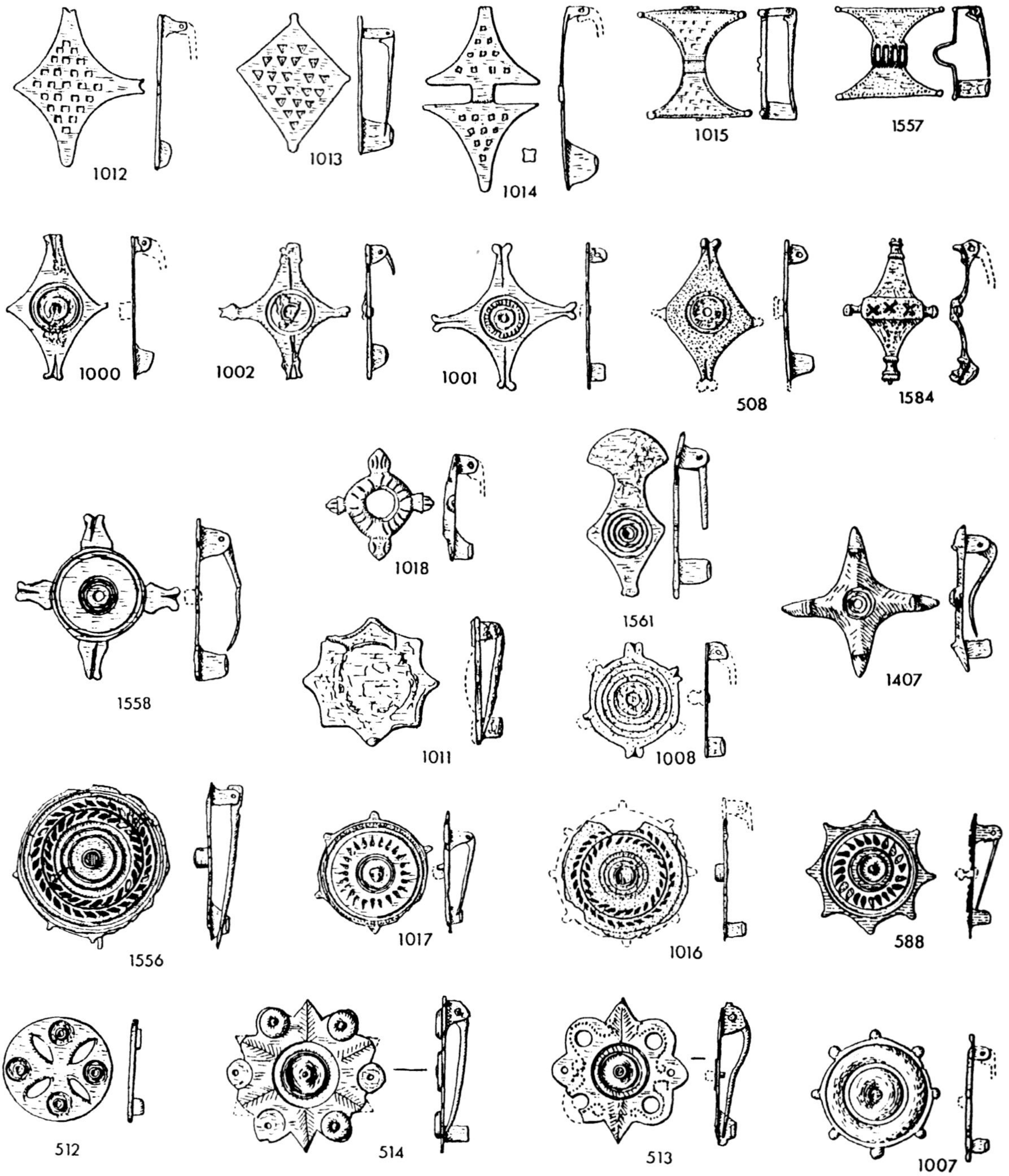

1–212 in **ARBB**
213–718 in **IARB**
719–1441 in **BoA**
1442–1729 in **ABOA**

Fig. 201 Plate brooches, early types, mid to late 1st century AD.

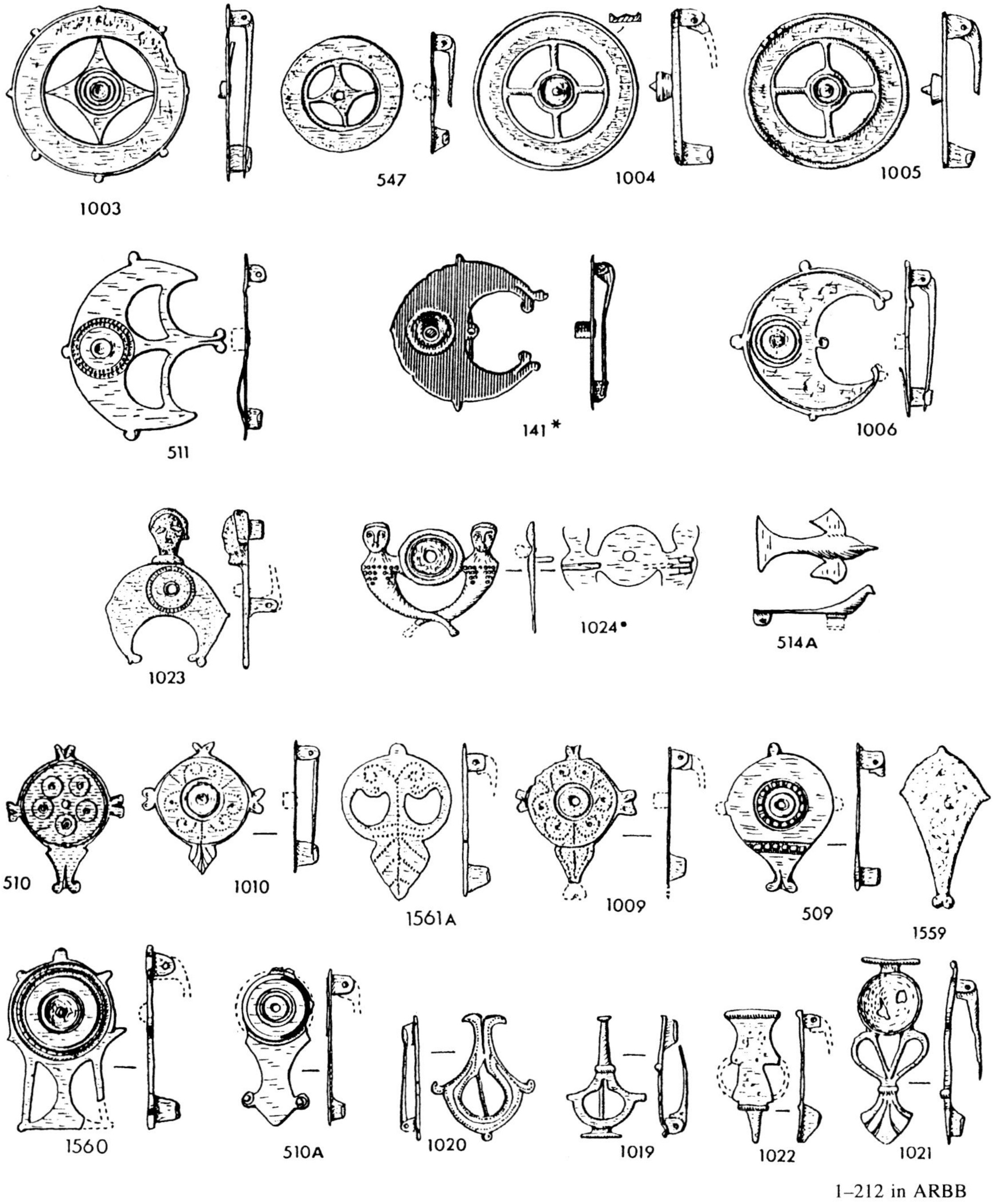

1–212 in ARBB
213–718 in IARB
719–1441 in BoA
1442–1729 in ABOA

Fig. 202 Plate brooches, early types, mid to late 1st century AD.

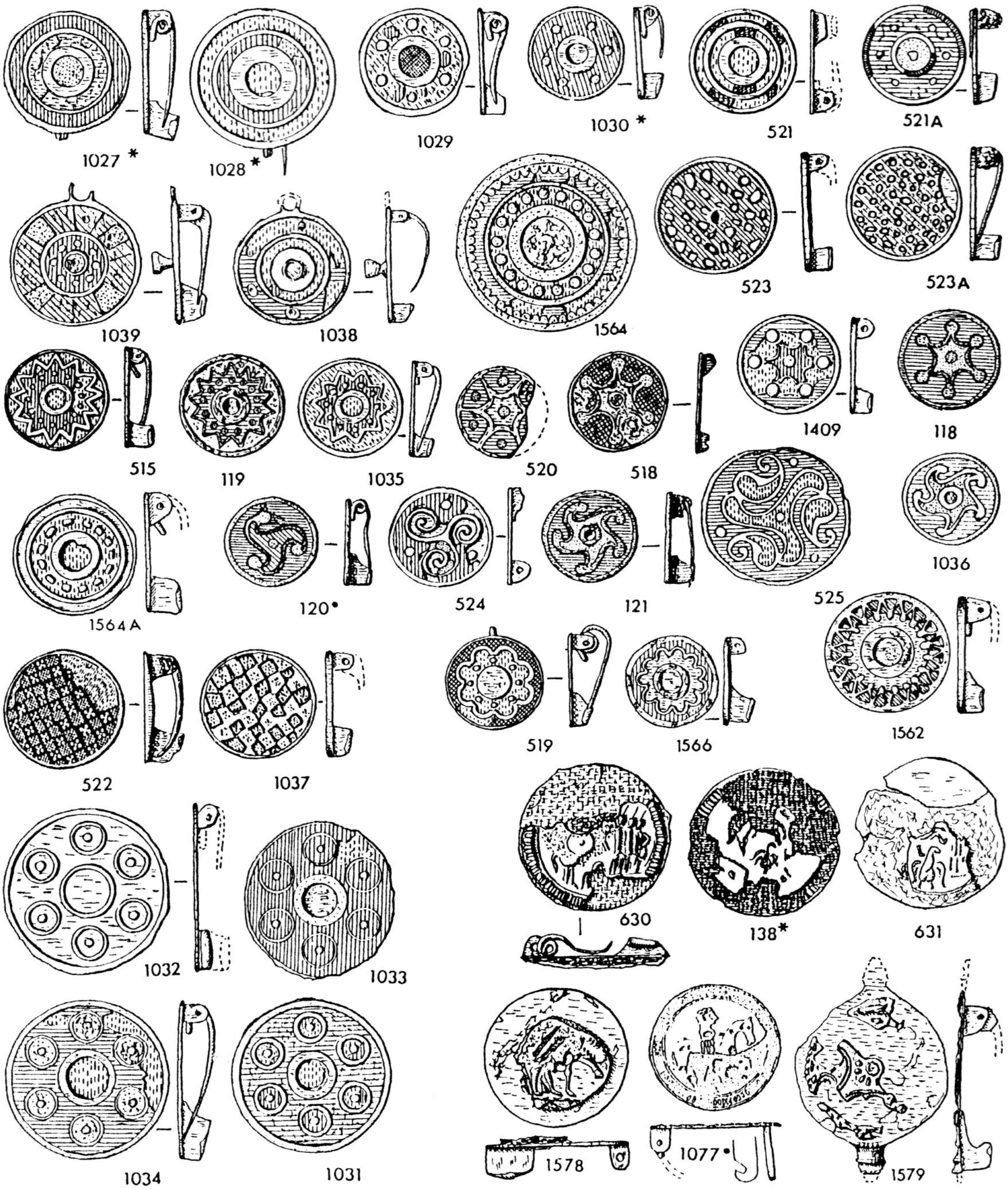

1–212 in ARBB
213–718 in IARB
719–1441 in BoA
1442–1729 in ABOA

Fig. 203 Disc brooches, flat and plain edged, 2nd century AD.

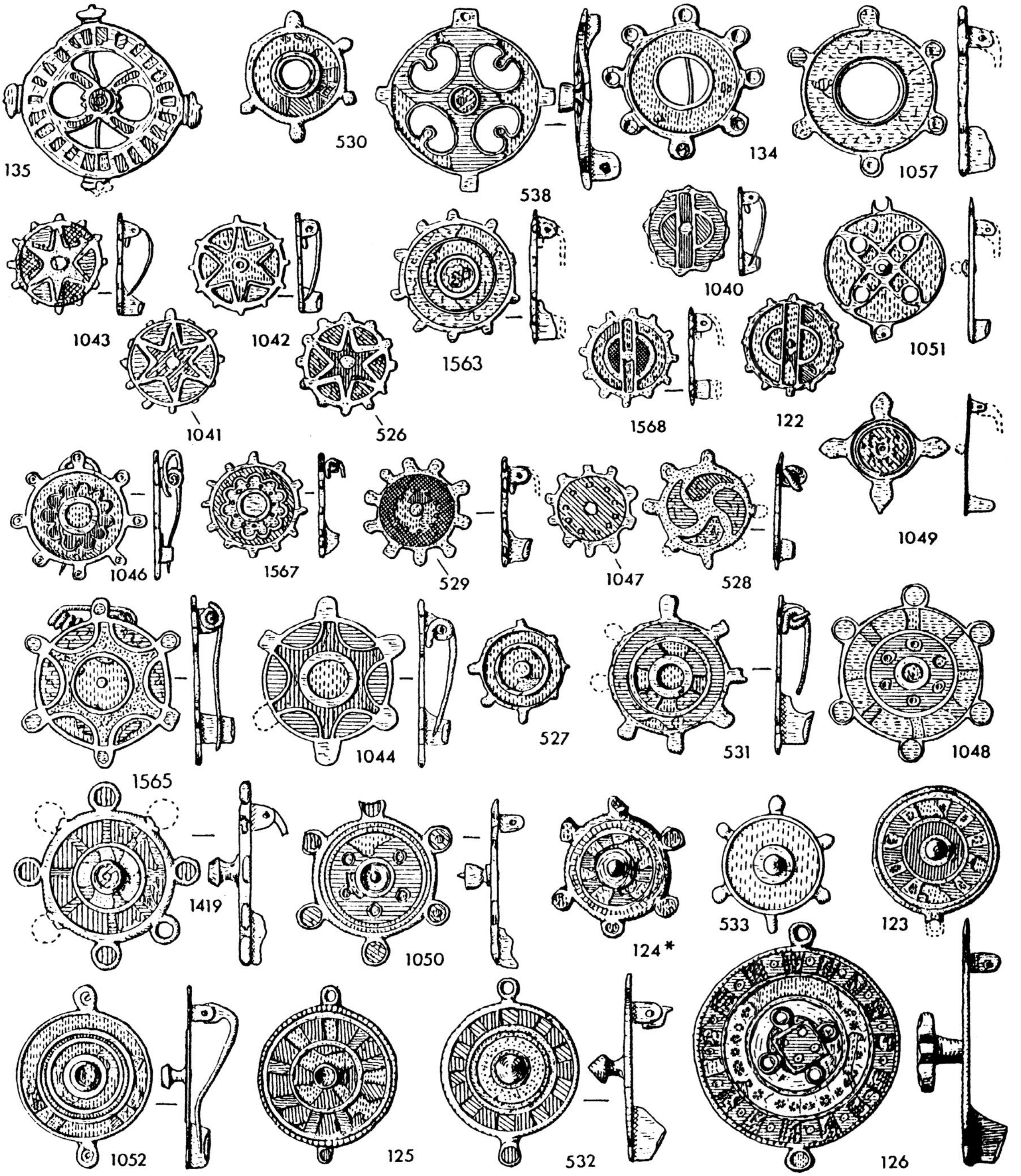

Fig. 204 Disc brooches, flat with peripheral lugs. Perforated above, with centre boss below. 2nd century AD.

1–212 in **ARBB**
213–718 in **IARB**
719–1441 in **BoA**
1442–1729 in **ABOA**

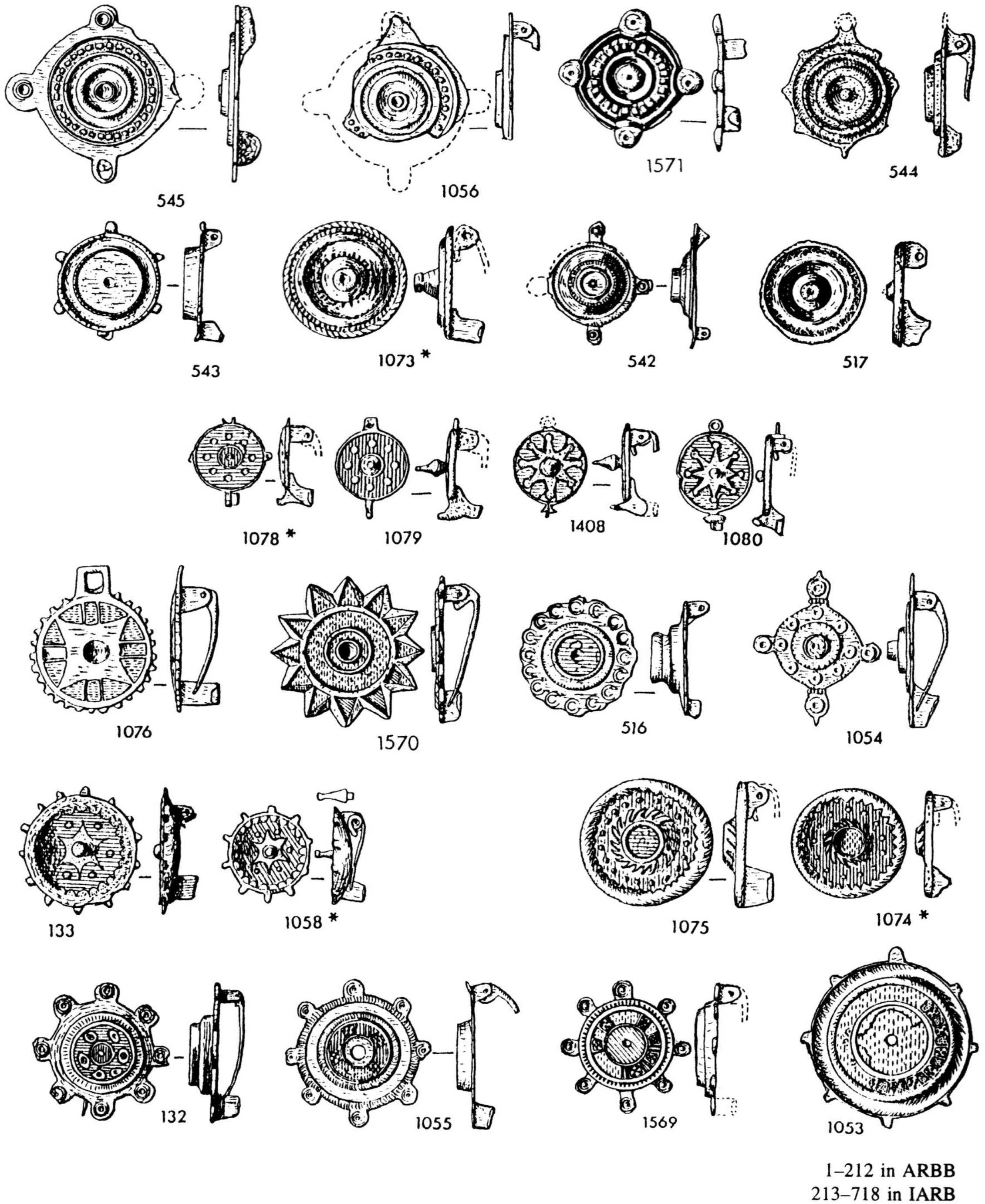

Fig. 205 Disc brooches, moulded types, 2nd century AD.

1–212 in **ARBB**
213–718 in **IARB**
719–1441 in **BoA**
1442–1729 in **ABOA**

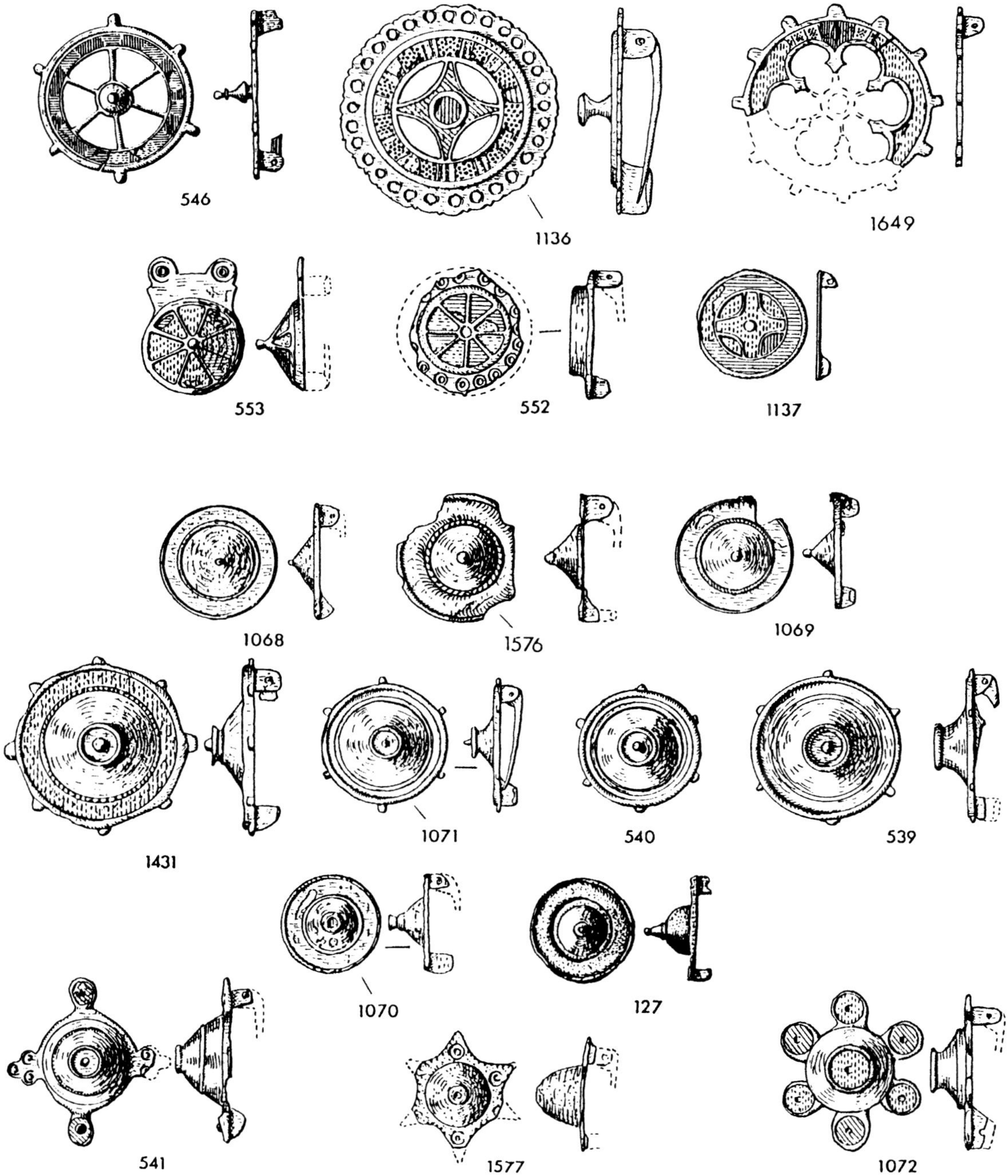

Fig. 206 Disc brooches, 2nd century AD. Above, later Wheel brooches and variants; below, Tutulus type and variants.

1–212 in ARBB
213–718 in IARB
719–1441 in BoA
1442–1729 in ABOA

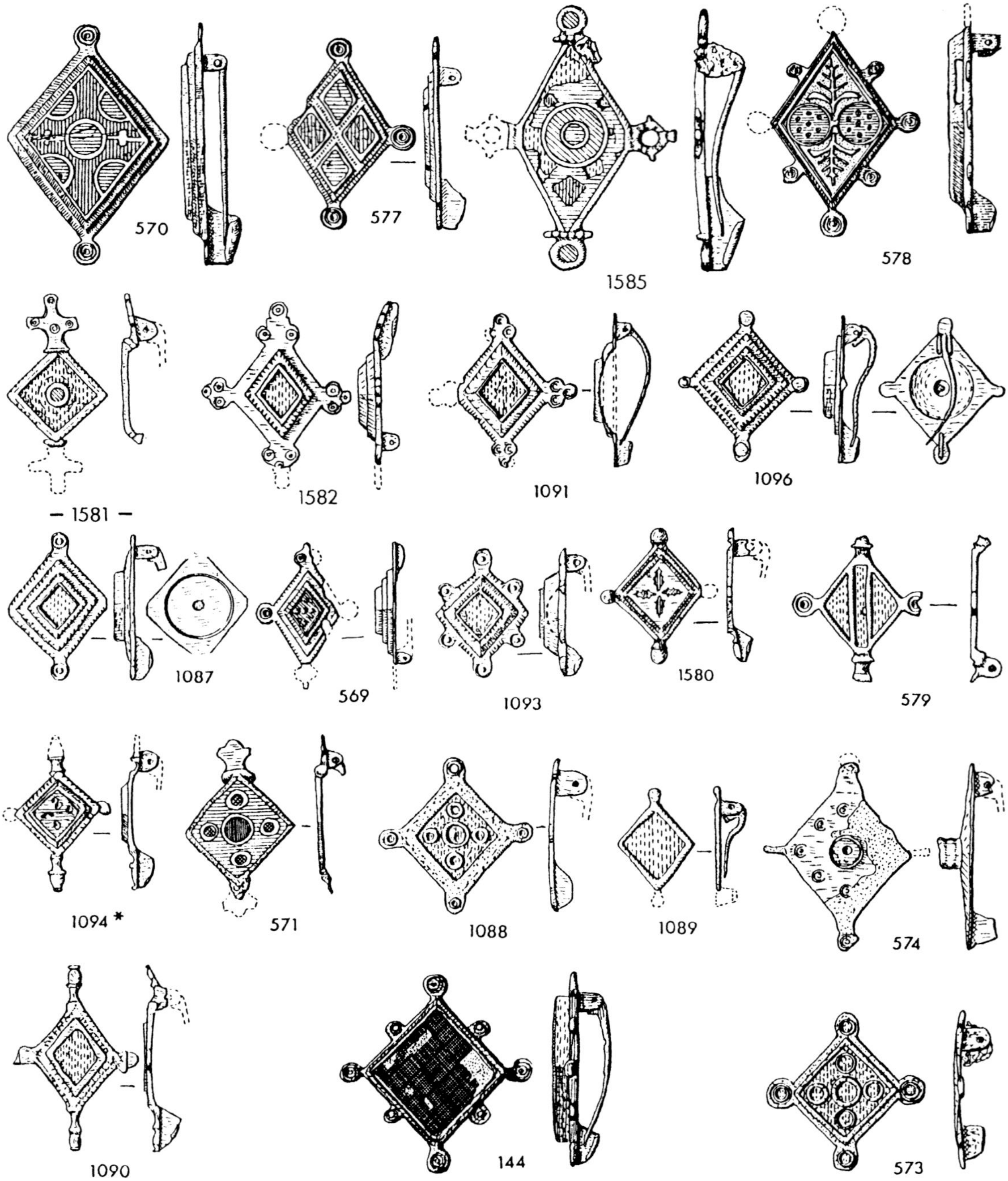

1–212 in ARBB
213–718 in IARB
719–1441 in BoA
1442–1729 in ABOA

Fig. 207 Plate brooches, lozenge shape with lugs, 2nd century AD.

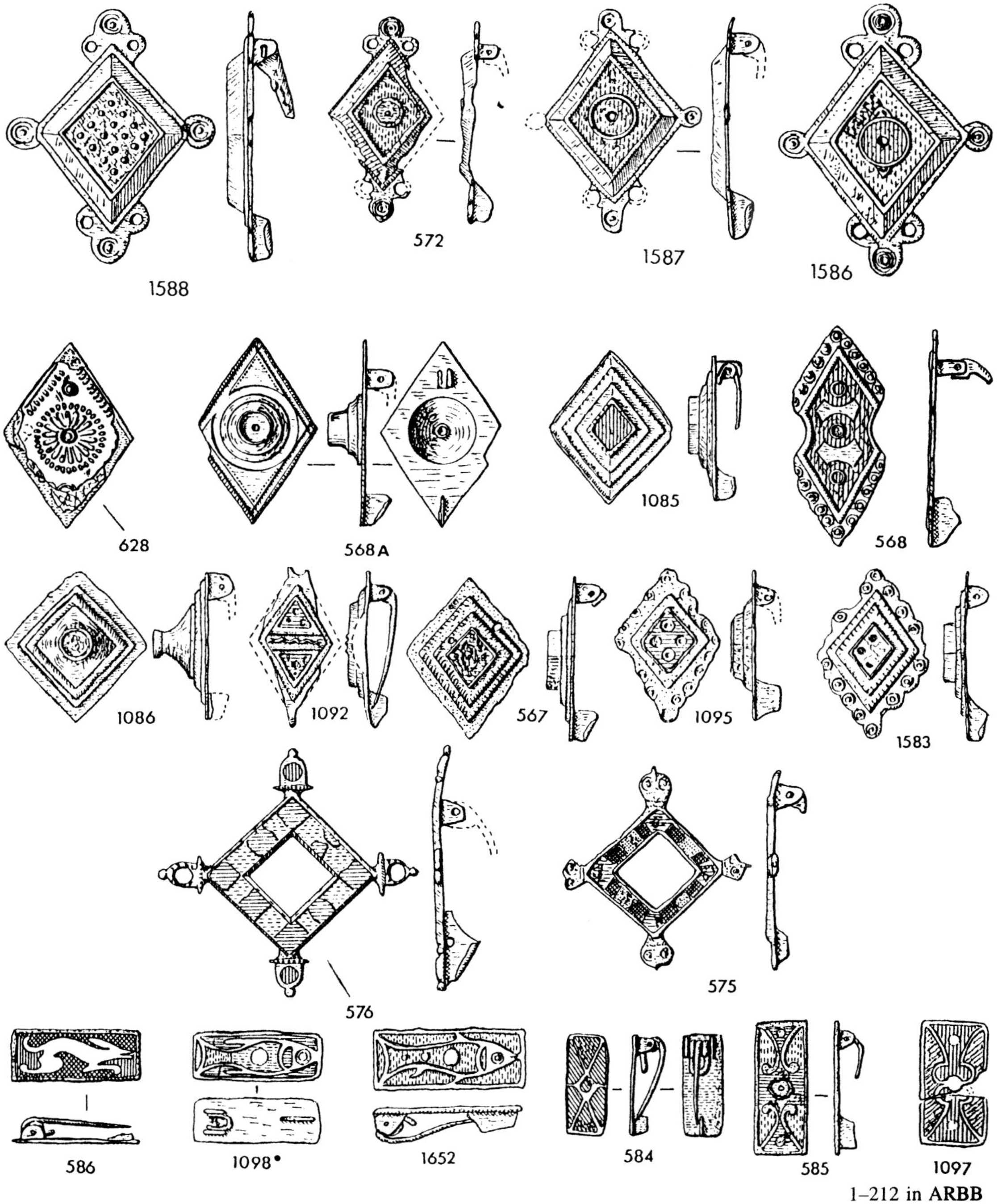

1–212 in **ARBB**
213–718 in **IARB**
719–1441 in **BoA**
1442–1729 in **ABOA**

Fig. 208 Plate brooches, lozenge shape various, and rectangular brooches. 2nd century AD.

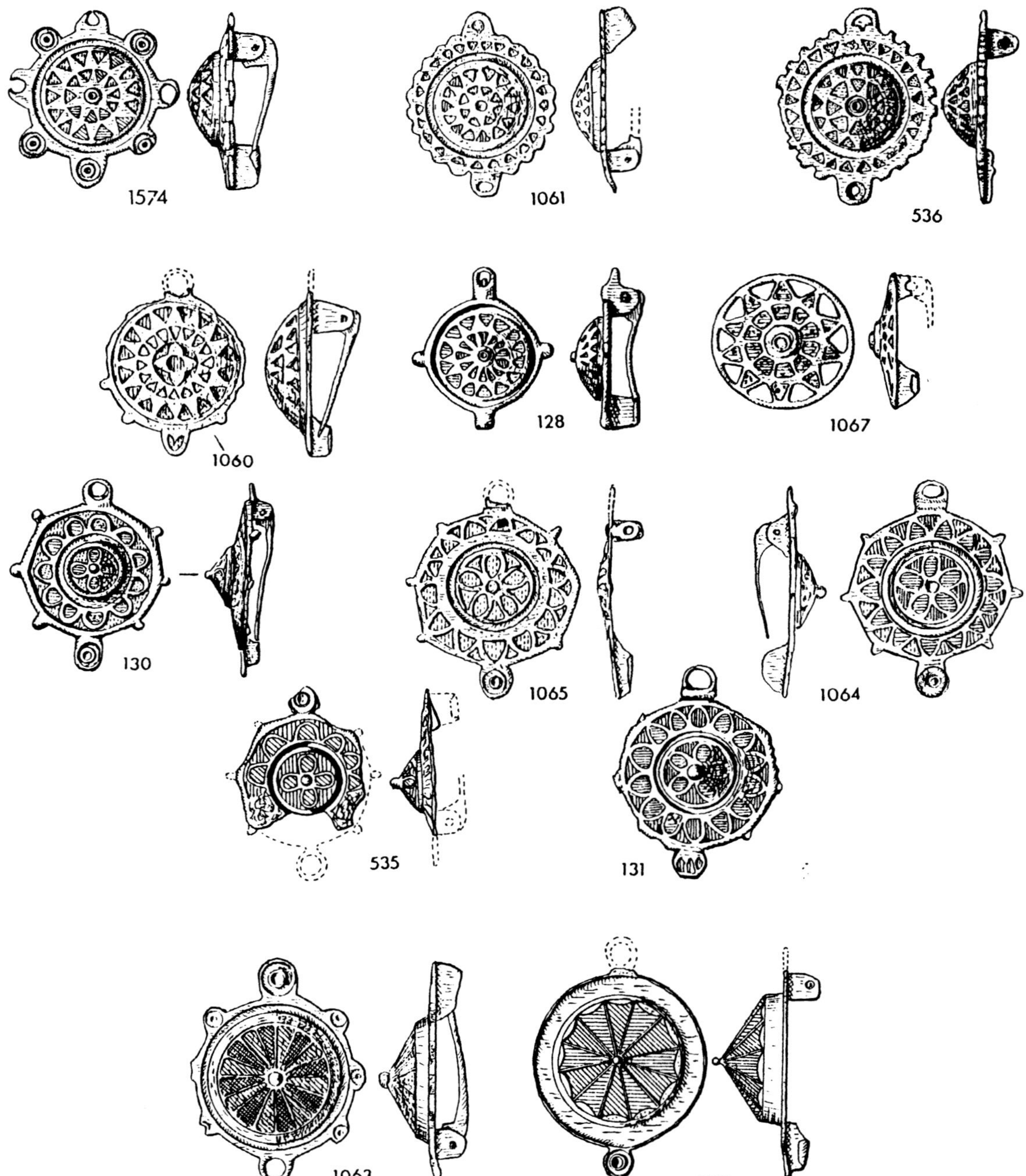

Fig. 209 Plate brooches, Umbonate type, 2nd century AD. Above, triangular enamel cells; centre, rounded cells; below, conical type.

1–212 in **ARBB**
213–718 in **IARB**
719–1441 in **BoA**
1442–1729 in **ABOA**

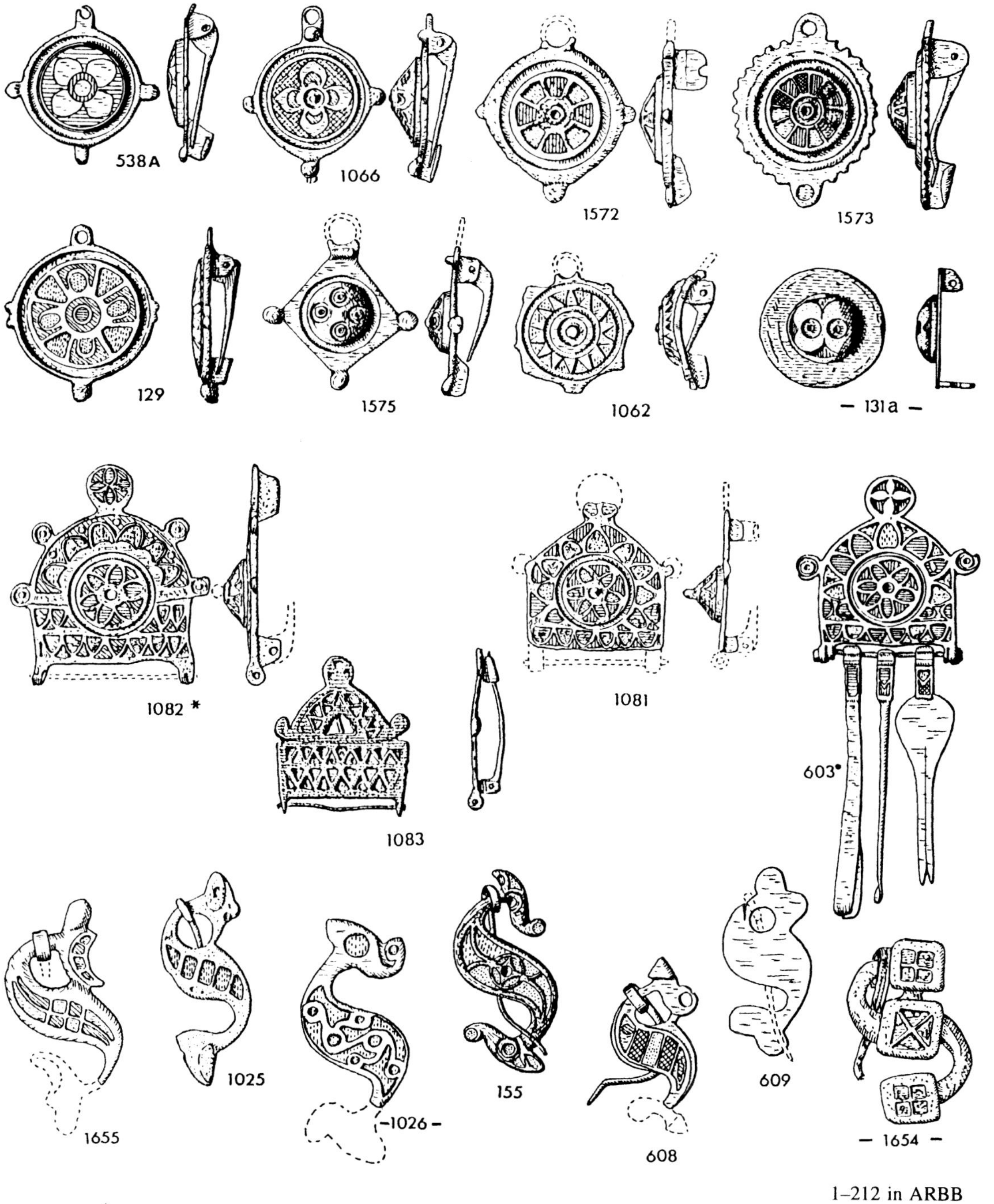

1–212 in ARBB
213–718 in IARB
719–1441 in BoA
1442–1729 in ABOA

Fig. 210 Plate brooches, 2nd century AD. Above, umbonate variants; centre, Chatelaine type; below Dragonesque brooches.

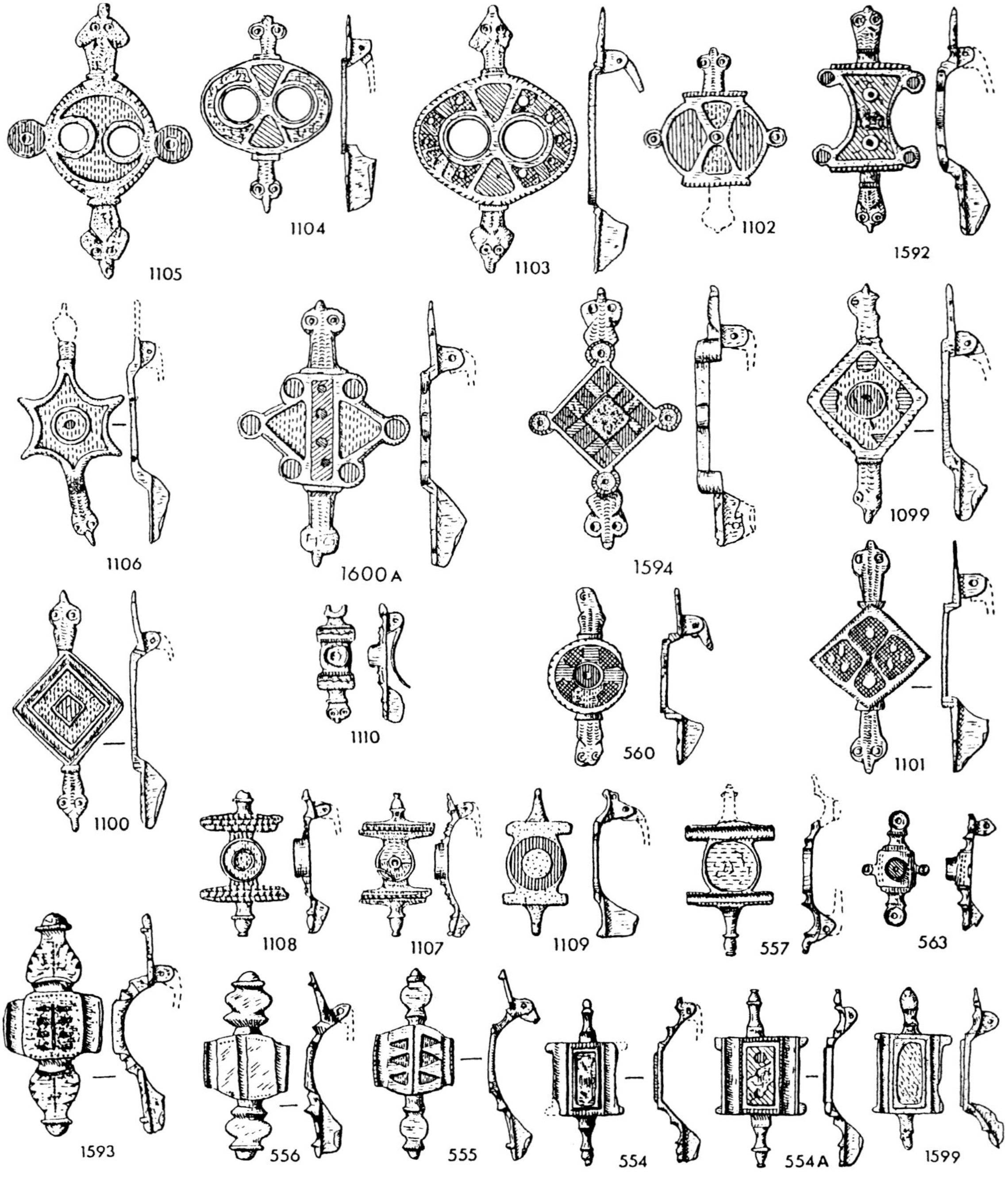

Fig. 211 Plate brooches, Equal-ended types, 2nd century AD. Above, zoomorphic terminals; below, Crossbar type and Side channel type.

1–212 in ARBB
213–718 in IARB
719–1441 in BoA
1442–1729 in ABOA

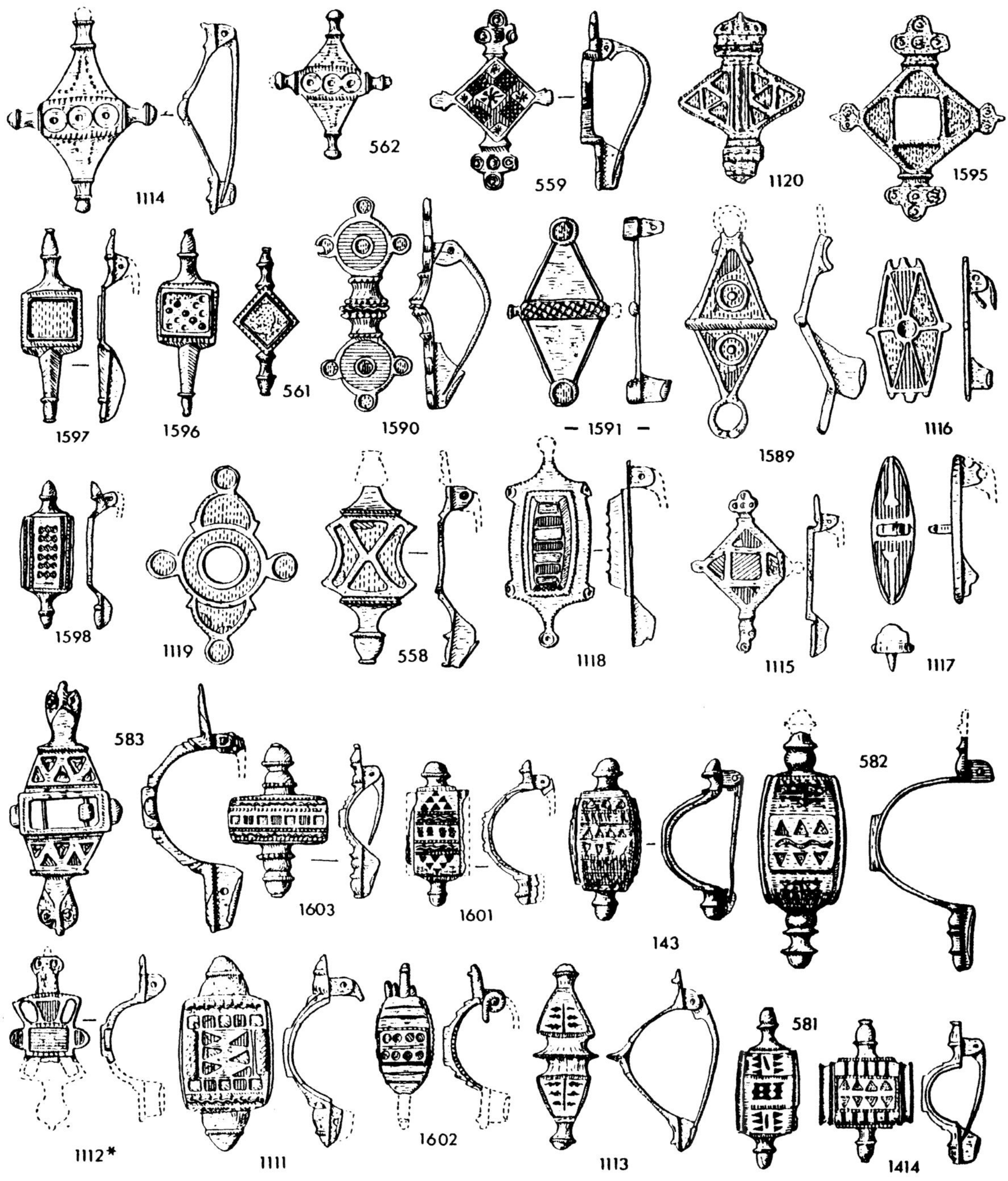

1–212 in **ARBB**
213–718 in **IARB**
719–1441 in **BoA**
1442–1729 in **ABOA**

Fig. 212 Plate brooches, Equal-ended types, 2nd century AD. Above, various shapes; below, Bridge type.

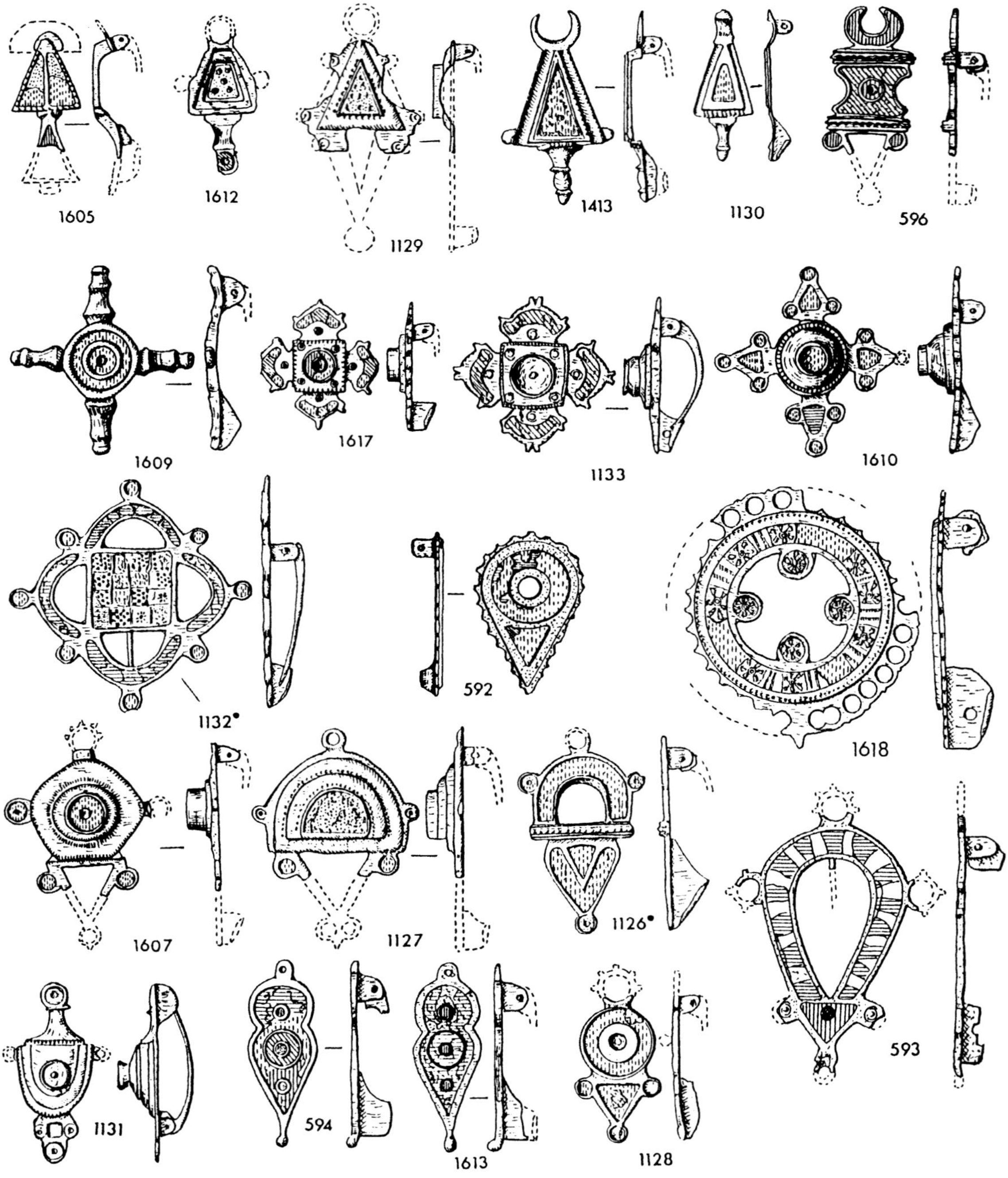

1–212 in ARBB
213–718 in IARB
719–1441 in BoA
1442–1729 in ABOA

Fig. 213 Composite Plate brooches, 2nd century AD.

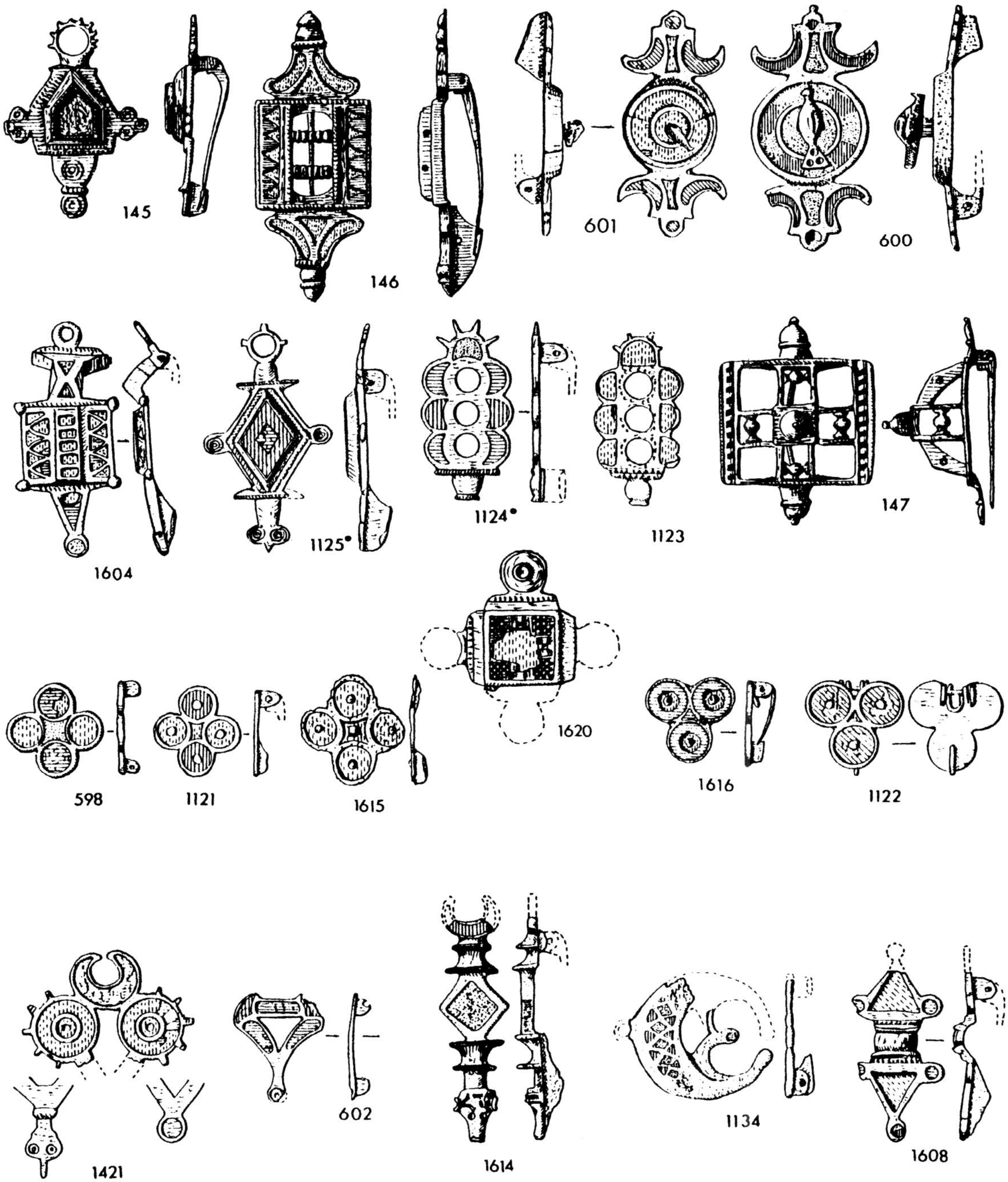

1–212 in ARBB
213–718 in IARB
719–1441 in BoA
1442–1729 in ABOA

Fig. 214 Composite Plate brooches, 2nd century AD.

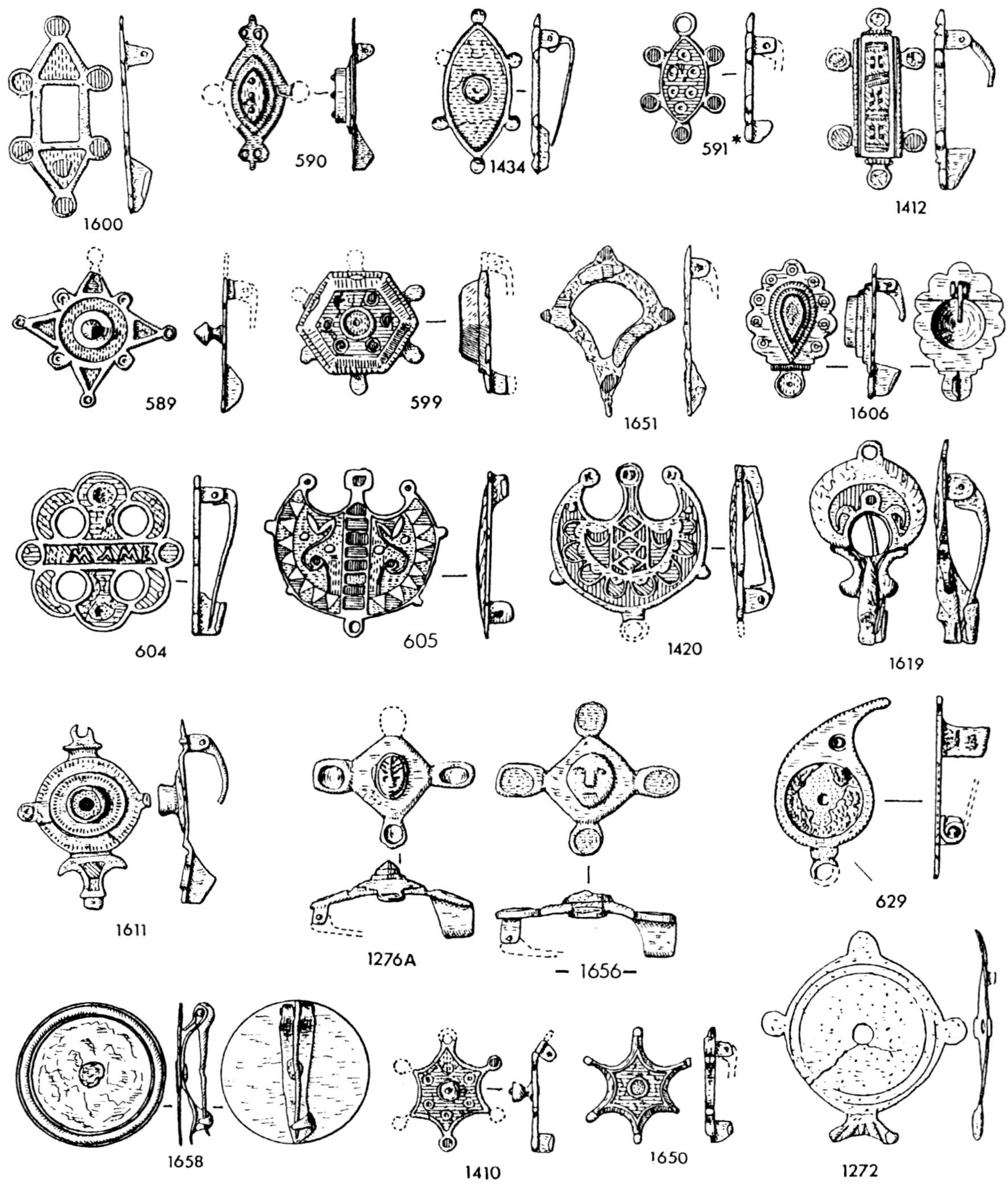

Fig. 215 Plate brooches, 2nd century AD. Various forms.

1–212 in ARBB
213–718 in IARB
719–1441 in BoA
1442–1729 in ABOA

1–212 in **ARBB**
213–718 in **IARB**
719–1441 in **BoA**
1442–1729 in **ABOA**

Fig. 216 Openwork non-enamelled brooches. 2nd into 3rd century AD.

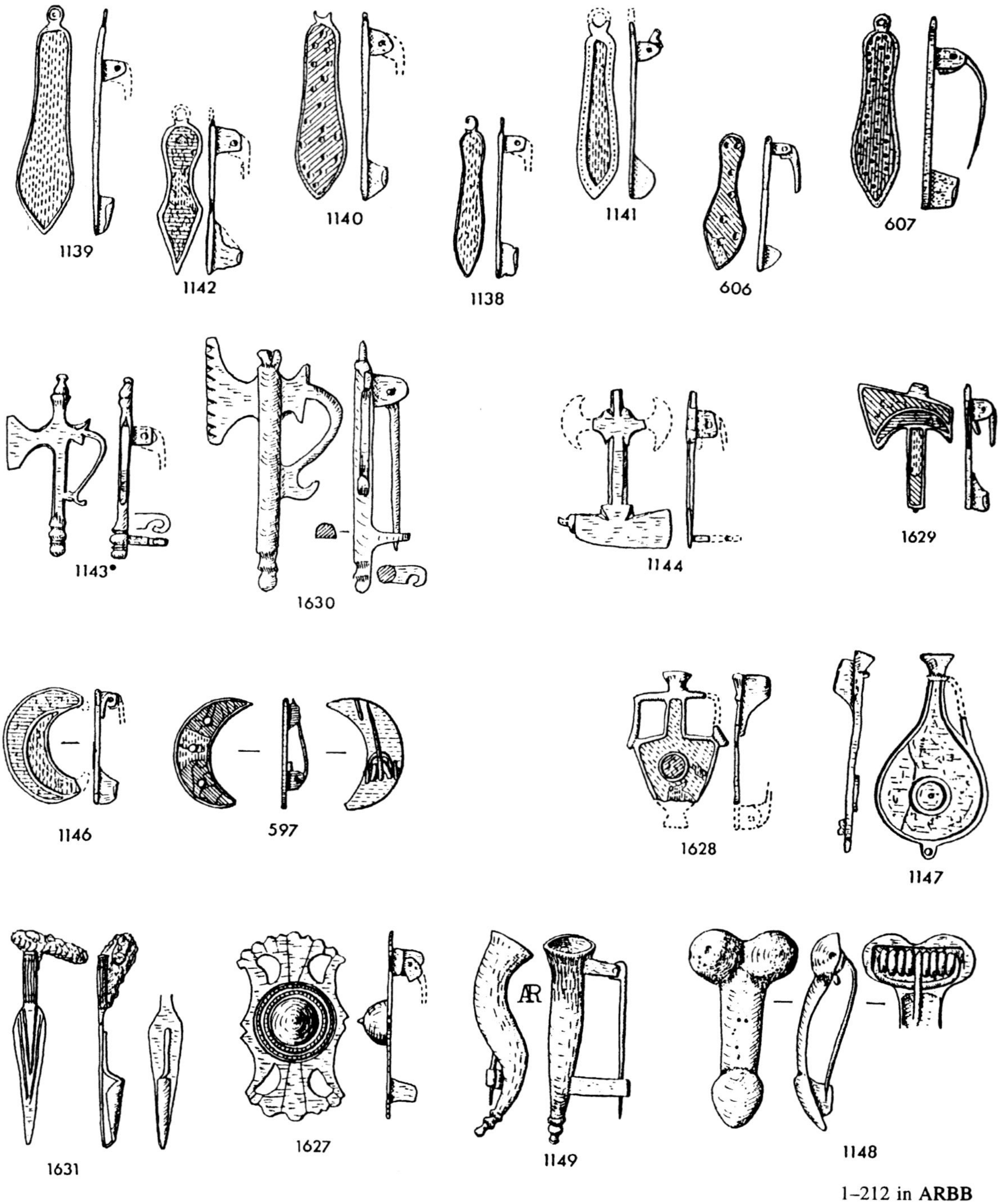

1–212 in **ARBB**
213–718 in **IARB**
719–1441 in **BoA**
1442–1729 in **ABOA**

Fig. 217 Skeuomorphic Plate brooches, 2nd century AD.

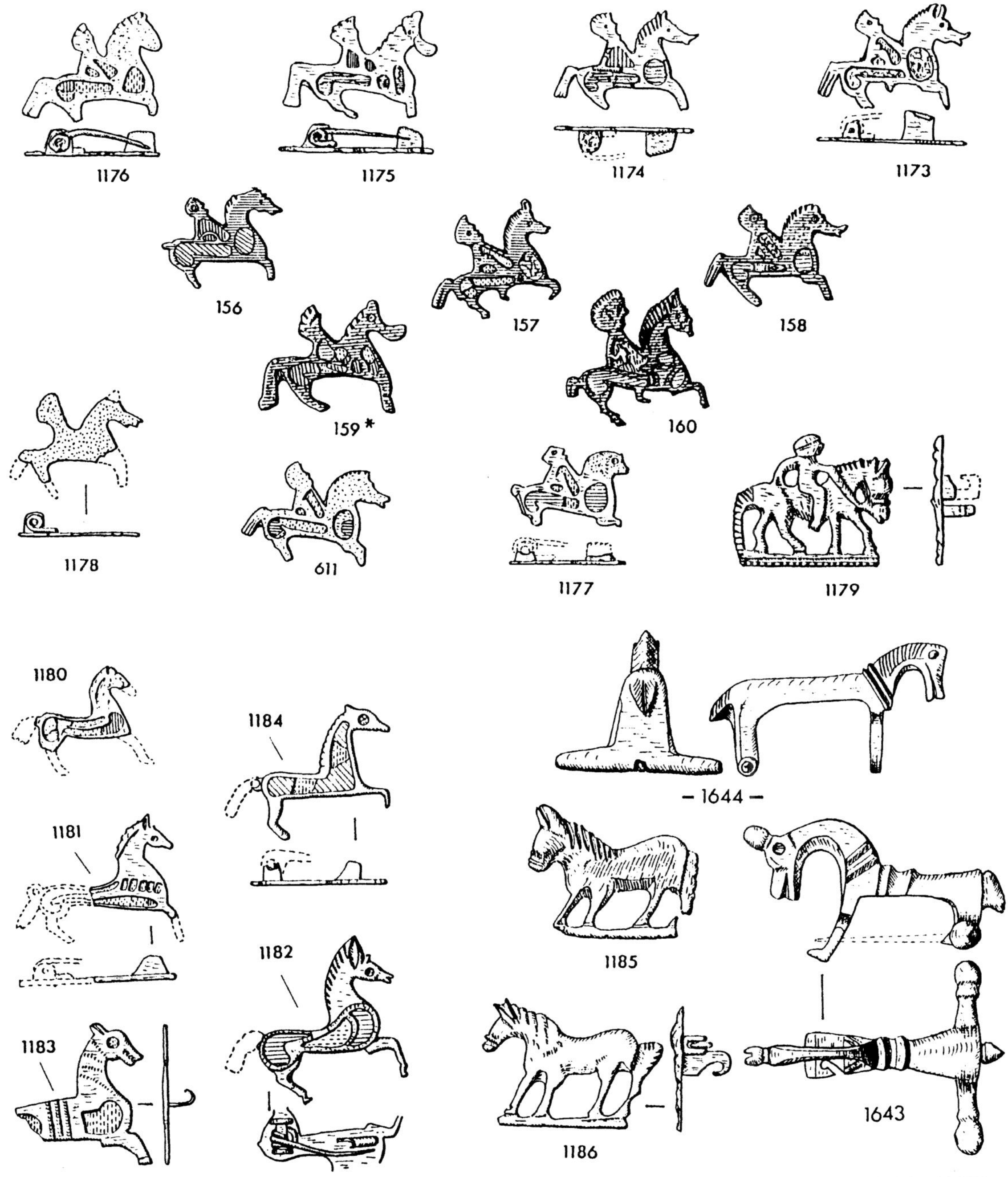

Fig. 218 Zoomorphic brooches, 2nd century AD. Above, Horse-and-rider type; below, horse brooches. Lower right, continental running into 3rd century.

1–212 in ARBB
213–718 in IARB
719–1441 in BoA
1442–1729 in ABOA

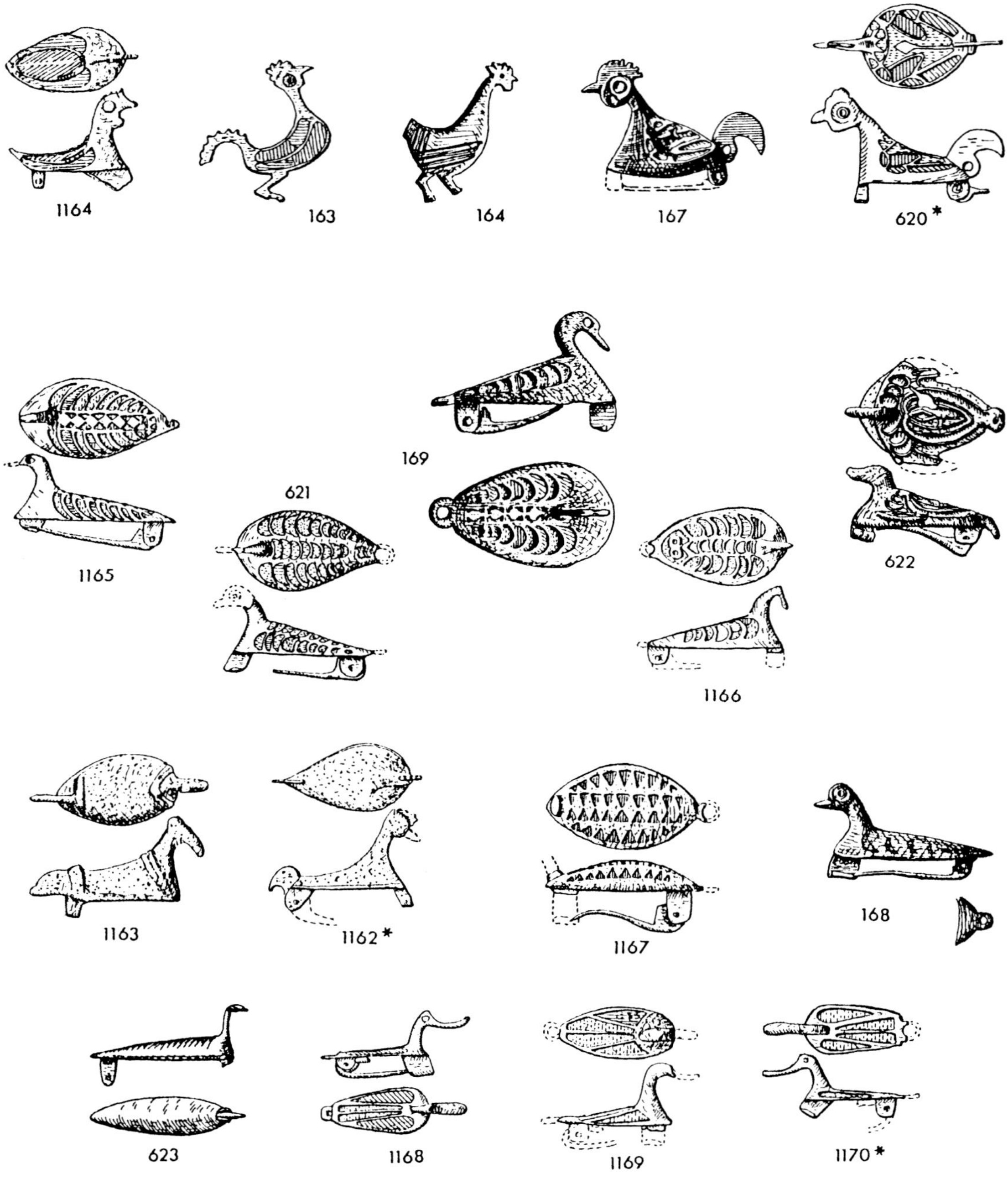

Fig. 219 Zoomorphic brooches, 2nd century AD. Domestic birds. Above, chicken; below, ducks. (1167 is problematic)

1–212 in ARBB
213–718 in IARB
719–1441 in BoA
1442–1729 in ABOA

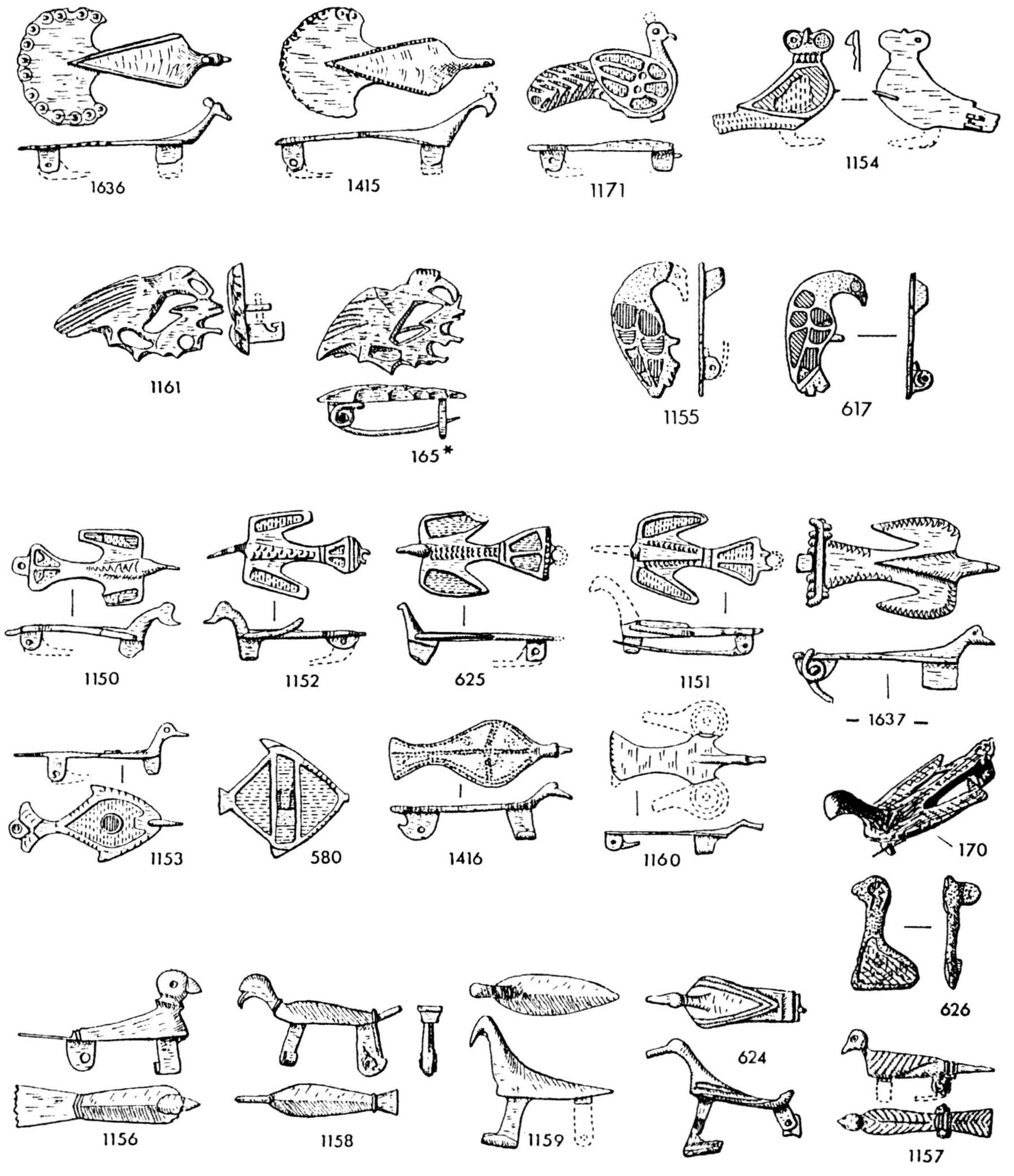

1–212 in **ARBB**
213–718 in **IARB**
719–1441 in **BoA**
1442–1729 in **ABOA**

Fig. 220 Zoomorphic brooches, 2nd century AD. Various bird types.

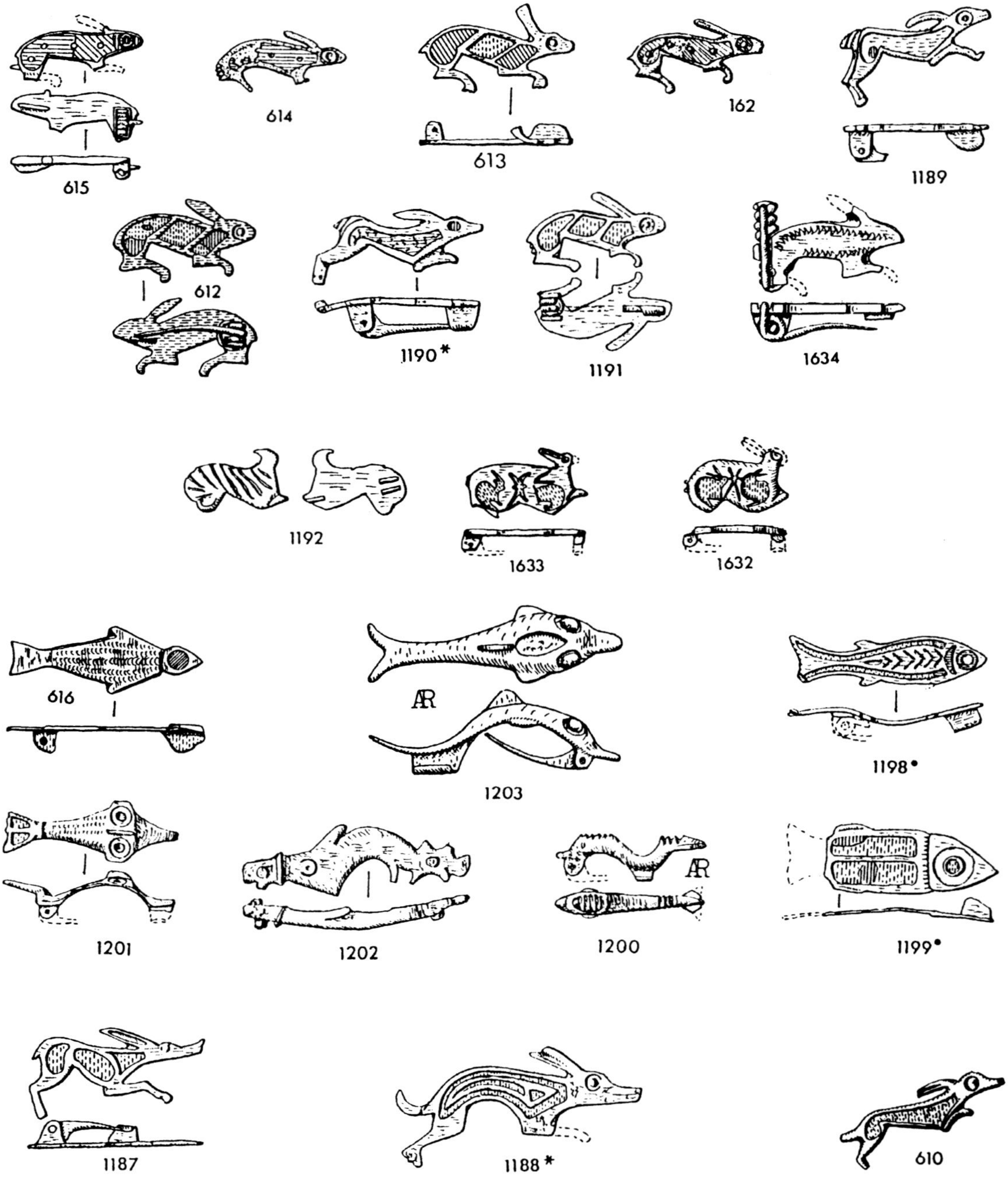

Fig. 221 Zoomorphic brooches, 2nd century AD. Hares, rabbits, fish and dogs.

1–212 in **ARBB**
213–718 in **IARB**
719–1441 in **BoA**
1442–1729 in **ABOA**

Fig. 222 Zoomorphic brooches, 2nd century AD. Wild animals, insects and fabulous creatures.

1–212 in ARBB
213–718 in IARB
719–1441 in BoA
1442–1729 in ABOA

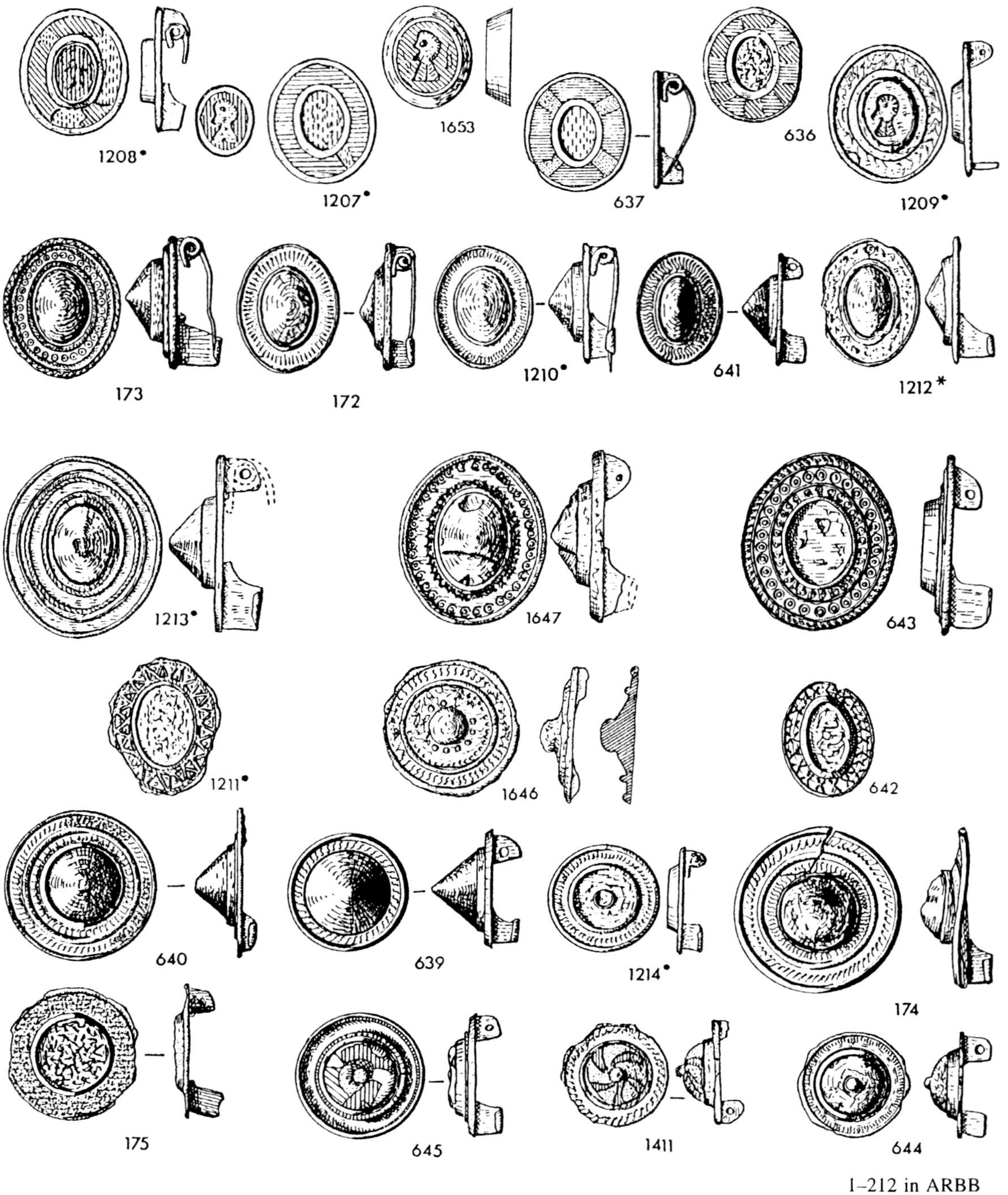

Fig. 223 Plate brooches, 2nd–3rd century AD. Above, enamelled oval with paste intaglio; remainder, gilded Glass Centre-boss type. 1646 is an aberration.

1–212 in ARBB
213–718 in IARB
719–1441 in BoA
1442–1729 in ABOA

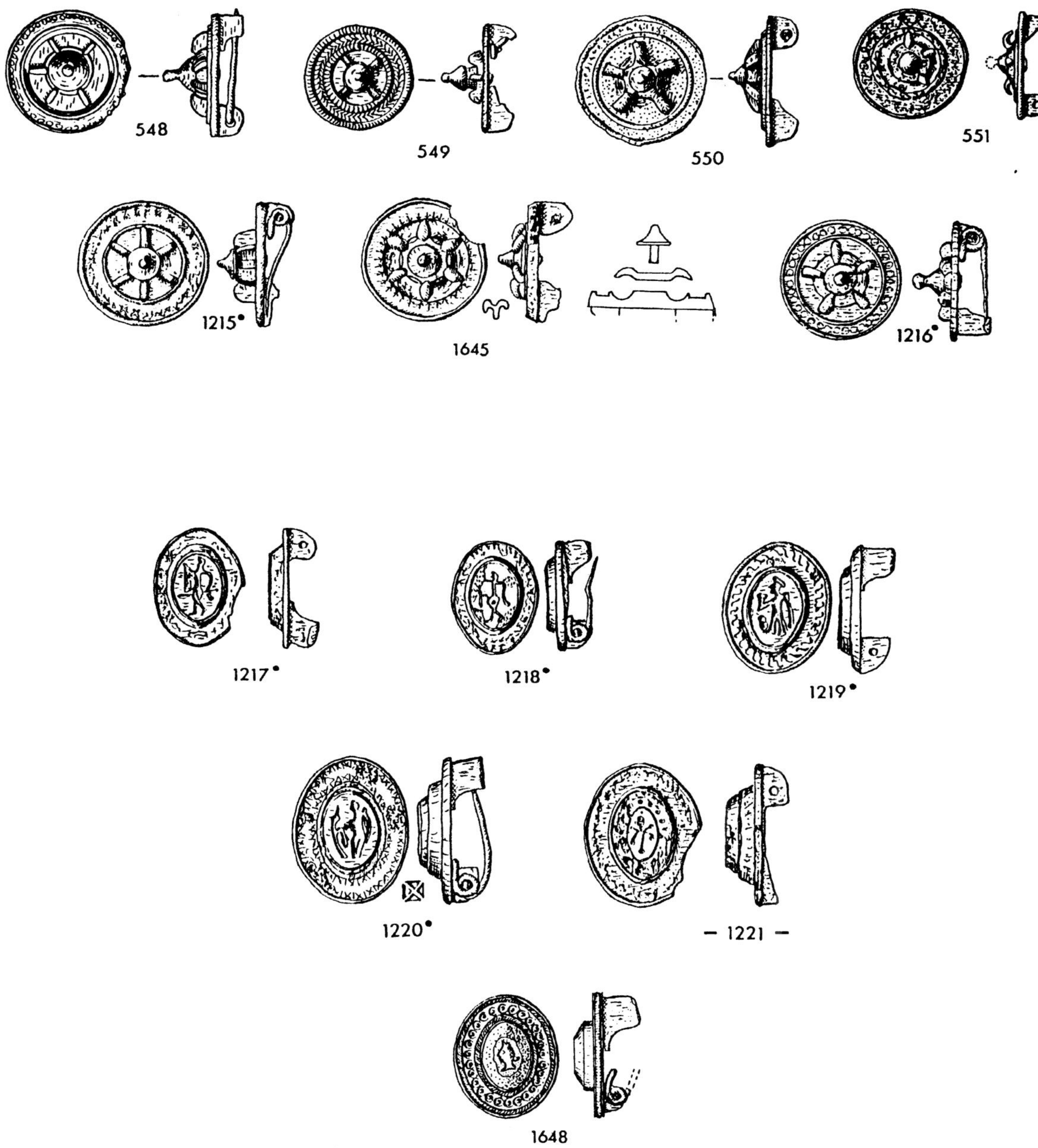

1–212 in **ARBB**
213–718 in **IARB**
719–1441 in **BoA**
1442–1729 in **ABOA**

Fig. 224 Plate brooches, 2nd–3rd century AD. Above, gilded spoked disc brooches; below, gilded oval brooches with intaglio gemstone.

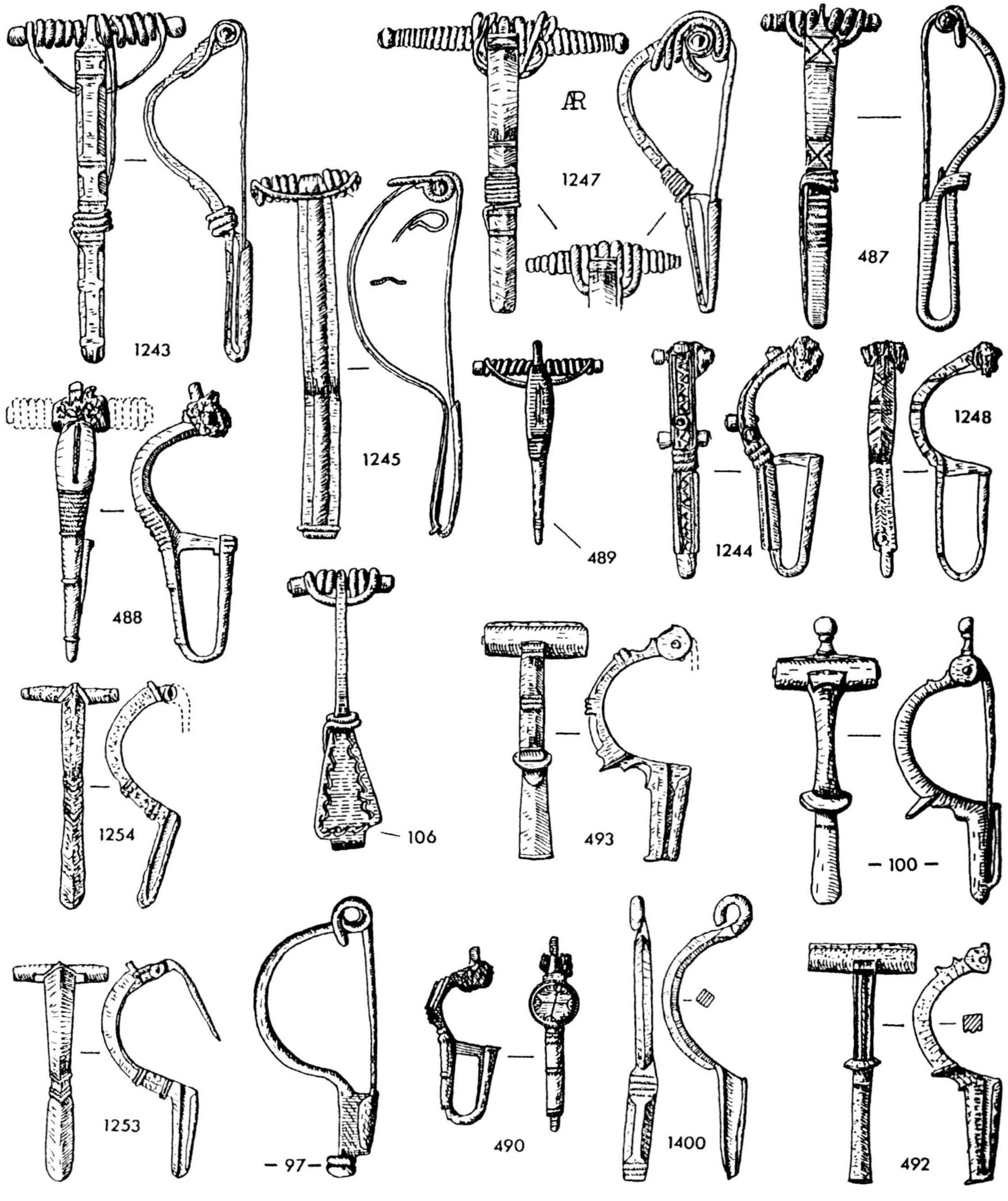

Fig. 225 P-shape bow brooches, 2nd–3rd century AD. Above, with returned foot; below, with solid foot.

1–212 in **ARBB**
213–718 in **IARB**
719–1441 in **BoA**
1442–1729 in **ABOA**

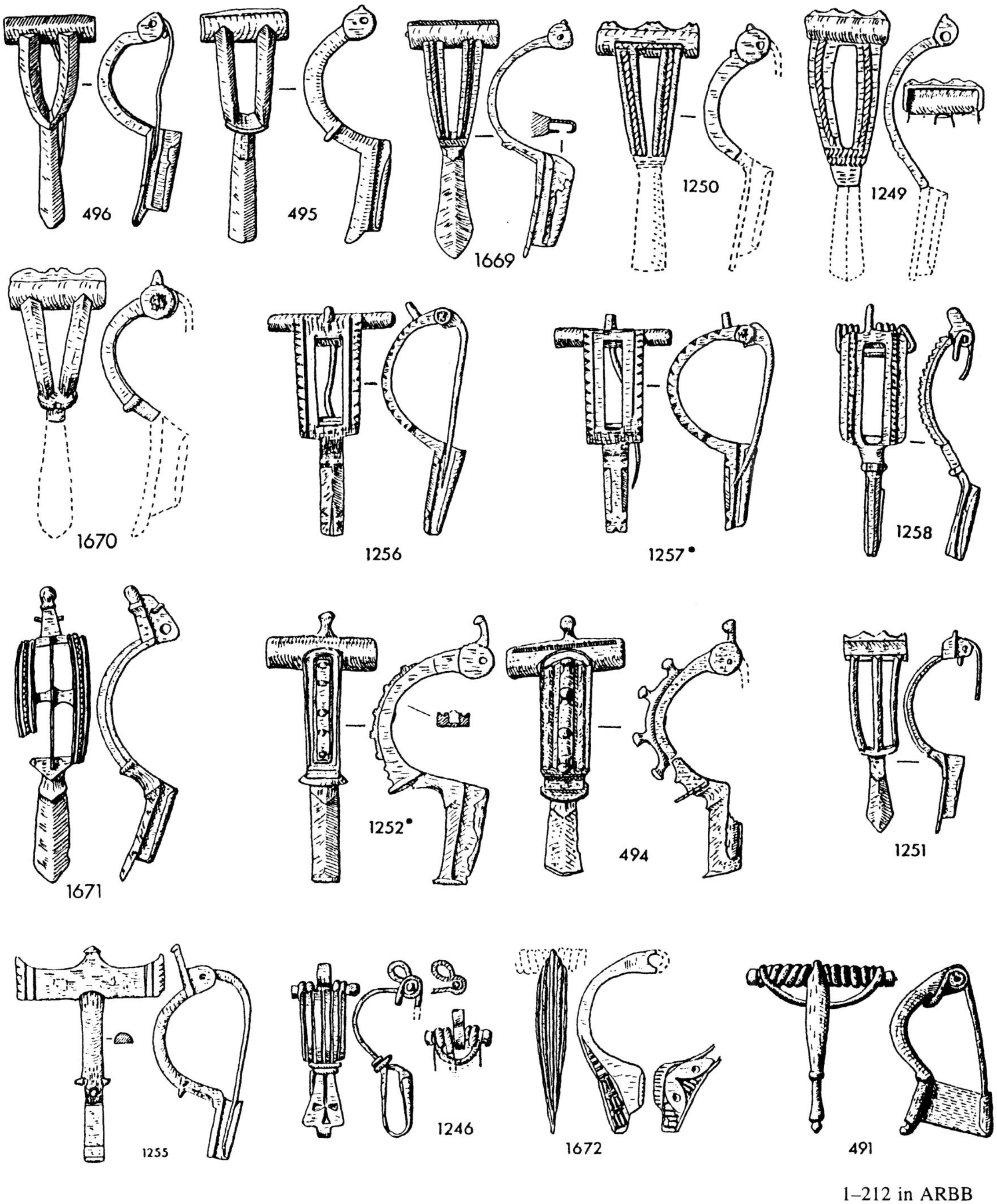

Fig. 226 P-shape bow brooches, 2nd–3rd century AD. Above, divided bow types; centre, with knobbed inset to bow; below, various.

1–212 in ARBB
213–718 in IARB
719–1441 in BoA
1442–1729 in ABOA

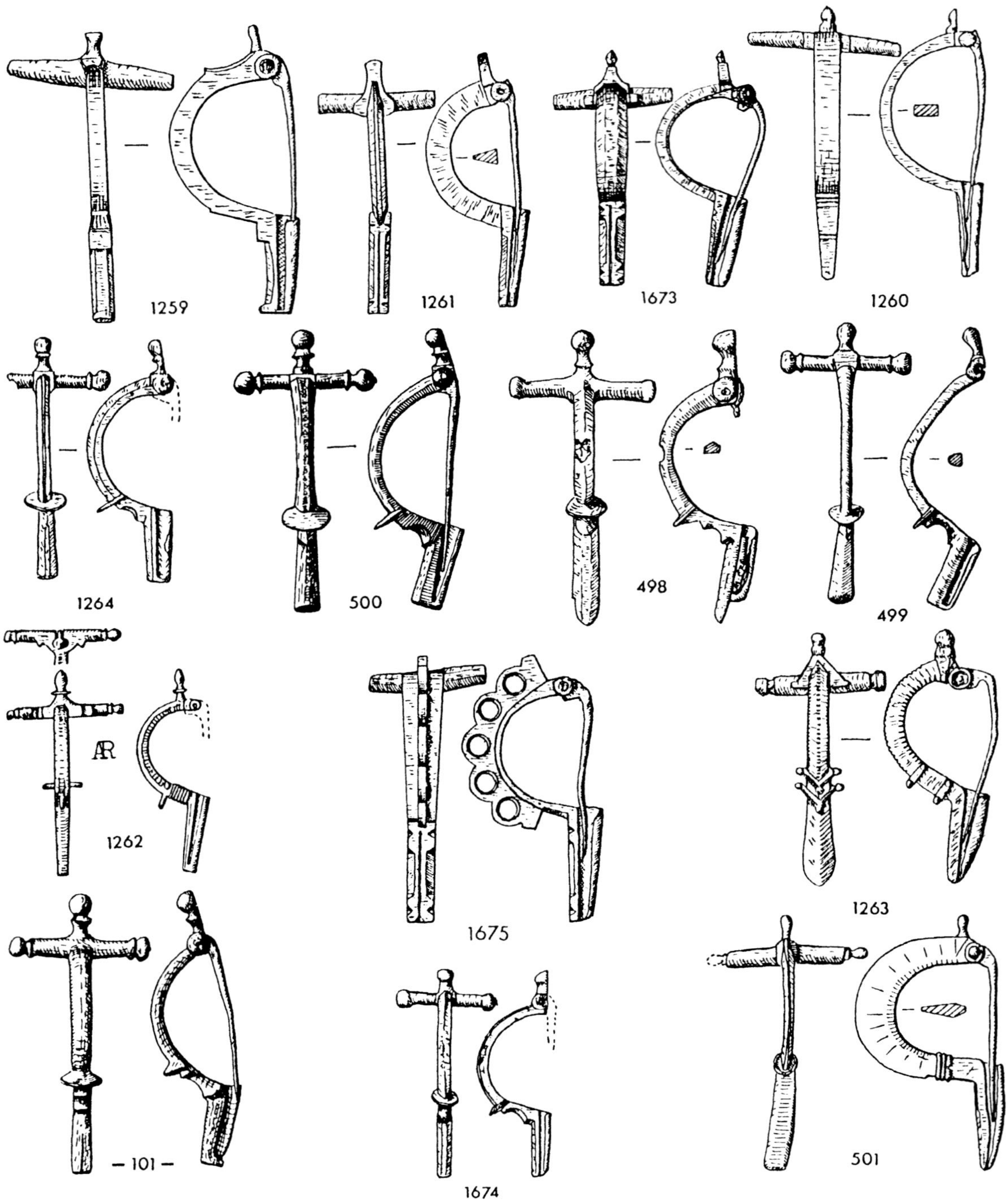

1–212 in ARBB
213–718 in IARB
719–1441 in BoA
1442–1729 in ABOA

Fig. 227 Crossbow brooches, early forms, 3rd century AD.

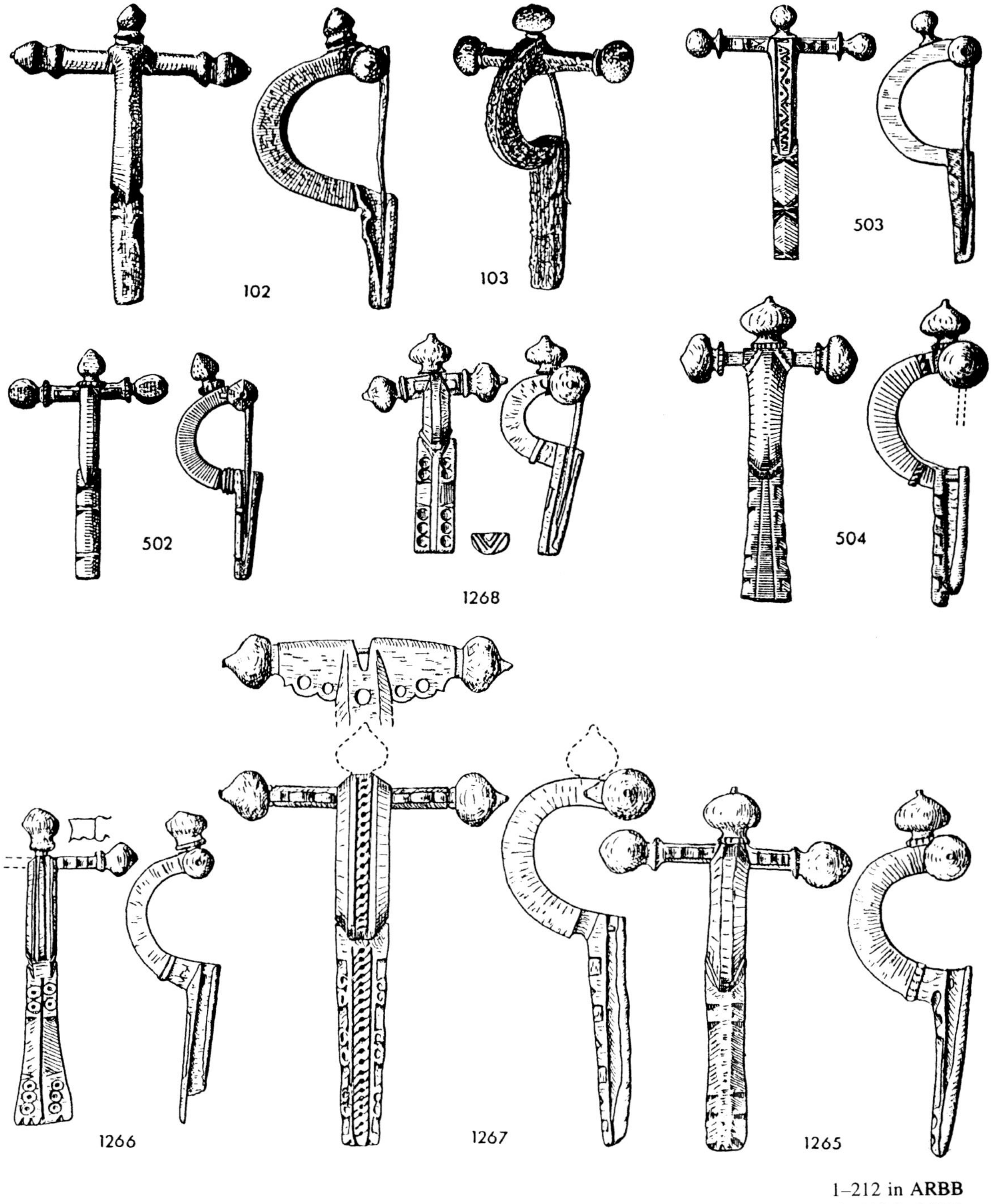

1–212 in **ARBB**
213–718 in **IARB**
719–1441 in **BoA**
1442–1729 in **ABOA**

Fig. 228 Crossbow brooches, 3rd–4th century AD.

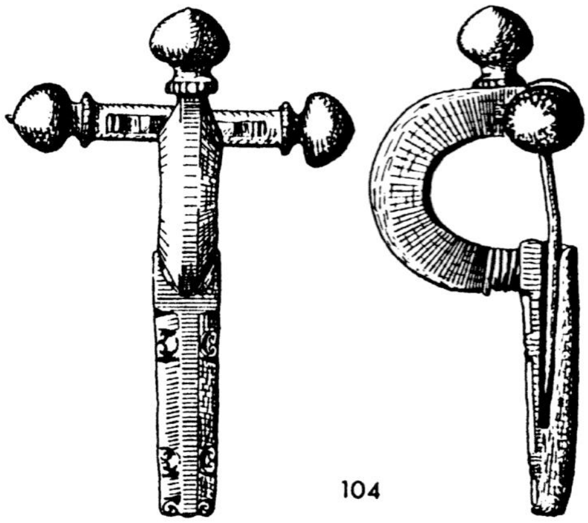

104

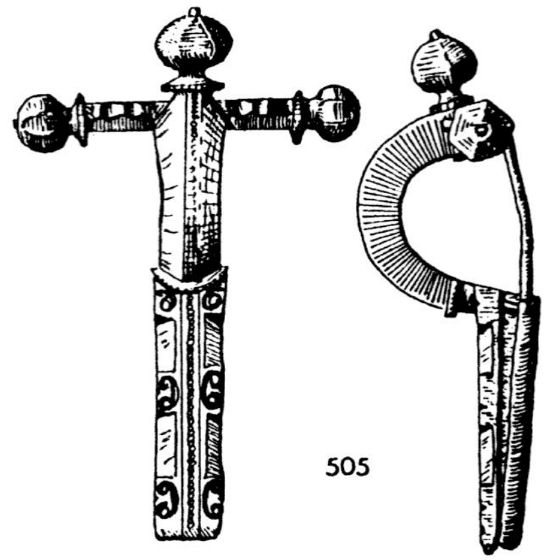

505

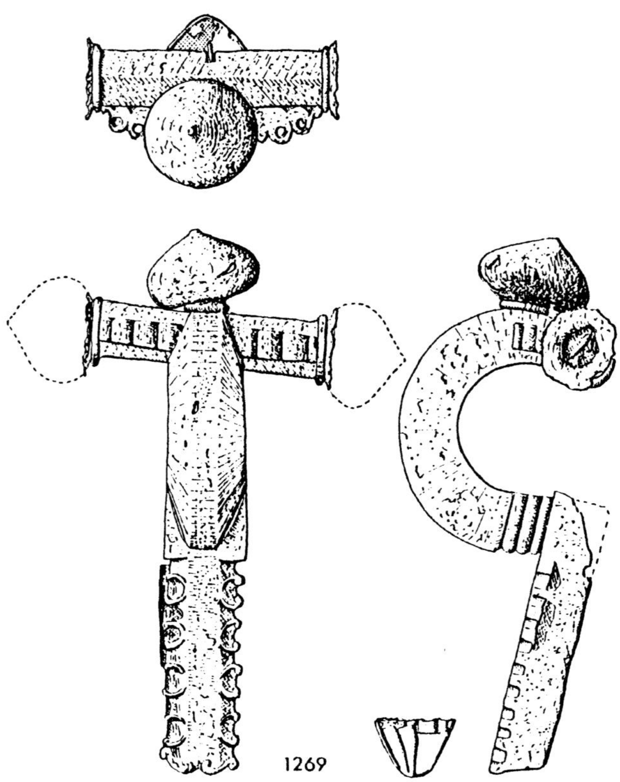

1269

1–212 in ARBB
213–718 in IARB
719–1441 in BoA
1442–1729 in ABOA

Fig. 229 Crossbow brooches, 4th century AD.

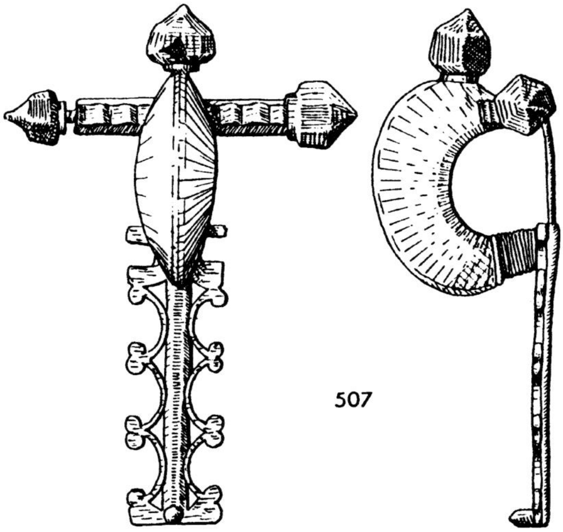

507

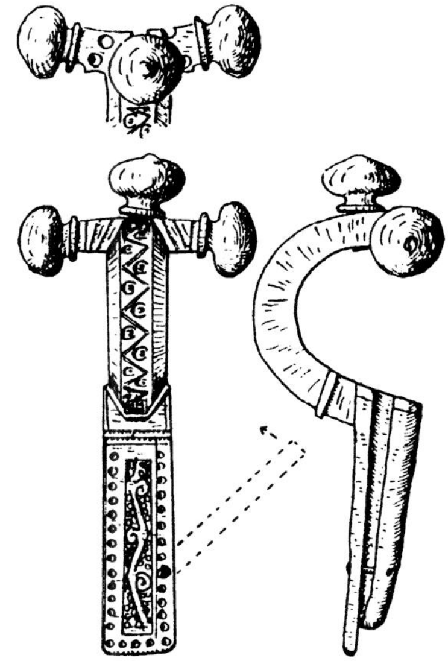

1676

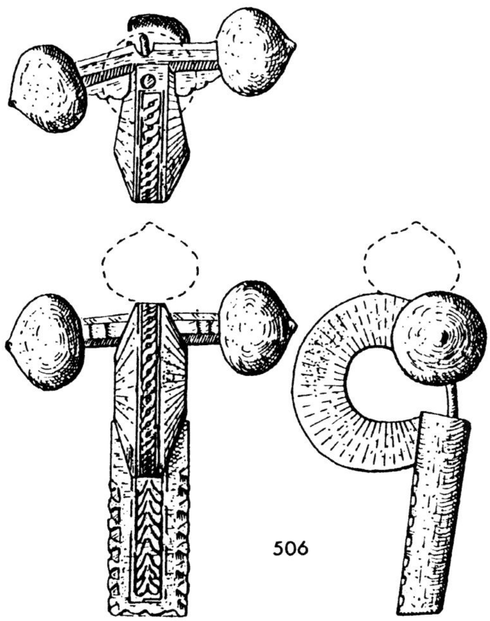

506

Fig. 230 Crossbow brooches, early 5th century AD.

1–212 in ARBB
213–718 in IARB
719–1441 in BoA
1442–1729 in ABOA

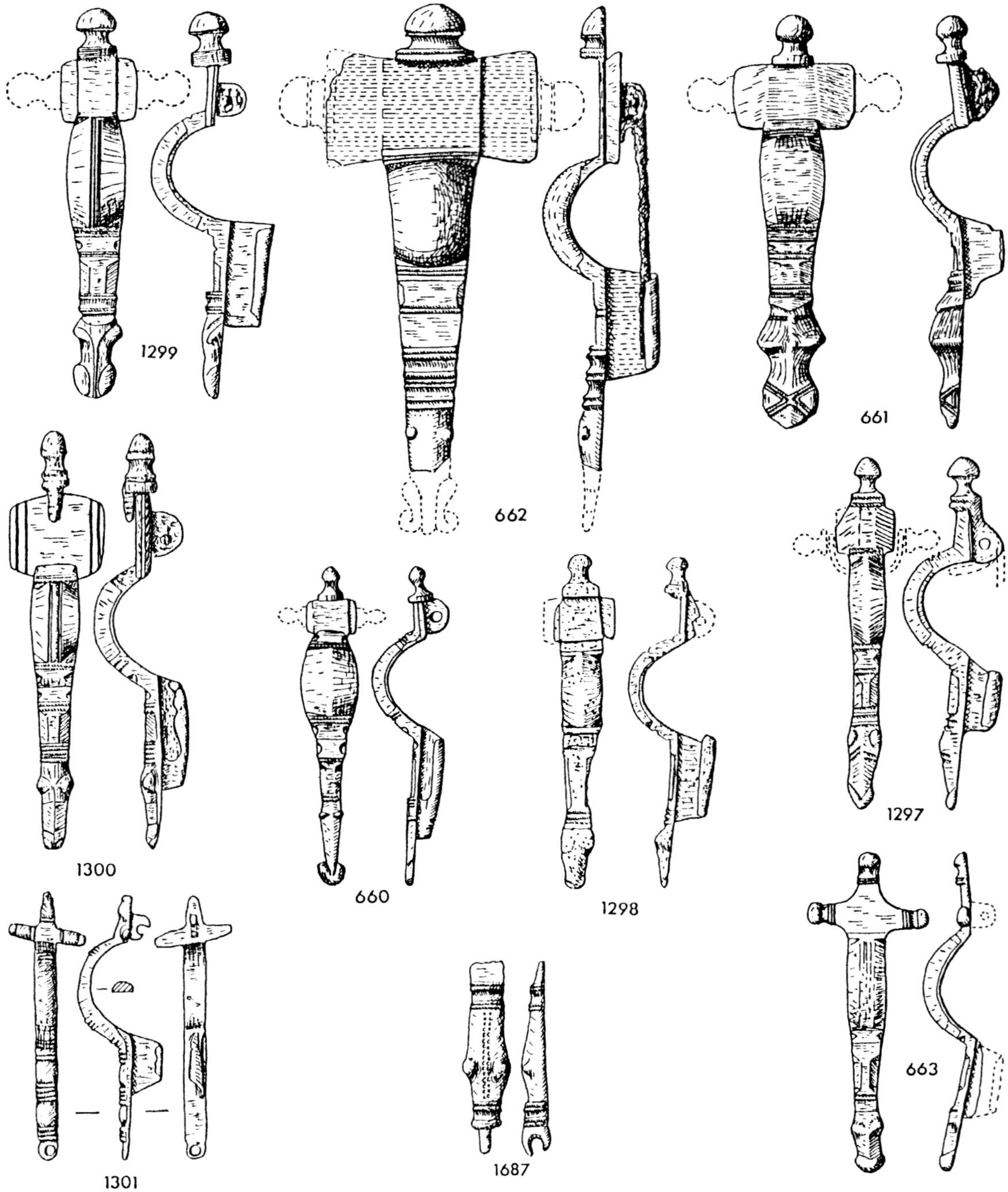

Fig. 231 Anglo-Saxon Cruciform Long brooches. Åberg Group I, 5th century AD; bottom row, Group II, AD 500–525, and a broken foot with unusual loop.

1–212 in ARBB
213–718 in IARB
719–1441 in BoA
1442–1729 in ABOA

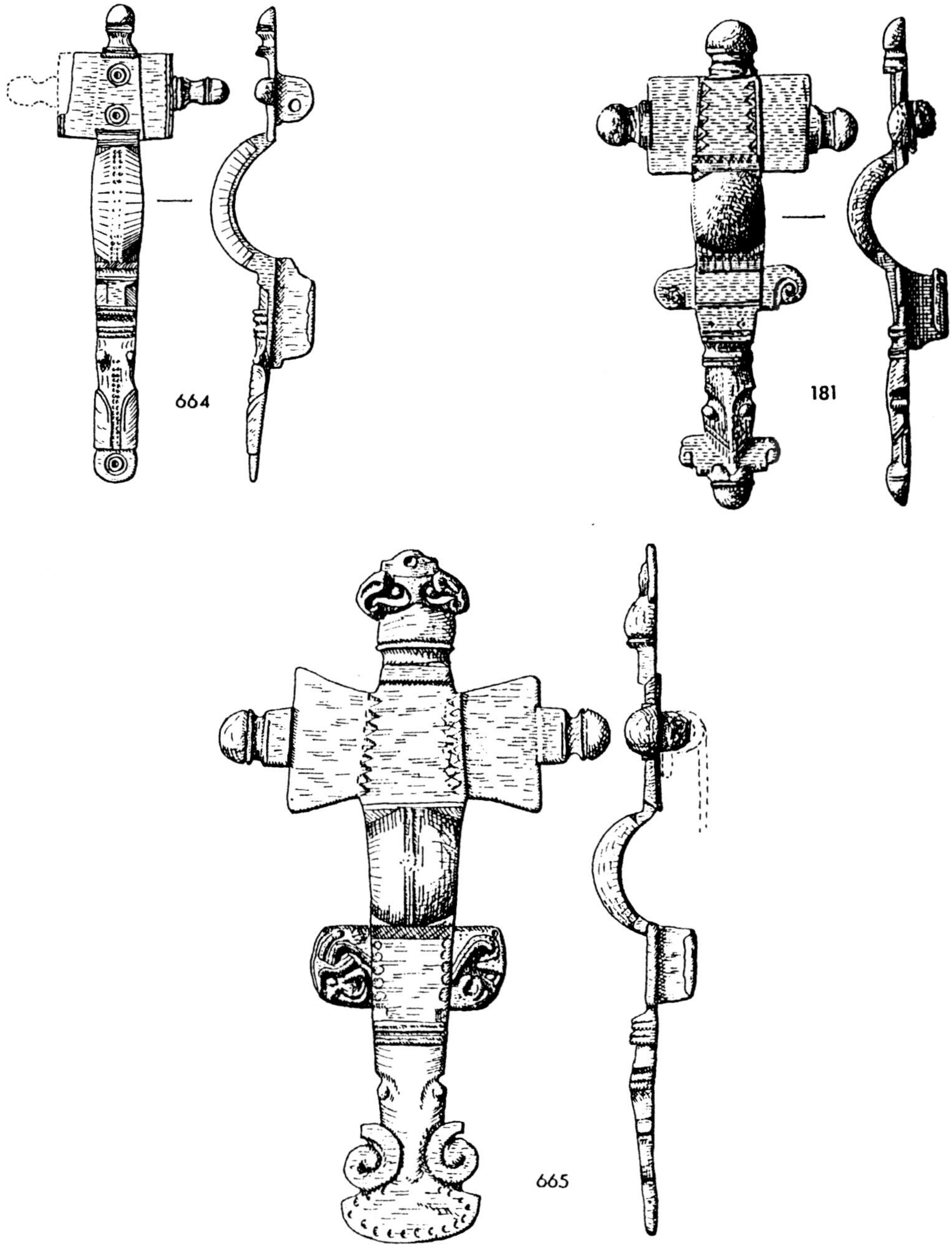

1–212 in ARBB
213–718 in IARB
719–1441 in BoA
1442–1729 in ABOA

Fig. 232 Anglo-Saxon Cruciform brooches. 6th century AD.

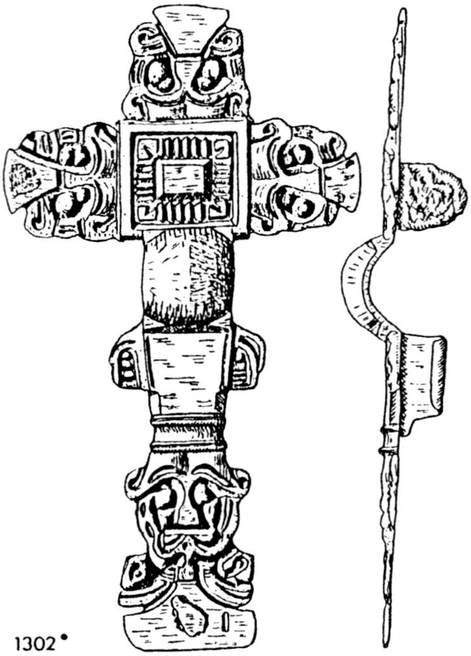

1302•

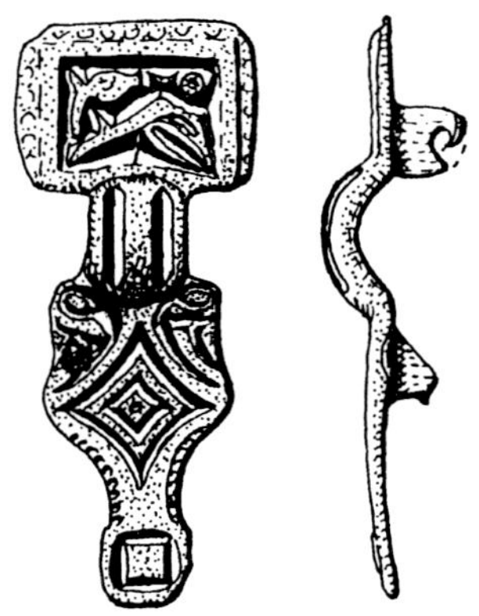

666

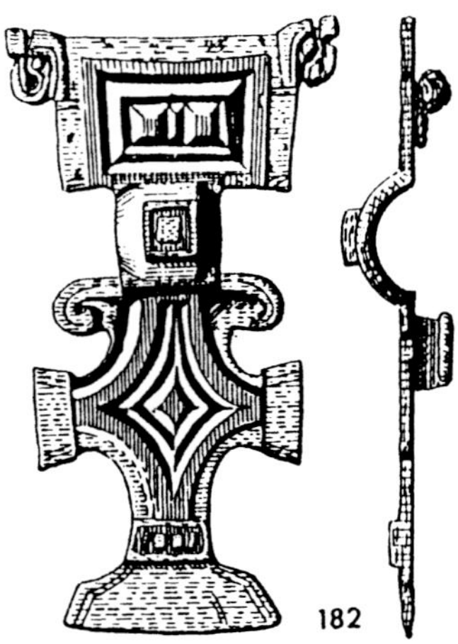

182

Fig. 233 Anglo-Saxon period brooches, c. 6th century AD. Above, a Florid Cruciform brooch; below, Square-headed type.

1–212 in ARBB
213–718 in IARB
719–1441 in BoA
1442–1729 in ABOA

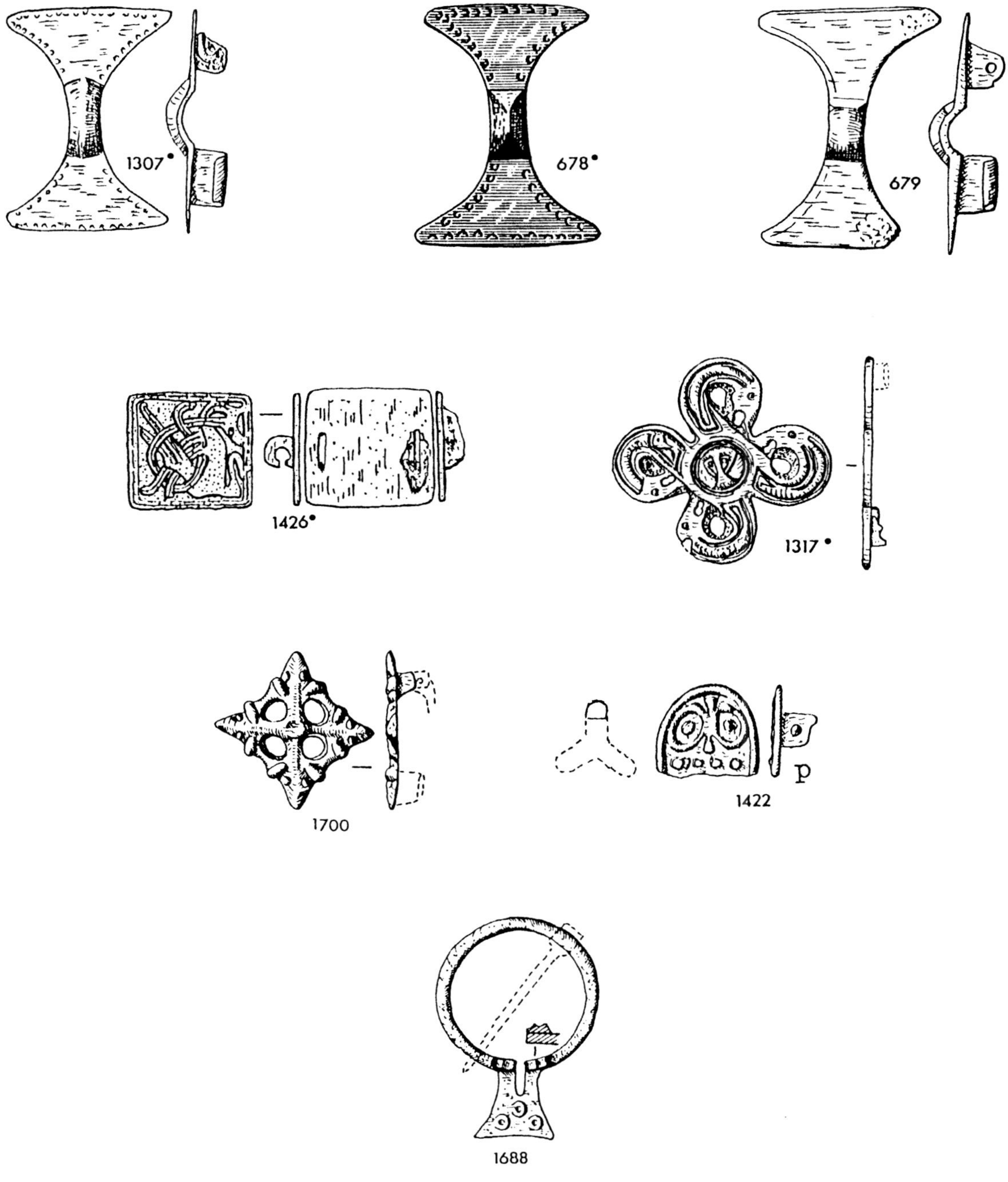

Fig. 234 Anglo-Saxon period brooches, 6th–10th century AD. Above, Equal-armed; centre, rare forms; below, Viking, Sub-penannular, and fragment of a Trefoil brooch.

1–212 in ARBB
213–718 in IARB
719–1441 in BoA
1442–1729 in ABOA

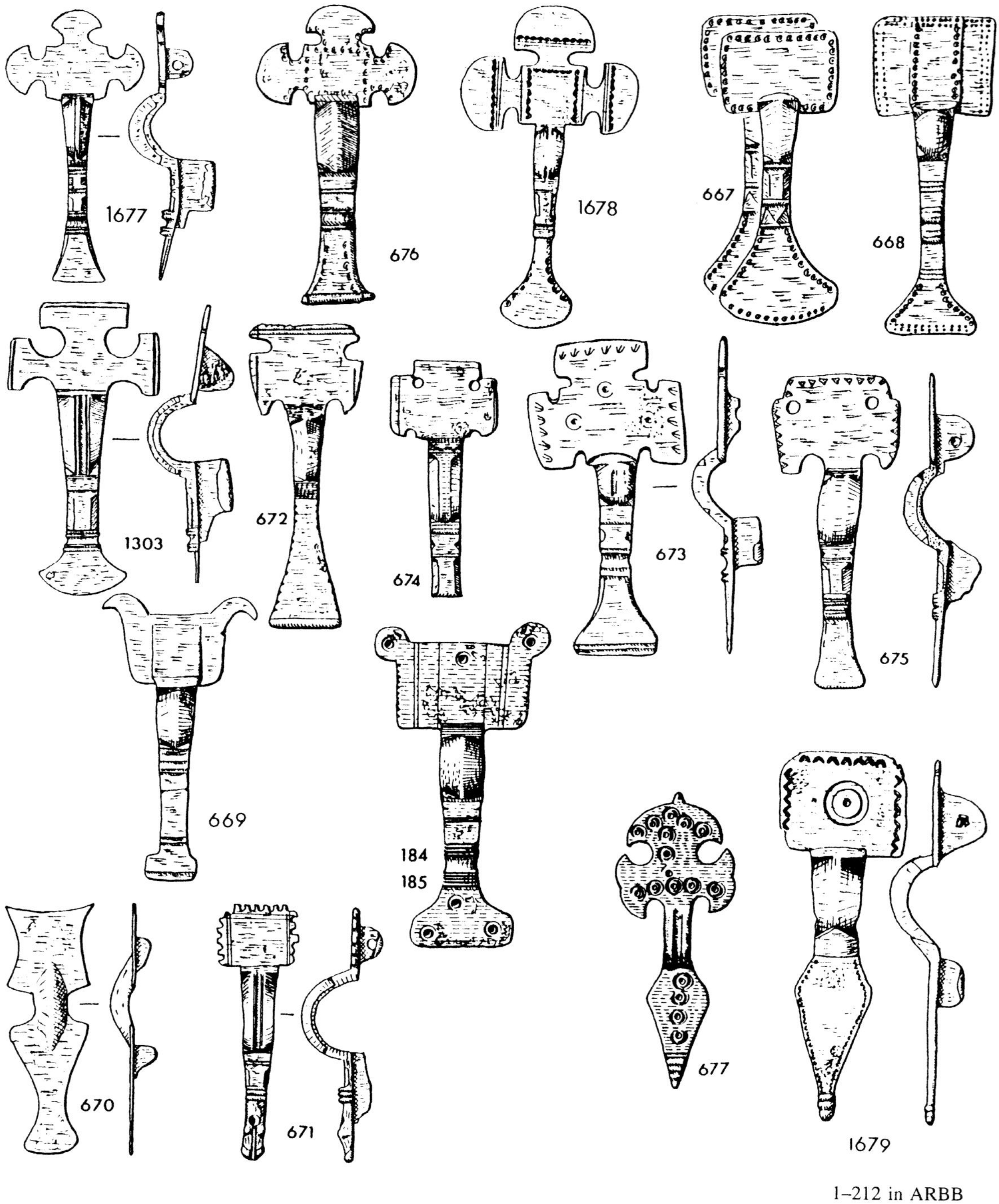

1–212 in ARBB
213–718 in IARB
719–1441 in BoA
1442–1729 in ABOA

Fig. 235 Anglo-Saxon Small-long brooches. 6th century AD.

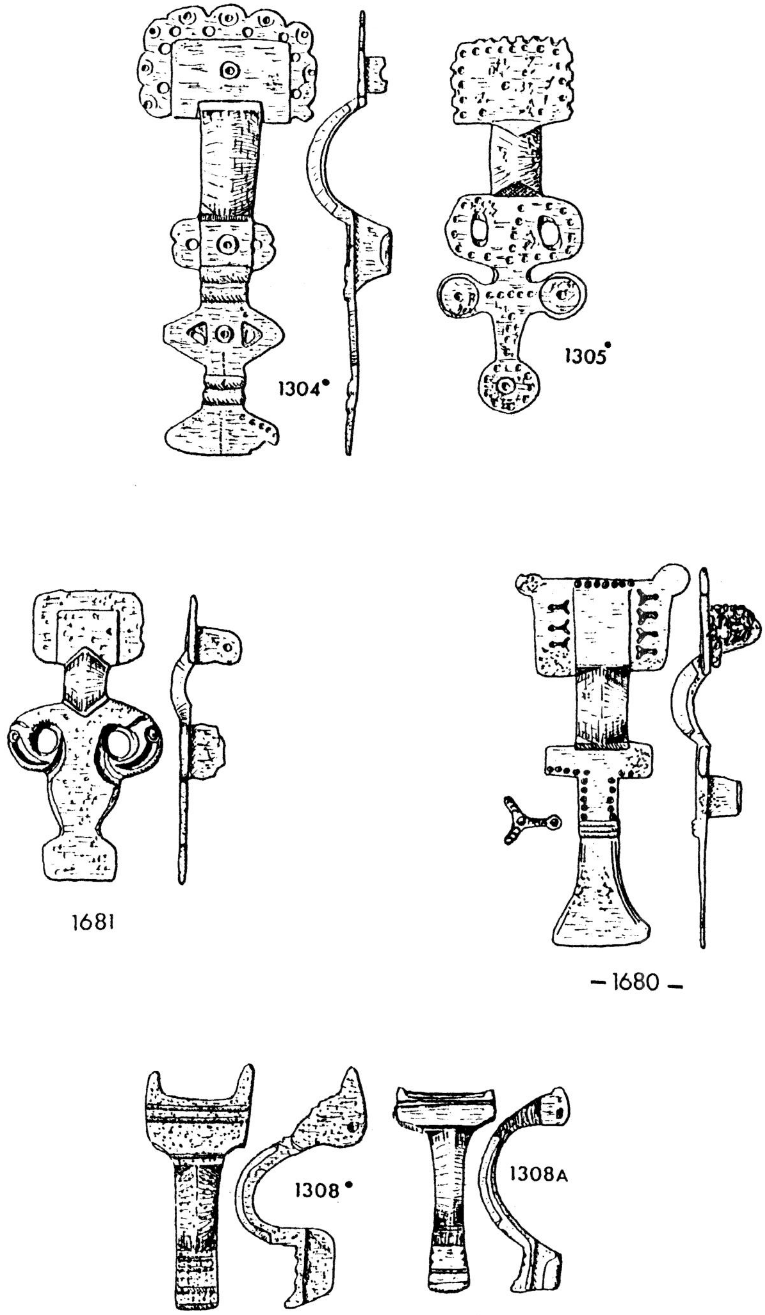

1–212 in **ARBB**
213–718 in **IARB**
719–1441 in **BoA**
1442–1729 in **ABOA**

Fig. 236 Anglo-Saxon Small-long brooches with lappets. 6th century AD. Below, Supporting-arm type.

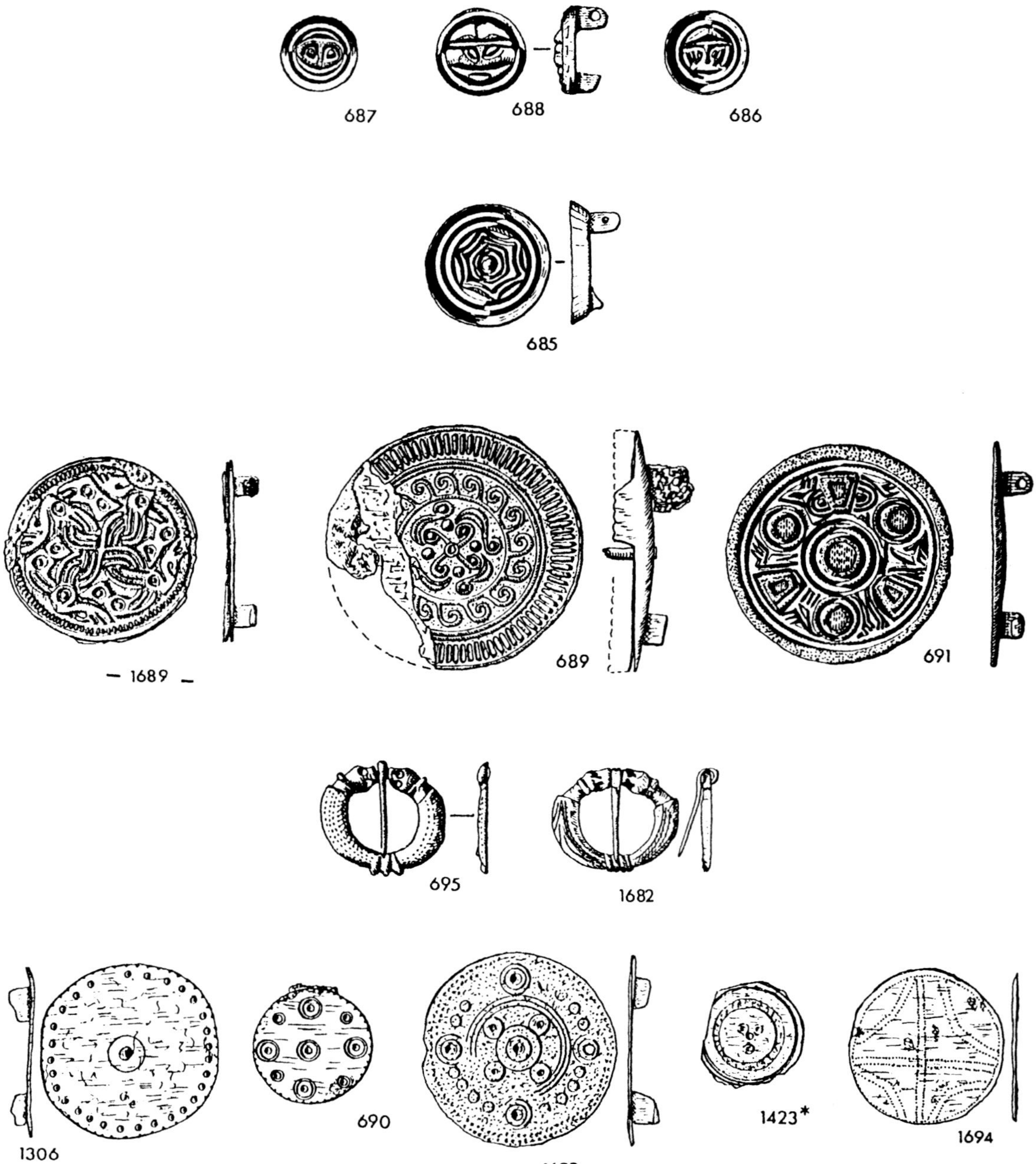

1–212 in **ARBB**
213–718 in **IARB**
719–1441 in **BoA**
1442–1729 in **ABOA**

Fig. 237 Anglo-Saxon round brooches of the Pagan period.

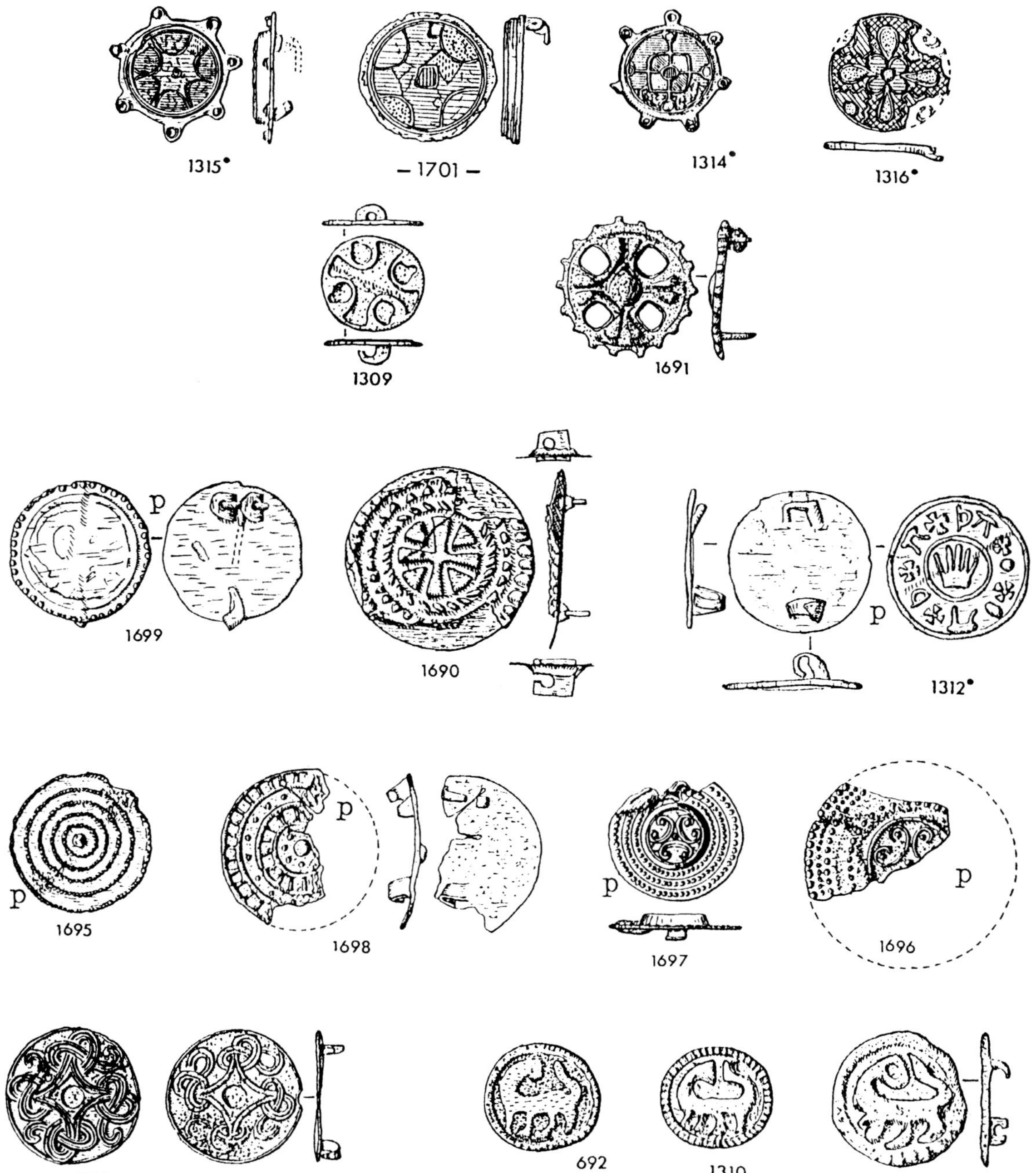

1–212 in ARBB
213–718 in IARB
719–1441 in BoA
1442–1729 in ABOA

Fig. 238 Anglo-Saxon disc brooches of the Middle to Late periods.

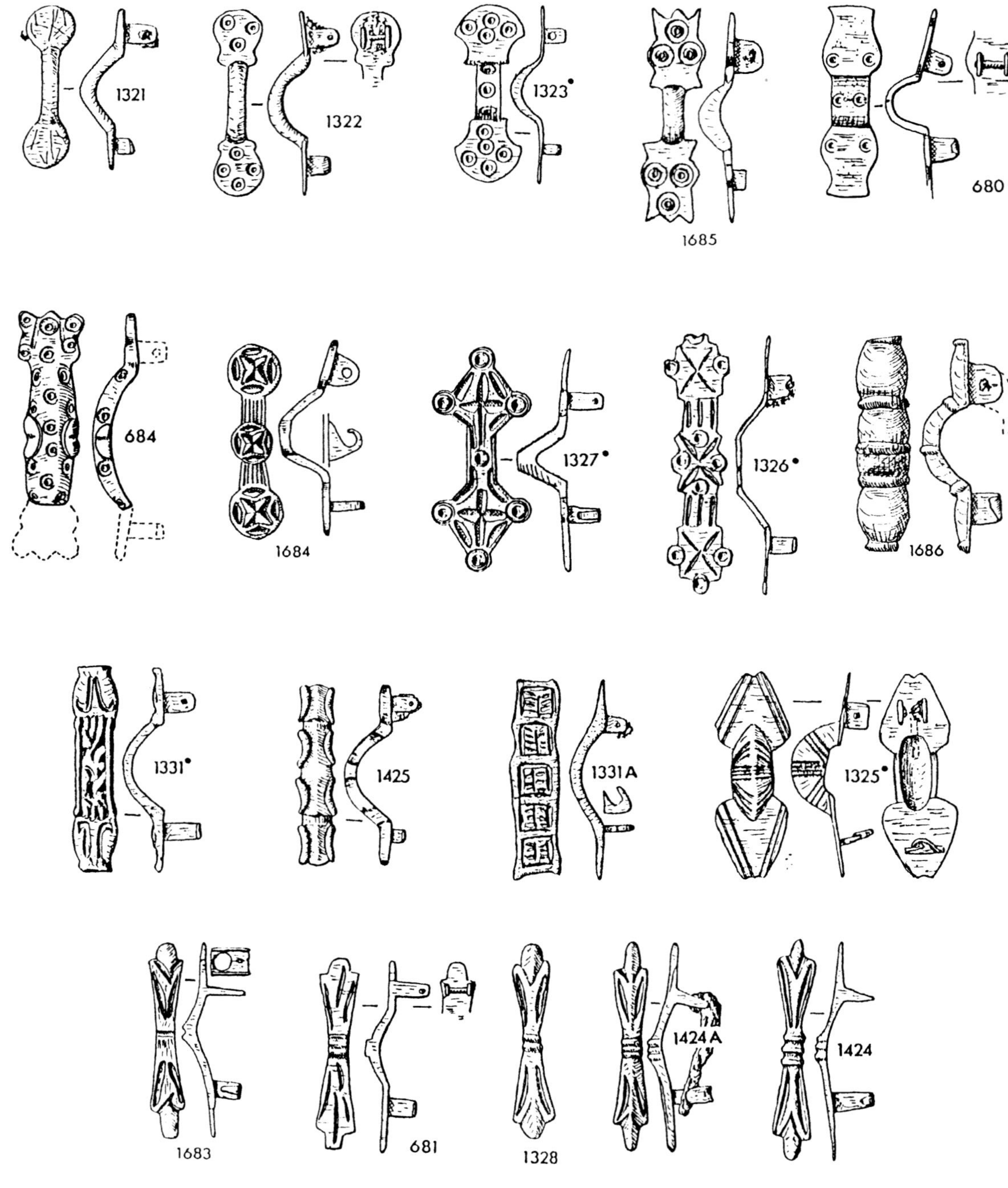

Fig. 239 Frankish Merovingian period Equal-armed brooches. Bottom row, English copies.

1–212 in ARBB
213–718 in IARB
719–1441 in BoA
1442–1729 in ABOA

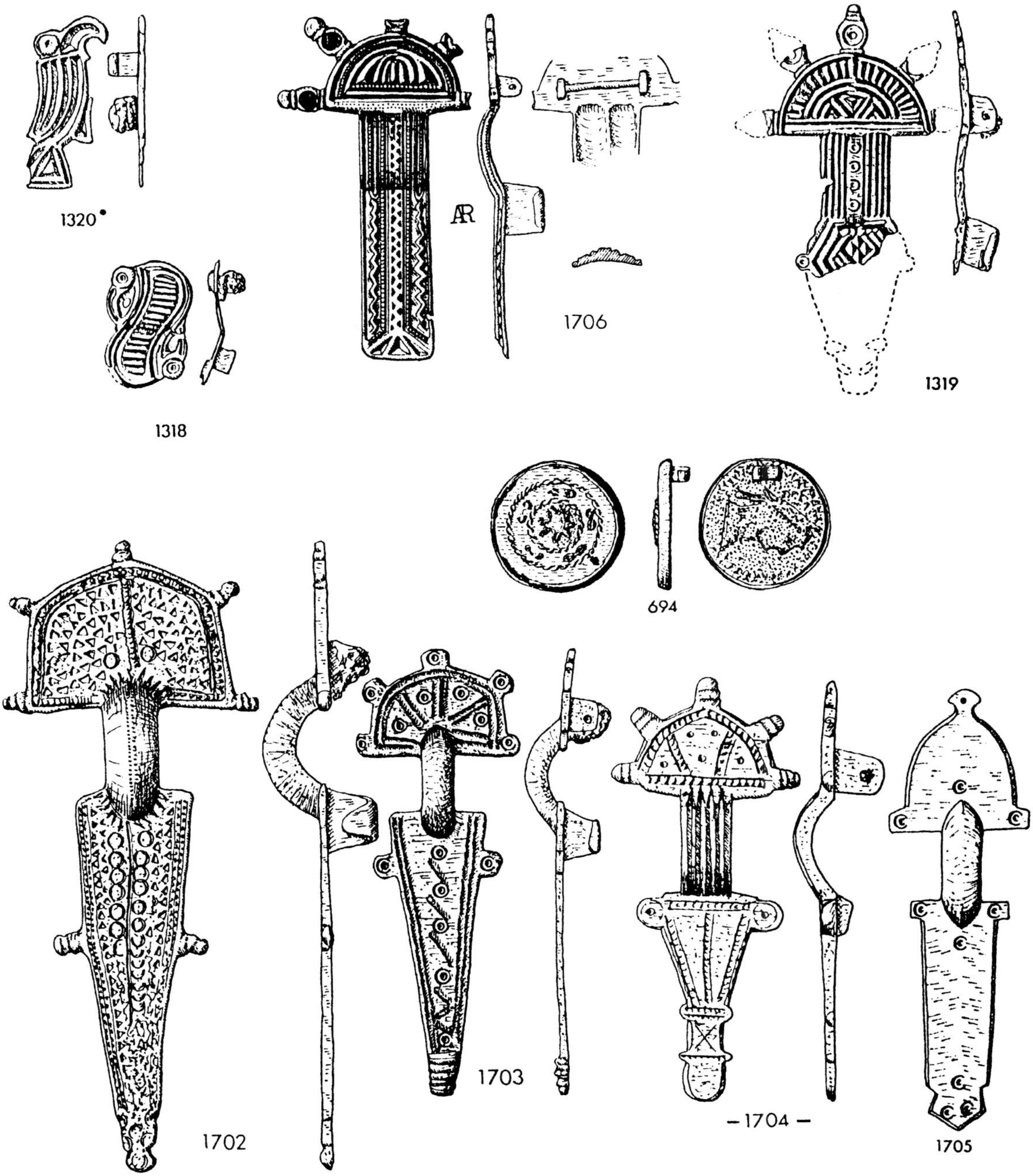

1–212 in **ARBB**
213–718 in **IARB**
719–1441 in **BoA**
1442–1729 in **ABOA**

Fig. 240 Anglo-Saxon period European brooches of 6th century AD. Above, Merovingian Frankish types; below, Visigothic.

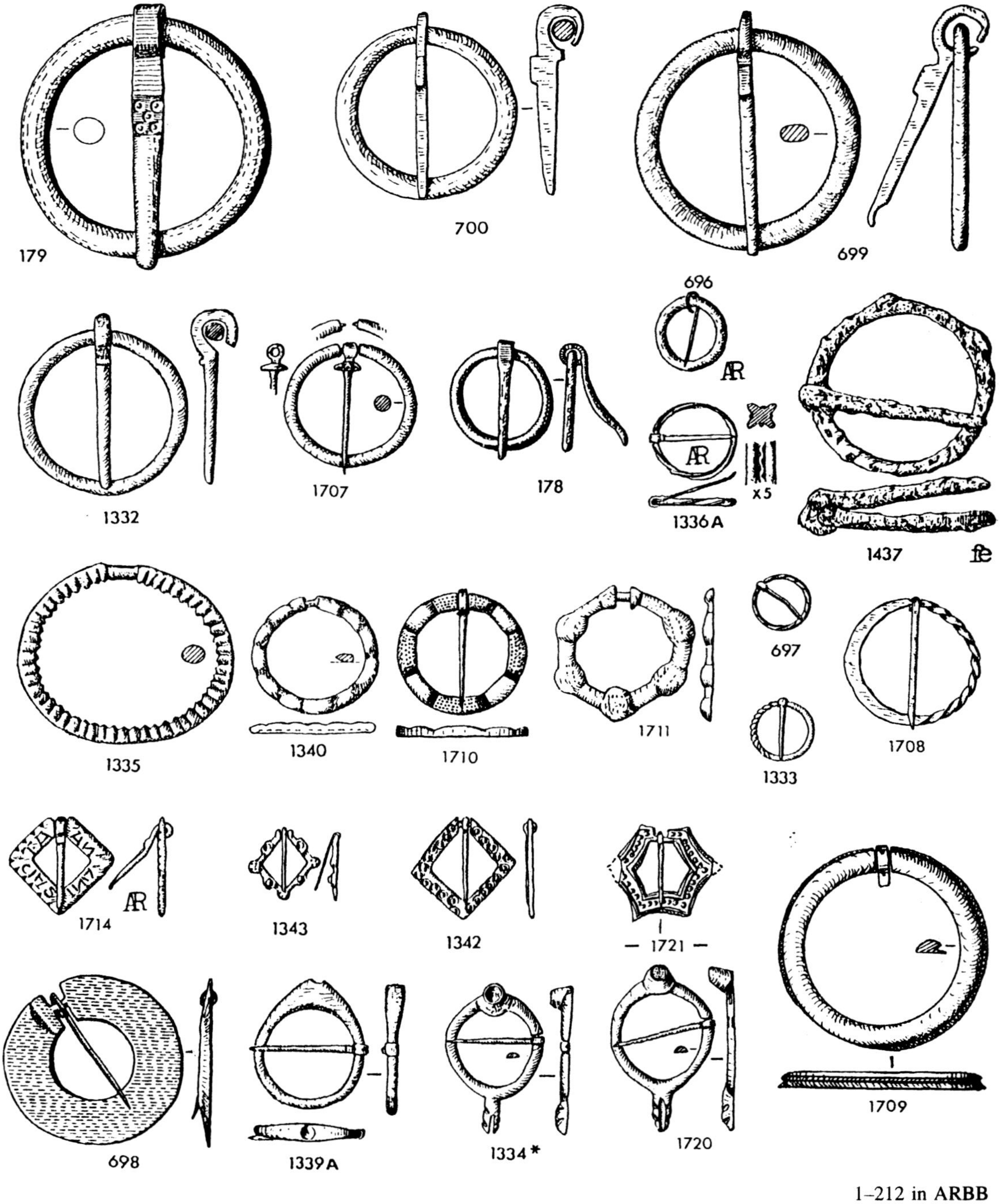

1–212 in **ARBB**
213–718 in **IARB**
719–1441 in **BoA**
1442–1729 in **ABOA**

Fig. 241 English Medieval Ring brooches, 13th–15th century AD.

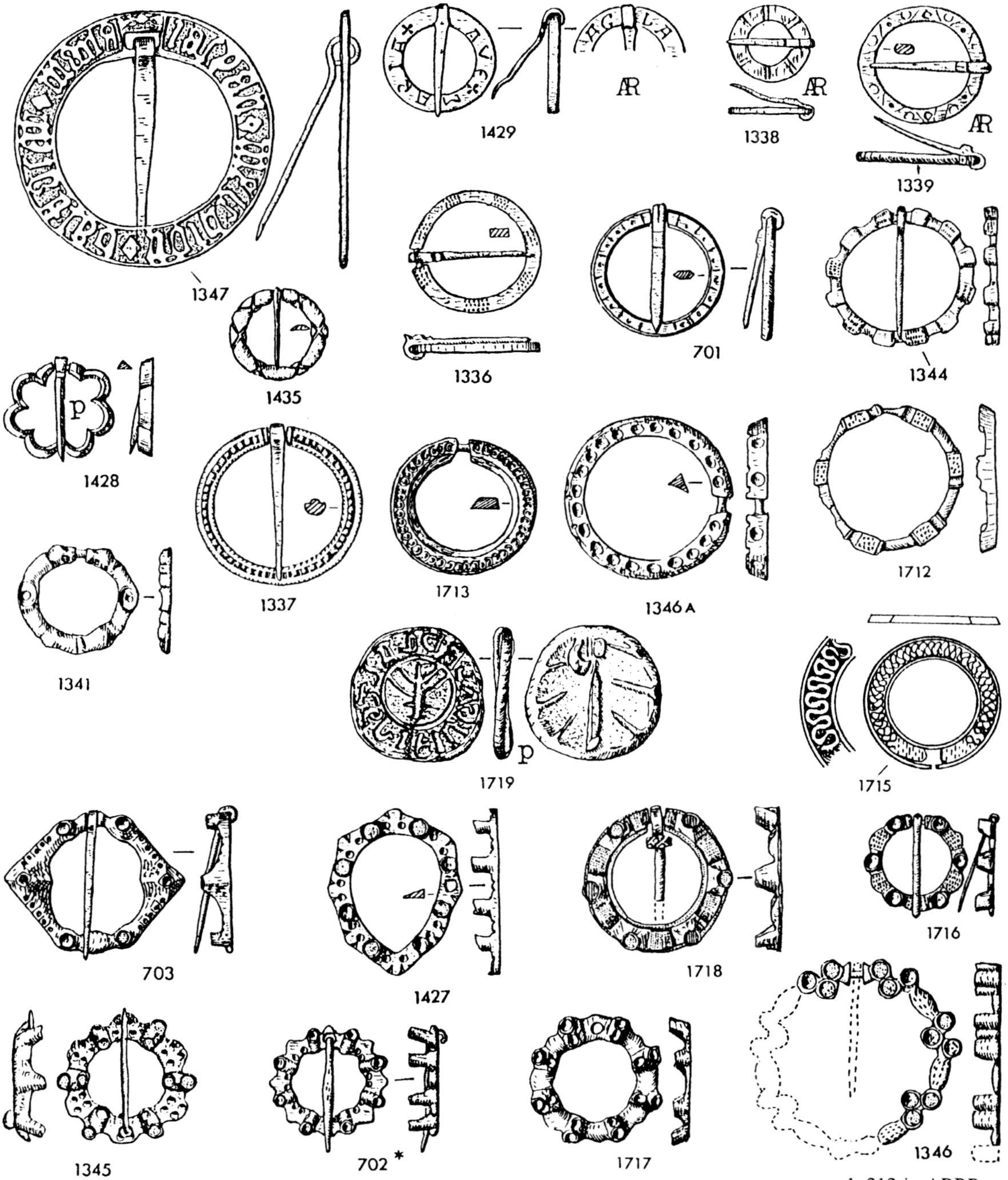

Fig. 242 English Medieval brooches, 13th–15th century AD.

1–212 in ARBB
213–718 in IARB
719–1441 in BoA
1442–1729 in ABOA

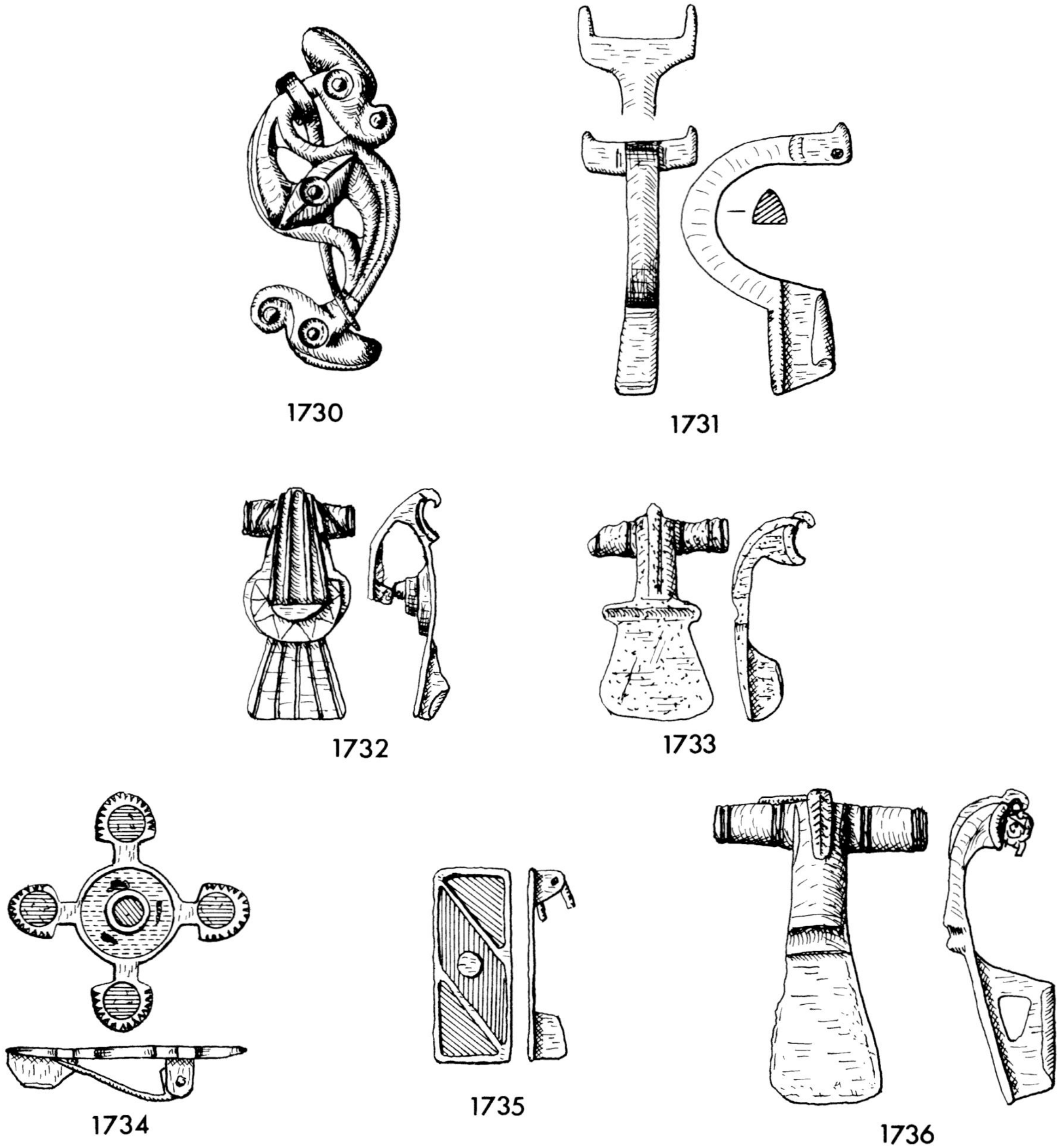

Addenda: Assorted brooches (late arrivals); described in ABOA.
1730, Dragonesque (see Fig. 210); 1731, Supporting-arm (compare Fig. 236); 1732 and 1733, Aesica variants (see Fig. 170); 1734, enamelled Plate brooch (compare Figs 210-214); 1735, enamelled Plate brooch (see Fig. 208); 1736, Wing-and-fanbow variant (compare Fig. 171).

Locations of brooches

This index provides the provenance of each brooch as recorded by Richard Hattatt at the time of purchase. Brooches not listed here have no recorded findspot.

1A	Italy
2	Pannonia
4	Cold Kitchen Hill, Wilts
5	Italy
7	France
8	Ipswich, Suffolk
9	Cold Kitchen Hill, Wilts
10	Kirmington, Humberside
11	London
12	Lincolnshire
14	Hemsworth, Dorset
15	Thetford, Norfolk
16A	Thistleton, Lincs
17	London
18	Thetford, Norfolk
20	Lincolnshire
21	Kirmington, Humberside
22	Kirmington, Humberside
23	Mildenhall, Suffolk
24	Stainfield, Lincs
25	London
26	London
27	Lincolnshire
28	Cold Kitchen Hill, Wilts
29	Kirmington, Humberside
31	Thetford, Norfolk
33	Owmby, Lincs
34	Broadstairs, Kent
35	Thetford, Norfolk
36	Owmby, Lincs
37	Ipswich, Suffolk
38	Thetford, Norfolk
39	Ipswich, Suffolk
40	Hod Hill, Dorset
41	Owmby, Lincs
42	Studland, Dorset
47	London
49	London
50	Mildenhall, Suffolk
51	Hod Hill, Dorset
52	Thetford, Norfolk
53	Lincolnshire
54	Lincolnshire
60	London
61	London
62	London
74	Kirmington, Humberside
75	Thetford, Norfolk
77	East Anglia
78	Pannonia
80	Adel, Yorks
81	Thetford, Norfolk
82	Ipswich, Suffolk
83	Thetford, Norfolk
87	Thetford, Norfolk
88A	Hexham, Northumberland
91	Somerset
92	Catterick, Yorks
94	Ancaster, Lincs
96	Easton Gray, Wilts
105	Studland, Dorset
106	St. Albans, Herts
107	Lincolnshire
108	Lincolnshire
109	Ipswich, Suffolk
110	Kirmington, Humberside
113	Oxton, Notts
114	Thistleton, Lincs
115	London
116	Lincolnshire

117	Thetford, Norfolk
119	Ipswich, Suffolk
120	Ipswich, Suffolk
121	Ipswich, Suffolk
122	Thistleton, Lincs
123	East Anglia
124	Cold Kitchen Hill, Wilts
125	Hampshire
127	Kirmington, Humberside
128	Owmby, Lincs
129	Thetford, Norfolk
130	Ipswich, Suffolk
131A	Kirmington, Humberside
132	Suffolk
133	Thetford, Norfolk
134	Ipswich, Suffolk
135	Levant
138	Cold Kitchen Hill, Wilts
141	Cold Kitchen Hill, Wilts
144	Oxford
145	Ipswich, Suffolk
146	Sussex
147	Lincolnshire
155	Kirmington, Humberside
156	Ipswich, Suffolk
157	Thetford, Norfolk
158	Ipswich, Suffolk
159	Cold Kitchen Hill, Wilts
160	Lincolnshire
162	Thistleton, Lincs
163	Ipswich, Suffolk
164	Ipswich, Suffolk
165	Cold Kitchen Hill, Wilts
166	Ham Hill, Somerset
167	Ipswich, Suffolk
168	Ipswich, Suffolk
169	Ipswich, Suffolk
170	Syria
171	Pannonia
172	Mildenhall, Suffolk
173	Ipswich, Suffolk
174	Thistleton, Lincs
175	Studland, Dorset
175C	Colchester, Essex
178	Bordon, Hampshire
179	Saxmundham, Suffolk
181	Lakenheath, Suffolk
182	Lakenheath, Suffolk
184	Lakenheath, Suffolk
185	Lakenheath, Suffolk
186	Greece
192	Italy
193	Italy
196	Italy
197	Italy
198	Italy
199	Italy
200	Italy
203	Italy
204	Italy
205	Italy
206	Turkey
207	Turkey
208	Turkey
209	Turkey
210	Turkey
211	Iran
212	Iran
217	Spain
220	Cold Kitchen Hill, Wilts
221	Cambridgeshire
226	Pannonia
227	Portsmouth, Hants
229	Maiden Bradley, Wilts
230	Cold Kitchen Hill, Wilts
237	Bury St. Edmunds, Suffolk
238	Bury St. Edmunds, Suffolk
239	Cheltenham, Glos
240	Bury St. Edmunds, Suffolk
241	Maiden Bradley, Wilts
242	Bournemouth, Dorset
243	Owmby, Lincs
244	Cambridgeshire
245	Worthy Down, Hants
249	Thetford, Norfolk
250	Thetford, Norfolk
253	East Midlands
255	Ashbury, Berks
256	Lakenheath, Suffolk
257	London
258	Thetford, Norfolk
259	Lakenheath, Suffolk
262	Britain
265	Farley Heath, Surrey
266	Lincolnshire
267	Bury St. Edmunds, Suffolk

269 Wimborne, Dorset
270 Cambridgeshire
273 Lincolnshire
276 Norfolk
277 Lower Hacheston, Suffolk
278 Essex
280 Bury St. Edmunds, Suffolk
281 Norfolk
282 Cambridgeshire
285 East Midlands
286 Stevenage, Herts
287 Farley Heath, Surrey
288 Cambridgeshire
289 Cambridgeshire
289A Suffolk
291 East Anglia
292 Norfolk
293 Norfolk
296 Norfolk
297 Berkshire
298 Reading, Berks
299 Suffolk
311 Norfolk
312 East Anglia
313 Norfolk
314 Norfolk
315 Suffolk
316 Suffolk
317 Worthy Down, Hants
318 Bury St. Edmunds, Suffolk
319 Italy
320 Norfolk
321 Cheltenham, Glos
322 Ashton Keynes, Wilts
324 Colchester, Essex
325 Dorset
326 Lower Hacheston, Suffolk
327 Cheltenham, Glos
328 Norfolk
329 Italy
330 Berkshire
334 Wroxeter, Salop
335 Norfolk
337 Pannonia
338 Pannonia
339 Suffolk
341 Wimborne, Dorset
341A Norfolk
341B Wiltshire
342 Stockton, Wilts
343 Cambridgeshire
346 Norfolk
349 Cambridgeshire
350 Badbury Rings, Dorset
352 Lincolnshire
353 Lincolnshire
355 Lincolnshire
356 Bournemouth, Dorset
357 East Anglia
358 Cambridgeshire
362 Suffolk
363 East Anglia
364 East Anglia
365 Farley Heath, Surrey
366 Co. Durham
366A Pakenham, Suffolk
367 East Anglia
368 Bournemouth, Dorset
369 Bournemouth, Dorset
370 Bournemouth, Dorset
373 Wimborne, Dorset
374 East Midlands
375 Wiltshire
377 Hadrian's Wall
378 Colchester, Essex
379 East Anglia
380 Petersfield, Hants
381 Norfolk
382 Upavon, Wilts
383 Maiden Bradley, Wilts
384 Somerton, Somerset
386 Wimborne, Dorset
388 Britain
389 Bath, Avon
390 Maiden Castle, Dorset
391 Britain
391A Blandford, Dorset
392 Britain
393 Wimborne, Dorset
395 Wimborne, Dorset
396 Norfolk
397 Suffolk
398 Norfolk
399 Essex
400 Wimborne, Dorset
401 Worthy Down, Hants

402	Wimborne, Dorset
403	Owmby, Lincs
404	Norfolk
405	Grimsby, Lincs
406	Cirencester, Glos
408	Bristol, Avon
409	Wimborne, Dorset
410	Suffolk
411	Northamptonshire
412	Bournemouth, Dorset
413	Bury St. Edmunds, Suffolk
414	Northamptonshire
415	Wiltshire
417	Maiden Bradley, Wilts
418	Adel, Yorks
419	Grimsby, Lincs
420	Hadrian's Wall
421	Northamptonshire
422	Norfolk
423	East Anglia
425	Bournemouth, Dorset
426	Northamptonshire
427	Cheltenham, Glos
428	Lower Hacheston, Suffolk
429	Suffolk
430	Lower Hacheston, Suffolk
431	Petersfield, Hants
432	East Anglia
433	Northamptonshire
434	Co. Durham
435	London
436	Norfolk
437	London
438	Cheltenham, Glos
438A	Blandford, Dorset
438B	Lambourn, Berks
439	Wall, Staffs
440	Owmby, Lincs
441	Suffolk
442	East Anglia
443	Worthy Down, Hants
444	Staffordshire
445	East Midlands
446	Peterborough, Cambs
447	Mildenhall, Suffolk
448	Norfolk
449	Thetford, Norfolk
450	Thetford, Norfolk
451	Shropshire
452	Suffolk
454	Bury St. Edmunds, Suffolk
455	Bury St. Edmunds, Suffolk
456	Northamptonshire
457	Bury St. Edmunds, Suffolk
458	Blandford, Dorset
459	Worthy Down, Hants
460	Norfolk
462	East Anglia
463	Lakenheath, Suffolk
466	Pannonia
467	Pannonia
468	Pannonia
469	Pannonia
470	Pannonia
471	Pannonia
472	Pannonia
473	Suffolk
474	Lincolnshire
475	Bristol, Avon
476	Hadrian's Wall
477	Hadrian's Wall
478	Cambridgeshire
479	Oxfordshire
480	Britain
481	East Anglia
482	Britain
483	Co. Durham
484	Britain
485	Ely, Cambs
488	Pannonia
491	Pannonia
492	Grimsby, Lincs
493	East Midlands
494	Bury St. Edmunds, Suffolk
495	Kent
496	Worthy Down, Hants
498	Suffolk
499	Basing, Hampshire
500	Oxford
503	Britain
506	Suffolk
507	Icklingham, Suffolk
508	Icklingham, Suffolk
509	Norfolk
510	Colchester, Essex
511	Suffolk

512	Blandford, Dorset
513	Northamptonshire
514	Northamptonshire
514A	Norfolk
515	Colchester, Essex
516	Suffolk
517	Suffolk
518	Britain
519	Suffolk
520	Britain
521	Britain
521A	Norfolk
522	Hampshire
523	Bury St. Edmunds, Suffolk
523A	Norfolk
524	Britain
525	Yorkshire
526	Norfolk
527	Britain
528	East Anglia
529	Lincolnshire
530	Colchester, Essex
531	Suffolk
532	East Anglia
533	Hod Hill, Dorset
535	Wall, Staffs
536	Saxlingham, Norfolk
537	Grimsby, Lincs
538	Suffolk
538A	Blandford, Dorset
539	Britain
540	Cirencester, Glos
541	East Anglia
542	Lincolnshire
543	London
544	Britain
545	Norfolk
547	Hadrian's Wall
548	Saxmundham, Suffolk
549	Norfolk
550	Norfolk
551	Britain
552	Wall, Staffs
553	Somerset
554	Britain
554A	Dorset
555	East Anglia
556	Lakenheath, Suffolk
557	Northamptonshire
558	Norfolk
559	East Anglia
560	Norfolk
561	Britain
562	Suffolk
563	London
564	Norfolk
565	Britain
566	Brighton, Sussex
567	Norfolk
568A	Suffolk
568	Hampshire
569	Norfolk
570	Bungay, Suffolk
571	Kent
572	Norfolk
573	Norfolk
574	Britain
575	St. Albans, Herts
576	Winchester, Hants
577	Norfolk
578	Norfolk
579	Norfolk
580	Norfolk
581	Kent
582	Hertfordshire
583	Norfolk
584	Suffolk
585	Norfolk
586	Old Sarum, Wilts
588	Harlow, Essex
589	Woodyates, Dorset
590	Suffolk
591	Wilton, Wilts
592	Northumberland
594	Norfolk
595	Northamptonshire
596	Wimborne, Dorset
597	Norfolk
598	Norfolk
599	Marlborough, Wilts
600	Syria
601	Northumberland
602	Hampshire
603	Epping Forest, Essex
604	Norfolk
605	Thetford, Norfolk

606	Suffolk
607	Winchester, Hants
608	Norfolk
609	Norfolk
610	Ipswich, Suffolk
611	Bury St. Edmunds, Suffolk
612	Suffolk
613	Britain
614	Bury St. Edmunds, Suffolk
615	Norfolk
616	Britain
617	Norwich
618	Faversham, Kent
619	Norfolk
621	Norfolk
622	Northamptonshire
623	Britain
624	Pannonia
625	Wimborne, Dorset
626	Norfolk
628	Norfolk
629	Norfolk
630	Bury St. Edmunds, Suffolk
631	Woodyates, Dorset
632	Norfolk
634	Icklingham, Suffolk
635	Suffolk
636	Colchester, Essex
637	Thetford, Norfolk
639	Cambridge
640	Thetford, Norfolk
641	Thetford, Norfolk
643	Dereham, Norfolk
644	Lincolnshire
645	Luton, Beds
646	Maidstone, Kent
647	Winchester, Hants
648	Britain
649	Bournemouth, Dorset
650	Oxford
651	Lincolnshire
652	Icklingham, Suffolk
653	Norfolk
654	Bury St. Edmunds, Suffolk
655	Bristol, Avon
656	Norfolk
657	Blandford, Dorset
660	Norfolk
661	Suffolk
662	Icklingham, Suffolk
663	East Anglia
664	Icklingham, Suffolk
665	Icklingham, Suffolk
666	Essex
667	Lakenheath, Suffolk
668	Icklingham, Suffolk
669	Suffolk
670	Norfolk
671	Bury St. Edmunds, Suffolk
672	Bury St. Edmunds, Suffolk
673	East Anglia
674	Hertfordshire
675	Bury St. Edmunds, Suffolk
676	King's Lynn, Norfolk
677	Essex
678	Brandon, Norfolk
679	East Anglia
680	Suffolk
681	East Anglia
684	East Anglia
685	Kent
686	Kent
687	Essex
688	Blandford, Dorset
689	East Anglia
690	Eastry, Kent
692	Icklingham, Suffolk
694	France
695	Lamyatt, Somerset
696	Winchester, Hants
697	Lincolnshire
699	Lincolnshire
701	Thetford, Norfolk
702	Westbury, Wilts
703	Greater London
704	Turkey
705	Turkey
706	Turkey
707	Turkey
708	Turkey
709	Turkey
710	Turkey
712	Greece
713	Greece
715	Italy
716	Italy

717	Italy
718	Iran
719	Bury St. Edmunds, Suffolk
720	Norfolk
721	Bledlow, Bucks
722	Bunwell, Norfolk
723	Britain
724	Britain
725	Britain
727	Dorset
728	Austria
729	Switzerland
730	Yugoslavia
733	Dorset
734	France
735	France
736	Dorset
737	Colchester, Essex
738	Bury St. Edmunds, Suffolk
739	Britain
740	Dorset
741	Dorset
742	Britain
743	East Anglia
745	Stockport, Lancs
746	Spain
747	London
748	Dorset
749	Hampshire
750	Norfolk
751	East Midlands
752	Northampton
753	London
757	Mildenhall, Suffolk
758	Austria
759	Austria
760	Littledean, Glos
761	Yugoslavia
762	Yugoslavia
763	Austria
764	Austria
768	Norfolk
769	Britain
770	France
771	France
772	Norfolk
774	Studland, Dorset
775	Suffolk
776	Norfolk
777	Turkey
779	London
780	Norfolk
782	East Anglia
783	Colchester, Essex
784	Cambridgeshire
785	Colchester, Essex
786	France
788	France
789	France
790	Norfolk
791	France
792	Dorset
793	Norfolk
794	Wiltshire
795	Blandford, Dorset
796	Britain
797	Salisbury, Wilts
798	East Anglia
799	Wiltshire
801	Suffolk
802	Suffolk
803	Suffolk
804	Norfolk
806	Weeting, Norfolk
807	Essex
810	Norfolk
811	Mildenhall, Suffolk
815	Owmby, Lincs
816	Wessex
817	Wiltshire
818	Wiltshire
819	Wessex
820	Wiltshire
823	Dorset
824	Spain
826	Italy
825	Syria
827	Mildenhall, Suffolk
828	France
829	Spain
830	Spain
830A	Levant
831	Syria
832	France
833	Yugoslavia
834	London

836	Yugoslavia
837	Caistor St. Edmunds, Norfolk
838	London
839	Dorset
840	Dorset
841	Stockport, Lancs
842	Lower Hacheston, Suffolk
843	Norfolk
844	Suffolk
845	Bury St. Edmunds, Suffolk
847	East Anglia
848	Lambourn, Berks
850	East Anglia
851	East Anglia
852	Silchester, Hants
854	East Anglia
855	Woodyates, Dorset
856	Norfolk
857	Hod Hill, Dorset
860	Salisbury, Wilts
861	Cambridgeshire
862	France
863	France
864	Norfolk
865	France
866	France
867	France
868	France
869	Norwich
870	Watton, Norfolk
871	Dorset
872	Suffolk
873	Britain
874	East Anglia
875	Wessex
876	Norfolk
877	Lakenheath, Suffolk
878	Suffolk
879	Kent
880	Suffolk
881	Maxey, Cambs
882	Wall, Staffs
883	Grimsby, Lincs
884	Suffolk
885	Wessex
886	Great Chesterford, Essex
887	East Anglia
889	Dorset
890	Suffolk
891	Norfolk
892	Dorset
894	Burgh Castle, Norfolk
895	Great Chesterford, Essex
896	South Cerney, Glos
897	Wroxeter, Salop
898	Norfolk
899	Norfolk
900	Wroxeter, Salop
901	Wiltshire
902	Lechlade, Glos
903	Wall, Staffs
904	Wroxeter, Salop
905	Langton Down, Dorset
906	Badbury Rings, Dorset
907	East Anglia
909	Salisbury, Wilts
910	Cirencester, Glos
911	Dorset
912	East Anglia
913	Sixpenny Handley
914	Tollard Royal, Dorset
915	Wiltshire
916	Wiltshire
917	Wiltshire
918	East Anglia
919	Wiltshire
920	Wiltshire
921	Dorset
921A	Dorset
921B	Dorset
922	Wiltshire
923	Bath, Avon
924	Dorset
925	Dorset
926	Salisbury, Wilts
927	Lechlade, Glos
928	Cirencester, Glos
930	Dorset
931	Bury St. Edmunds, Suffolk
932	Dorset
933	Lechlade, Glos
934	Dorset
935	Lechlade, Glos
937	Cirencester, Glos
938	Brettenham, Norfolk
939	East Anglia

940	Lechlade, Glos
941	Cirencester, Glos
942	Wall, Staffs
943	East Anglia
944	Doncaster, Yorks
946	Dorset
947	Wall, Staffs
948	Wall, Staffs
949	Wroxeter, Salop
950	Wroxeter, Salop
951	East Anglia
952	Wall, Staffs
953	Wiltshire
954	East Anglia
956	Norfolk
957	Cirencester, Glos
958	London
959	Wall, Staffs
960	Winchester, Hants
961	Salisbury, Wilts
962	Salisbury, Wilts
963	Cirencester, Glos
964	Lechlade, Glos
966	East Anglia
967	Wall, Staffs
968	East Anglia
969	Wroxeter, Salop
970	Mildenhall, Suffolk
971	France
972	Britain
973	East Anglia
974	Britain
975	Thetford, Norfolk
976	Norfolk
977	Badbury Rings, Dorset
978	Wiltshire
979	Norfolk
980	France
981	Cirencester, Glos
982	Dorset
983	Norfolk
984	Wiltshire
985	Mildenhall, Suffolk
986	Norfolk
987	Co. Durham
988	Bury St. Edmunds, Suffolk
989	Norfolk
990	King's Lynn, Norfolk
991	Bury St. Edmunds, Suffolk
992	Mere, Wilts
994	Austria
995	Suffolk
996	France
998	Yugoslavia
999	Levant
1000	Bicester, Oxon
1002	Dorset
1004	Oxfordshire
1005	Oxfordshire
1006	France
1007	France
1008	East Anglia
1009	Bicester, Oxon
1010	France
1011	Britain
1012	Shapwick,Dorset
1013	Dorset
1014	Essex
1015	Spain
1016	Grimsby, Lincs
1017	Levant
1018	France
1019	Abbotsbury, Dorset
1020	France
1021	France
1022	St. Albans, Herts
1023	Spain
1024	France
1025	London
1026	Lincolnshire
1027	Wiltshire
1028	Codford, Wilts
1029	Lincolnshire
1030	Salisbury, Wilts
1031	Norfolk
1032	Kent
1033	Bury St. Edmunds, Suffolk
1034	Britain
1035	Britain
1036	Ipswich, Suffolk
1037	Ely, Cambs
1038	Mildenhall, Wilts
1039	Britain
1040	Britain
1041	Britain
1043	London

1044	Britain
1045	Salisbury, Wilts
1046	Dorset
1047	Dorset
1049	Bicester, Oxon
1050	Thetford, Norfolk
1051	Dover, Kent
1052	Dover, Kent
1053	Norfolk
1054	Levant
1056	Wroxeter, Salop
1057	Kent
1058	Salisbury, Wilts
1060	Britain
1061	Britain
1062	Suffolk
1063	Britain
1064	Britain
1065	Britain
1066	Northamptonshire
1067	Norfolk
1068	Dorset
1069	Kent
1070	Wessex
1071	Hengistbury Head, Dorset
1072	Dorset
1073	Salisbury, Wilts
1074	Wiltshire
1075	Britain
1076	Norfolk
1077	London
1078	Mildenhall, Wilts
1079	Suffolk
1080	Great Chesterford, Essex
1081	Kent
1082	Wiltshire
1083	Suffolk
1085	Britain
1086	Lamyatt, Somerset
1087	Norfolk
1088	Brighton, Sussex
1089	Winchester, Hants
1090	Littledean, Glos
1091	Bicester, Oxon
1092	Dorset
1093	Lambourn, Berks
1094	Wiltshire
1095	Dorset
1096	France
1097	Great Chesterford, Essex
1098	Faversham, Kent
1099	Oxford
1101	London
1102	Cambridgeshire
1103	Levant
1104	Spain
1105	France
1106	Suffolk
1108	France
1109	Bicester, Oxon
1110	France
1111	Bury St. Edmunds, Suffolk
1113	Levant
1114	Norfolk
1115	Corfe Castle, Dorset
1116	Dorset
1117	Oxford
1118	Ipswich, Suffolk
1119	Britain
1120	France
1121	Brighton, Sussex
1122	Bury St. Edmunds, Suffolk
1124	Spain
1125	Levant
1126	Britain
1127	Kent
1128	Maidenhead, Berks
1129	Bicester, Oxon
1130	France
1131	Bury St. Edmunds, Suffolk
1132	King's Lynn, Norfolk
1134	Wall, Staffs
1136	East Anglia
1137	Brighton, Sussex
1138	Britain
1139	Norfolk
1140	Lincolnshire
1141	Mildenhall, Suffolk
1142	Britain
1143	Turkey
1144	London
1145	Syria
1146	Norwich
1147	Cirencester, Glos
1148	Yorkshire
1149	Turkey

1150	Oxford
1151	Britain
1152	Bicester, Oxon
1153	France
1154	Norfolk
1155	Kent
1157	Spain
1160	Norfolk
1161	Norfolk
1162	Mere, Wilts
1163	Norwich
1164	Britain
1165	East Anglia
1166	Berkshire
1167	Colchester, Essex
1168	Spalding, Lincs
1169	Norfolk
1170	Wiltshire
1171	France
1172	Britain
1173	Norfolk
1174	Ipswich, Suffolk
1175	Norfolk
1176	Norfolk
1177	Mildenhall, Suffolk
1178	Shapwick, Dorset
1179	Norfolk
1180	Hungerford, Berks
1181	Norfolk
1182	Norfolk
1183	Britain
1184	Winchester, Hants
1186	Austria
1187	Norfolk
1188	Wiltshire
1189	Wiltshire
1190	Wiltshire
1191	Hungerford, Berks
1192	Britain
1193	Woodyates, Dorset
1194	France
1195	Levant
1196	France
1197	Turkey
1198	Lincolnshire
1199	Woodyates, Dorset
1200	East Anglia
1201	Pentridge, Dorset
1203	Yorkshire
1204	Bicester, Oxon
1205	France
1206	Britain
1209	Bury St. Edmunds, Suffolk
1210	Northamptonshire
1211	Wall, Staffs
1212	Salisbury, Wilts
1213	East Anglia
1214	Bicester, Oxon
1215	Northamptonshire
1217	Britain
1218	East Anglia
1219	Northumberland
1220	Bath, Avon
1222	Silchester, Hants
1223	Bicester, Oxon
1224	East Anglia
1225	Dorset
1226	Wessex
1227	Norfolk
1228	Dorset
1229	Salisbury, Wilts
1230	France
1231	France
1233	Levant
1234	Yugoslavia
1235	Austria
1236	Austria
1238	Levant
1240	Austria
1241	Austria
1242	Austria
1243	Austria
1244	Greece
1245	Yugoslavia
1246	Yugoslavia
1248	Yugoslavia
1249	Mildenhall, Suffolk
1250	Dorset
1251	Norfolk
1252	Cirencester, Glos
1253	Wessex
1254	Littledean, Glos
1258	Austria
1259	London
1260	Austria
1261	Austria

1262 France
1263 Cirencester, Glos
1264 Wroxeter, Salop
1265 Levant
1266 East Anglia
1268 Norfolk
1269 Bury St. Edmunds, Suffolk
1270 Greece
1272 Yugoslavia
1273 Wall, Staffs
1274 Bury St. Edmunds, Suffolk
1275 Wiltshire
1276 Norfolk
1276A Hampshire
1277 King's Lynn, Norfolk
1278 Merrow Down, Surrey
1279 Wroxeter, Salop
1280 Lincolnshire
1281 Norfolk
1282 Lechlade, Glos
1283 Levant
1285 Bicester, Oxon
1286 Norfolk
1288 Burgh Castle, Norfolk
1289 Lechlade, Glos
1290 Norfolk
1291 Burgh Castle, Norfolk
1292 Dorset
1293 Tunisia
1295 Caistor St. Edmunds, Norfolk
1295A Norfolk
1297 Norfolk
1298 Suffolk
1299 Norfolk
1300 East Anglia
1301 Icklingham, Suffolk
1303 Norfolk
1305 Icklingham, Suffolk
1306 Colchester, Essex
1306 Harrogate, Yorks
1307 Norfolk
1308 Bergh Apton, Norfolk
1308A Chelmsford, Essex
1309 Norfolk
1310 Norfolk
1311 Suffolk
1312 Bury St. Edmunds, Suffolk
1313 Bury St. Edmunds, Suffolk
1314 Faversham, Kent
1315 Mildenhall, Suffolk
1316 Dunstable, Beds
1317 Harrogate, Yorks
1318 East Anglia
1319 East Anglia
1320 Eastry, Kent
1321 Norfolk
1322 Wiltshire
1323 France
1325 France
1326 Norfolk
1327 France
1328 Thetford, Norfolk
1331 France
1331A France
1332 Dorset
1333 London
1334 Sutton Veny, Wilts
1335 Burgh Castle, Norfolk
1336 Dover, Kent
1336A Britain
1337 Somerset
1338 Cambridgeshire
1339 Newmarket, Cambs
1339A Bury St. Edmunds, Suffolk
1340 Wiltshire
1341 Kent
1342 Norfolk
1343 Dorchester, Dorset
1344 Somerset
1345 Dorset
1346 Yorkshire
1346A Fritton, Norfolk
1347 Norfolk
1348 Italy
1349 Italy
1350 Italy
1351 Italy
1352 Italy
1353 Italy
1354 Italy
1355 Merrow Down, Surrey
1356 Italy
1357 Italy
1358 Italy
1359 Spain
1360 Spain

1361	Spain
1362	Spain
1363	Spain
1364	Spain
1365	Spain
1366	Spain
1367	Spain
1368	Spain
1372	Turkey
1373	Turkey
1374	Syria
1375	Syria
1385	Norfolk
1386	Suffolk
1387	France
1388	Bergh Apton, Norfolk
1389	Bergh Apton, Norfolk
1390	Norfolk
1391	Burgh Castle, Norfolk
1392	Great Dunham, Norfolk
1393	Bergh Apton, Norfolk
1394	Great Dunham, Norfolk
1395	Thurleton, Norfolk
1396	Austria
1397	Austria
1398	Burgh Castle, Norfolk
1399	Syria
1400	Dorset
1401	Salisbury, Wilts
1402	Austria
1403	Iran
1404	Iran
1405	Iran
1406	Iran
1407	Austria
1408	Norfolk
1409	Brampton, Norfolk
1410	Great Dunham, Norfolk
1411	Brampton, Norfolk
1412	Syria
1413	Dorset
1414	Suffolk
1415	France
1416	Britain
1417	Norfolk
1418	Iran
1419	Lincolnshire
1420	Lincolnshire
1421	Bury St. Edmunds, Suffolk
1422	Thurleton, Norfolk
1423	Wiltshire
1424	Caistor St. Edmunds, Norfolk
1424A	East Harling, Norfolk
1425	Bury St. Edmunds, Suffolk
1426	Bergh Apton, Norfolk
1427	Winchester, Hants
1428	Canterbury, Kent
1429	Winchester, Hants
1430	Necton, Norfolk
1431	Burgh Castle, Norfolk
1432	Bergh Apton, Norfolk
1433	Switzerland
1434	East Anglia
1435	Winchester, Hants
1436	Dorset
1437	Bath, Avon
1438	Levant
1439	Maiden Bradley, Wilts
1440	Upavon, Wilts
1441	Upavon, Wilts
1442	Stoke-by-Nayland, Essex
1444	Suffolk
1446	Belton, Norfolk
1447	Belton, Norfolk
1447A	Belton, Norfolk
1449	Bicester, Oxon
1450	Turkey
1450A	Caistor St. Edmunds, Norfolk
1451	Guildford, Surrey
1452	Suffolk
1453	France
1454	Hanging Langford, Wilts
1456	Brooke, Norfolk
1457	Lincolnshire
1458	Bradwell, Norfolk
1459	Brooke, Norfolk
1460	Bradwell, Norfolk
1461	Burgh Castle, Norfolk
1462	Burgh Castle, Norfolk
1463	Norfolk
1464	East Anglia
1465	Turkey
1466	Thetford, Norfolk
1467	Bradwell, Norfolk
1468	Ashby de la Launde, Lincs
1469	Bergh Apton, Norfolk

1470 East Anglia
1471 France
1472 Brooke, Norfolk
1473 Norfolk
1474 Caister-on-sea, Norfolk
1475 Fareham, Hants
1476 Lechlade, Glos
1477 Wiltshire
1478 Ancaster, Lincs
1479 Caistor St. Edmunds, Norfolk
1480 Belton, Norfolk
1481 Belton, Norfolk
1481A East Anglia
1482 Bradwell, Norfolk
1483 Britain
1484 Faversham, Kent
1485 Belton, Norfolk
1486 Arminghall, Norfolk
1487 Bergh Apton, Norfolk
1488 Tunisia
1489 Peterborough, Cambs
1490 Tunisia
1491 Burgh Castle, Norfolk
1492 Bradwell, Norfolk
1494 France
1495 Newbury, Berks
1496 Hampshire
1497 Dorset
1498 Bergh Apton, Norfolk
1498A Caistor St. Edmunds, Norfolk
1499 Britain
1500 Watton, Norfolk
1501 Saham Toney, Norfolk
1502 Eartham, West Sussex
1503 Belton, Norfolk
1504 Dorset
1506 Norfolk
1507 Caister-on-sea, Norfolk
1508 Norfolk
1509 Britain
1510 East Anglia
1511 East Anglia
1512 Brooke, Norfolk
1513 Brooke, Norfolk
1514 Ashby de la Launde, Lincs
1515 Norfolk
1516 Ireland
1517 Dorset
1518 Bergh Apton, Norfolk
1519 Wilton, Wilts
1520 Norfolk
1521 Salisbury, Wilts
1522 Dorchester, Dorset
1523 Winchester, Hants
1524 Kirkby Stephen, Cumbria
1526 Norfolk
1527 Yorkshire
1528 Yorkshire
1529 Castleford, West Yorks
1530 Burgh Castle, Norfolk
1531 Norfolk
1532 Gloucester
1533 Faringdon, Oxon
1534 Norfolk
1535 Britain
1536 Brooke, Norfolk
1537 Wareham, Dorset
1538 Eye, Suffolk
1539 Suffolk
1540 Thetford, Norfolk
1541 Peterborough, Cambs
1542 Dorset
1543 Thetford, Norfolk
1544 Swanpool, Lincs
1546 Malton, Yorks
1547 Bergh Apton, Norfolk
1548 Caister-on-sea, Norfolk
1549 Wiltshire
1550 Grimsby, Lincs
1551 Saham Toney, Norfolk
1551A East Anglia
1552 East Anglia
1553 Cambridgeshire
1554 Suffolk
1555 Ixworth, Suffolk
1556 France
1557 France
1558 Norfolk
1559 Belton, Norfolk
1560 Bury St. Edmunds, Suffolk
1561 Lincolnshire
1561A Wiltshire
1562 Thetford, Norfolk
1563 Belton, Norfolk
1564 Thrapston, Northants
1564A Market Deeping, Lincs

1565 France
1566 Bedfordshire
1567 Norfolk
1568 Bedfordshire
1569 Cambridgeshire
1570 France
1571 Kent
1571 Grimsby, Lincs
1572 Watton, Norfolk
1573 Peterborough, Cambs
1574 Ashby de la Launde, Lincs
1576 Caister-on-sea, Norfolk
1577 Belton, Norfolk
1578 Bury St. Edmunds, Suffolk
1579 Belton, Norfolk
1580 Suffolk
1580 Hadrian's Wall
1581 Kent
1582 Belton, Norfolk
1583 Levant
1584 Norfolk
1585 Peterborough, Cambs
1587 Levant
1588 Hadrian's Wall
1589 Belton, Norfolk
1590 Kent
1591 Wiltshire
1592 Lincolnshire
1593 Levant
1594 Turkey
1595 Levant
1596 Suffolk
1597 Norfolk
1598 Norfolk
1599 Bradwell, Norfolk
1600 Levant
1600A Great Chesterford, Essex
1601 France
1602 Dorchester, Dorset
1603 France
1604 Yorkshire
1605 Norfolk
1607 Bradwell, Norfolk
1608 Bergh Apton, Norfolk
1609 Cambridgeshire
1610 Suffolk
1611 Levant
1612 Eartham, West Sussex
1613 Watton, Norfolk
1614 Catterick, Yorks
1615 Yorkshire
1616 Bergh Apton, Norfolk
1617 France
1618 Catterick, Yorks
1619 Digby, Lincs
1620 Belton, Norfolk
1621 Peterborough, Cambs
1622 Yugoslavia
1623 Levant
1624 Yugoslavia
1625 Yugoslavia
1625A France
1625B France
1626 Levant
1626A Saham Toney, Norfolk
1626B Co. Durham
1627 East Anglia
1628 Bedfordshire
1629 East Anglia
1630 Yugoslavia
1631 Levant
1632 Loddon, Norfolk
1633 France
1634 Britain
1635 Yugoslavia
1636 France
1637 Yugoslavia
1638 Dorset
1639 Wiltshire
1640 Turkey
1641 Yugoslavia
1642 France
1643 Austria
1644 Yugoslavia
1645 Brettenham, Norfolk
1646 Gissing, Norfolk
1647 Caistor St. Edmunds, Norfolk
1648 Abbotts Ann, Hampshire
1649 Watton, Norfolk
1650 Levant
1651 Norfolk
1652 Newbury, Berks
1653 Burgh Castle, Norfolk
1654 Yorkshire
1655 Humberside
1656 Thetford, Glos

1657 Carlton Rode, Norfolk
1658 Levant
1659 Austria
1660 Guildford, Surrey
1661 Yorkshire
1662 Brooke, Norfolk
1663 Belton, Norfolk
1664 Bradwell, Norfolk
1665 Brockenhurst, Hants
1666 Belton, Norfolk
1667 Yugoslavia
1668 Norfolk
1669 Dorset
1670 Thetford, Norfolk
1671 Great Yarmouth, Norfolk
1672 Belton, Norfolk
1673 Kent
1674 Newark, Notts
1675 Yugoslavia
1676 Austria
1677 Cambridge
1678 Yorkshire
1679 Lincolnshire
1680 Norfolk
1681 Norfolk
1682 Sleaford, Lincs
1683 Hales, Norfolk
1684 Co. Durham
1685 France
1686 Dover, Kent
1687 Geldeston, Norfolk
1688 Burgh Castle, Norfolk
1689 Wiltshire
1690 East Harling, Norfolk
1691 Sleaford, Lincs
1692 Costessey, Norfolk
1693 Essex
1694 Suffolk
1695 Suffolk
1696 Thwaite St. Mary, Norfolk
1697 York
1698 Geldeston, Norfolk
1699 Ashby de la Launde, Lincs
1700 Kirby Cane, Norfolk
1701 Sussex
1702 France
1703 France
1704 France
1705 Kent
1706 East Anglia
1707 King's Lynn, Norfolk
1708 Norfolk
1709 Fritton, Norfolk
1710 Haddiscoe, Norfolk
1711 Norfolk
1712 Norfolk
1713 Dorset
1714 East Anglia
1715 Fritton, Norfolk
1716 Britain
1717 Blythborough, Suffolk
1718 France
1719 East Anglia
1720 Norfolk
1721 Haddiscoe, Norfolk
1722 Spain
1723 Spain
1724 Spain
1725 Greece
1727 Levant
1728 Turkey
1729 Turkey
1730 Co. Durham
1731 Burgh Castle, Norfolk
1732 Norfolk
1734 Dorset
1735 Dorset
1736 Norfolk